Suzuki RM Motocross Owners Workshop Manual

by Pete Shoemark

Models covered
RM50N (1979) RM50T (1980)
RM60N (1979) RM60T (1980)
RM80N (1979) RM80T (1980)
RM100N (1979) RM100T (1980)
RM125N (1979) RM125T (1980)
RM250N (1979) RM250T (1980)
RM400N (1979) RM400T (1980)

ISBN 0 85696 534 0

Printed in England

HAYNES PUBLISHING GROUP
SPARKFORD YEOVIL SOMERSET ENGLAND
distributed in the USA by
HAYNES PUBLICATIONS INC
861 LAWRENCE DRIVE
NEWBURY PARK
CALIFORNIA 91320
USA

Acknowledgements

Our thanks are due to Beamish Suzuki, the UK distributors for the Suzuki competition range, who kindly supplied the RM80, 100 and 400 featured throughout this manual. Particular thanks must go to Nick Beamish, Tony Barnard, Andy Foulkes and George Russell of the above company for their patience and enthusiasm in providing much of the necessary data and advice during the preparation of the book. Thanks are also due to Heron Suzuki (GB) Ltd for permission to reproduce their line drawings and to Spalding Public Relations for the black and white model photographs.

Brian Horsfall assisted with the stripdown and rebuilding of the three machines, and devised ingenious methods for overcoming problems created by the lack of service tools. Les Brazier arranged and took the photographs; Mansur Darlington edited the text.

Finally, we would also like to thank the Avon rubber company, who supplied information and technical assistance on tyre fitting; NGK Spark Plugs (UK) Ltd for information on sparking plug maintenance and electrode conditions, and Renold Ltd for advice on chain care and renewal.

About this manual

The purpose of this manual is to present the owner with a concise and graphic guide which will enable him to tackle any operation from basic routine maintenance to a major overhaul. It has been assumed that any work will be undertaken without the luxury of a well-equipped workshop and a range of manufacturers service tools.

To this end, the three machines featured in the manual were stripped and rebuilt in our own workshop, by a team comprising a mechanic, a photographer and the author. The resulting photographic sequence depicts events as they took place, the hands shown being those of the author and the mechanic.

The use of specialised, and expensive, service tools was avoided unless their use was considered to be essential due to risk of breakage or injury. There is usually some way of improvising a method of removing a stubborn component, provided that a suitable degree of care is exercised.

The author learnt his motorcycle mechanics over a number of years, faced with the same difficulties and using similar facilities to those encountered by most owners. It is hoped that this practical experience can be passed on through the pages of this manual.

Where possible, a well-used example of the machine is chosen for a workshop project, as this highlights any areas which might be particularly prone to giving rise to problems. In this way, any such difficulties are encountered and resolved before the text is written, and the techniques used to deal with them can be incorporated in the relevant Section. Armed with a working knowledge of the machine, the author undertake a considerable amount of research in order that the maximum amount of data can be included in the manual.

Each Chapter is divided into numbered sections. Within these Sections are numbered paragraphs. Cross reference throughout the manual is quite straightforward and logical. When reference is made 'See Section 6.10' it means Section 6, paragraph 10, in the same Chapter. If another Chapter were intended, the reference would read, for example, 'See Chapter 2, Section 6.10'. All the photographs are captioned with a section/paragraph number to which they refer and are relevant to the Chapter text adjacent. Furthermore, most captions are followed by a model number in brackets which identifies the machine photographed. In most cases components fitted to other models within the same group will be identical or similar to those shown.

Figures (usually line illustrations) appear in a logical but numerical order, within a given Chapter. Fig. 1.1 therefore refers to the first figure in Chapter 1.

Left-hand and right-hand descriptions of the machines and their components refer to the left and right of a given machines when the rider is seated normally.

Whilst every care is taken to ensure that the information in this manual is correct no liability can be accepted by the author or publishers for loss, damage or injury caused by any errors in or omissions from the information given.

Contents

Note: General descriptions and specifications are given in each Chapter immediately after the list of contents. Fault diagnosis is given at the end of each Chapter.

1980 Suzuki RM50T

1980 Suzuki RM80T

1979 Suzuki RM100N

1979 Suzuki RM125N

1980 Suzuki RM250T

1980 Suzuki RM400T

Introduction to the Suzuki RM motocross models

Suzuki's first excursion into the motocross field came in 1968, when their RH250 model was launched into what was then a sport dominated by the European manufacturers. Although this machine was built on traditional lines, it had the advantage of more engine power and less weight than the established machines, and quickly established itself as a potential winner. By 1970, the Suzuki works machines had won the first of a series of World championship victories. Suzuki paid careful attention to the numerous innovations being pioneered by other manufacturers, incorporating and developing those which promised to be advantageous to them.

With seven years of motocross experience behind them, Suzuki launched the first of the RM models during 1975. These were production machines which followed closely the general lines of the works machines, thus bringing genuinely competitive motocross machinery within the grasp of amateur riders. Needless to say, this was a popular move, and the RM series has become the best known and most competitive motocross range to come out of Japan.

Predictably, Suzuki have realised the need to update and modify the range on a regular and frequent basis, thus maintaining the RM's competitiveness over the years. The basic machine remains very similar to the original layout, but has evolved by way of numerous detail changes each season.

This manual deals with the 1979 (N) and 1980 (T) ranges. This has been done to ensure that coverage was kept accurate and specific, rather than offer too vague a coverage of the entire range. It follows that owners of pre-1979 models will find that although specific coverage of their machines is not given, much of the text and the various procedures will be applicable.

Ordering spare parts

When ordering spare parts for any Suzuki, it is advisable to deal direct with an official Suzuki agent who should be able to supply most of the parts ex-stock. Parts cannot be obtained from Suzuki direct and all orders must be routed via an approved agent even if the parts required are not held in stock. Always quote the engine and frame numbers in full, especially if parts are required for earlier models.

The frame and engine numbers are stamped on a Manufacturer's Plate riveted to the frame downtube. The frame number is also stamped on the frame itself on the right-hand side of the steering head. The engine number is stamped on the upper crankcase.

Use only genuine Suzuki spares. Some pattern parts are available that are made in Japan and may be packed in similar looking packages. They should only be used if genuine parts are hard to obtain or in an emergency, for they do not normally last as long as genuine parts, even though there may be a price advantage.

Some of the more expendable parts such as spark plugs, bulbs, tyres, oils and greases etc., can be obtained from accessory shops and motor factors, who have convenient opening hours and can often be found not far from home. It is also possible to obtain parts on a Mail Order basis from a number of specialists who advertise regularly in the motorcycle magazines.

Frame number location

Engine number location

Safety first!

Professional motor mechanics are trained in safe working procedures. However enthusiastic you may be about getting on with the job in hand, do take the time to ensure that your safety is not put at risk. A moment's lack of attention can result in an accident, as can failure to observe certain elementary precautions.

There will always be new ways of having accidents, and the following points do not pretend to be a comprehensive list of all dangers; they are intended rather to make you aware of the risks and to encourage a safety-conscious approach to all work you carry out on your vehicle.

Essential DOs and DON'Ts

DON'T start the engine without first ascertaining that the transmission is in neutral.

DON'T suddenly remove the filler cap from a hot cooling system – cover it with a cloth and release the pressure gradually first, or you may get scalded by escaping coolant.

DON'T attempt to drain oil until you are sure it has cooled sufficiently to avoid scalding you.

DON'T grasp any part of the engine, exhaust or silencer without first ascertaining that it is sufficiently cool to avoid burning you.

DON'T syphon toxic liquids such as fuel, brake fluid or antifreeze by mouth, or allow them to remain on your skin.

DON'T inhale brake lining dust – it is injurious to health.

DON'T allow any spilt oil or grease to remain on the floor – wipe it up straight away, before someone slips on it.

DON'T use ill-fitting spanners or other tools which may slip and cause injury.

DON'T attempt to lift a heavy component which may be beyond your capability – get assistance.

DON'T rush to finish a job, or take unverified short cuts.

DON'T allow children or animals in or around an unattended vehicle.

DON'T inflate a tyre to a pressure above the recommended maximum. Apart from overstressing the carcase and wheel rim, in extreme cases the tyre may blow off forcibly.

DO ensure that the machine is supported securely at all times. This is especially important when the machine is blocked up to aid wheel or fork removal.

DO take care when attempting to slacken a stubborn nut or bolt. It is generally better to pull on a spanner, rather than push, so that if slippage occurs you fall away from the machine rather than on to it.

DO wear eye protection when using power tools such as drill, sander, bench grinder etc.

DO use a barrier cream on your hands prior to undertaking dirty jobs – it will protect your skin from infection as well as making the dirt easier to remove afterwards. Before starting the job ensure that the cream has dried and your hands are not slippery.

DO keep loose clothing (cuffs, tie etc) and long hair well out of the way of moving mechanical parts, and always remove your watch and any rings before starting the job.

DO work tidily, keeping the floor space uncluttered by removed components and tools; there is less likelihood of tripping over if this approach is adopted.

DO exercise caution when compressing springs for removal or installation. Ensure that the tension is applied and released in a controlled manner, using suitable tools which preclude the possibility of the spring escaping violently.

DO ensure that any lifting tackle used has a safe working load rating adequate for the job.

DO get someone to check periodically that all is well, when working alone on the vehicle.

DO carry out work in a logical sequence and check that everything is correctly assembled and tighten afterwards.

DO remember that your vehicle's safety affects that of yourself and others. If in doubt on any point, get specialist advice.

IF, in spite of following these precautions, you are unfortunate enough to injure yourself, seek medical attention as soon as possible.

Fire

Remember at all times that petrol (gasoline) is highly flammable. Never smoke, or have any kind of naked flame around, when working on the vehicle. But the risk does not end there – a spark caused by an electrical short-circuit, by two metal surfaces contacting each other, or even by static electricity built up in your body under certain conditions, can ignite petrol vapour, which in a confined space is highly explosive.

Always disconnect the battery earth (ground) terminal before working on any part of the fuel system, and never risk spilling fuel on to a hot engine or exhaust.

It is recommended that a fire extinguisher of a type suitable for fuel and electrical fires is kept handy in the garage or workplace at all times. Never try to extinguish a fuel or electrical fire with water.

Fumes

Certain fumes are highly toxic and can quickly cause unconsciousness and even death if inhaled to any extent. Petrol (gasoline) vapour comes into this category, as do the vapours from certain solvents such as trichlorethylene. Any draining or pouring of such volatile fluids should be done in a well ventilated area.

When using cleaning fluids and solvents, read the instructions carefully. Never use materials from unmarked containers – they may give off poisonous vapours.

Never run the engine of a motor vehicle in an enclosed space such as a garage. Exhaust fumes contain carbon monoxide which is extremely poisonous; if you need to run the engine, always do so in the open air or at least have the rear of the vehicle outside the workplace.

If you are fortunate enough to have the use of an inspection pit, never drain or pour petrol over it; the fumes, being heavier than air, will concentrate in the pit with possibly lethal results.

The battery

Never cause a spark, or allow a naked light, near the vehicle's battery. It will normally be giving off a certain amount of hydrogen gas, which is highly explosive.

Always disconnect the battery earth (ground) terminal before working on the fuel or electrical systems.

If possible, loosen the filler plugs or cover when charging the battery from an external source. Do not charge at an excessive rate or the battery may burst.

Take care when topping up and when carrying the battery. The acid electrolyte, even when diluted, is very corrosive and should not be allowed to contact the eyes or skin.

If you ever need to prepare electrolyte yourself, always add the acid slowly to the water, and never the other way round. Protect against splashes by wearing rubber gloves and goggles.

Mains electricity

When using an electric power tool, inspection light etc which works from the mains, always ensure that the appliance is correctly connected to its plug and that, where necessary, it is properly earthed (grounded). Do not use such appliances in damp conditions and, again, beware of creating a spark or applying excessive heat in the vicinity of fuel or fuel vapour.

Ignition HT voltage

A severe electric shock can result from touching certain parts of the ignition system, such as the HT leads, when the engine is running or being cranked, paticularly if components are damp or the insulation is defective. Where an electronic ignition system is fitted, the HT voltage is much higher and could prove fatal.

Routine and competition maintenance

Like any other motorcycle, motocross machines require regular and methodical maintenance if they are to be expected to perform competitively. A poorly maintained and consequently unreliable machine will inevitably lose races, thus it is vitally important to develop a routine for checking the machine over between heats and at the end of each race.

It is not practical to advise precisely when each operation should be tackled, because this depends entirely upon the prevailing conditions, the age of the machine, and the riding style adopted. Ultimately, each rider will develop a sequence based on past experience, and will check all the areas that are known to be likely to require attention. This is a practice to be encouraged, because a systematic checking sequence will save time and help avoid unexpected failures during the next race.

The maintenance operations listed below are intended as a guide for the rider until a regular checking sequence has been developed. It should be noted that in particularly adverse conditions, some operations, such as drive chain lubrication and air filter cleaning, should be attended to more frequently.

Maintenance check 1: between each race, or every 60 miles (100 km)

---

1 Cleaning

Remove any heavy accumulation of mud or dust so that the various controls and moving parts can be checked for adjustment and tightness. A thorough cleaning is not necessary at this stage, but it is important to restore the tyres, suspension etc. to a competitive state before the next race.

2 Nuts and bolts

Check all accessible nuts and bolts for tightness, and if necessary re-tighten to the specified torque setting. This operation is less important if the machine has been stripped and reassembled with self-locking nuts, thread locking compound or with wire-locked nuts. This latter course of action is recommended, as it will save time between races. It will be found in practice, that only those nuts and bolts overlooked during the check will work loose during the next race. Locking the various threads can add greatly to peace of mind during racing.

3 Spoke tension

Give the spokes a cursory inspection looking for broken, bent or loose items. Run a screwdriver around the spokes noting the sound made as each spoke is struck. A sound spoke will make a characteristic 'ping' noise, whilst a slack or damaged spoke will sound dead. If a spoke breaks in service, it can cause a considerable amount of damage to the rim and inner tube. This problem can be minimised by wiring the spokes together where they cross. In this way, the sound spokes will support any broken ones, preventing any tendency for the broken end to flail outwards. Thread locking wire, preferably stainless steel, is recommended.

4 Tyres and rims

Remove any dirt from the rims and tyres, and inspect both for damage. In particular, look for cuts or splits in the tyres, not forgetting the side walls which can be ripped by rocks on the track. The rims should be free from cracks or bruising due to impact damage.

5 Final drive chain

Wipe off the drive chain, checking for damaged sideplates or pins. Check the security of the joining link. Many professional riders favour the more secure type of joining link which employs locking nuts or some similar arrangement to secure the side plate. The conventional spring link can become displaced if it drags against the frame or chain tensioners during use. Lubricate the chain with an aerosol chain grease, and adjust the chain tension if necessary.

6 Controls and cables

Check and reset the adjustment of the brake and clutch controls where required. If frequent adjustment is required between races, make a note that that area of the machine will require particular attention after the event has finished. Check the exposed portions of all control cable inners for kinks or fraying. If in doubt, play safe and renew the cable before the next race.

7 Suspension and steering

Ensure that the suspension works smoothly and effectively, and that no play has developed in the steering or swinging arm pivot. If wear is detected, this should be investigated as soon as is practicable, because it will worsen rapidly under competition conditions.

8 Air cleaner

Remove and clean the air filter element. Re-impregnate with engine or air-cleaner oil before installing the element in the air cleaner chamber. To save time, obtain a number of elements which can be cleaned and oiled before the event, and can then be installed as required. The dirty elements can then be cleaned and re-oiled at home. This arrangement can be very useful if an element becomes torn in use, because there is always a sound spare available.

9 Sparking plug

Remove the sparking plug, and note its condition before cleaning, comparing it with the colour sparking plug condition photographs in Chapter 3. The colour of the plug electrodes can give a good indication of the general condition of the engine, and indicates whether carburettor adjustment is required.

Remove any carbon deposits using a brass wire brush. Clean the electrodes and check the gap setting against the specified settings listed under Routine Maintenance settings and capacities, at the end of this Section.

Ensure chain link clip is correctly secured with closed end facing direction of normal travel

Lubricate the chain with an aerosol chain grease

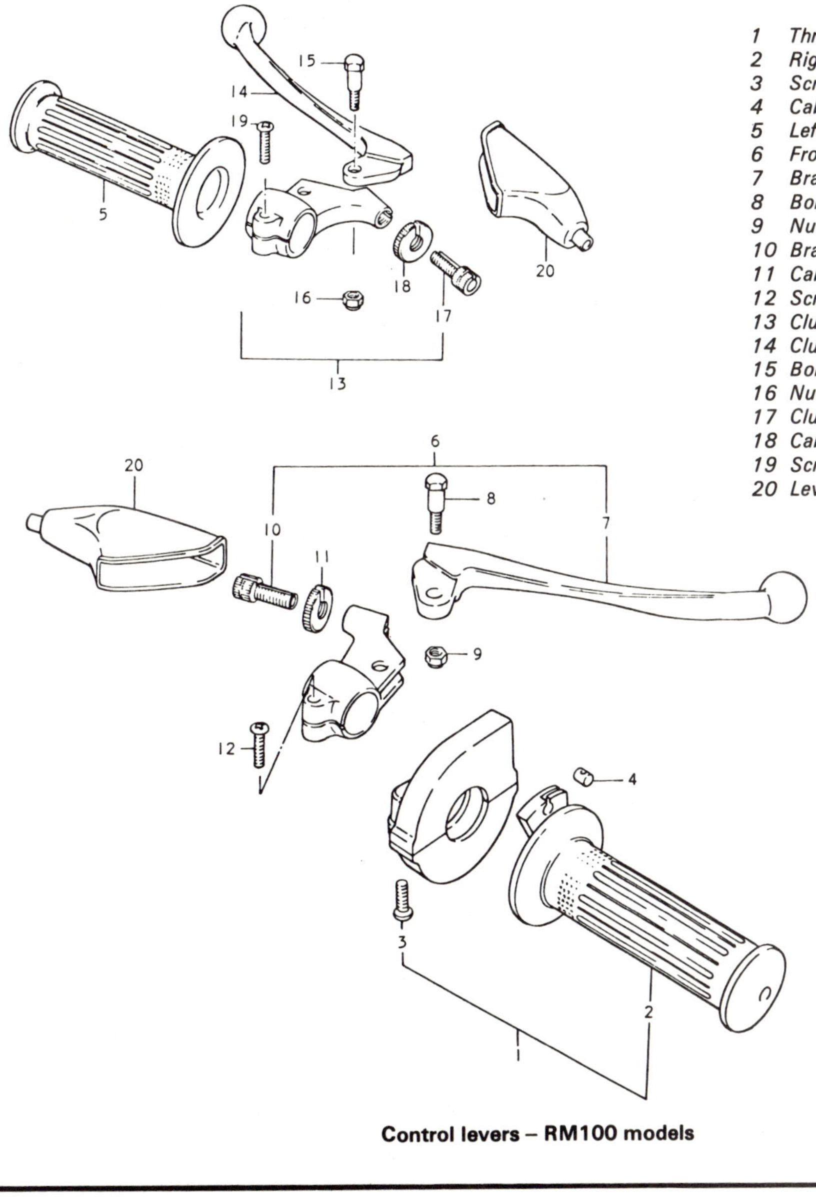

1 Throttle grip assembly
2 Right-hand throttle grip
3 Screw – 2 off
4 Cable trunnion
5 Left-hand throttle grip
6 Front brake lever assembly
7 Brake lever
8 Bolt
9 Nut
10 Brake cable adjuster
11 Cable adjuster lock nut
12 Screw
13 Clutch lever assembly
14 Clutch lever
15 Bolt
16 Nut
17 Clutch cable adjuster
18 Cable adjuster lock nut
19 Screw
20 Lever cover

Control levers – RM100 models

Displace protective boots and loosen locknut prior to adjusting clutch cable tension

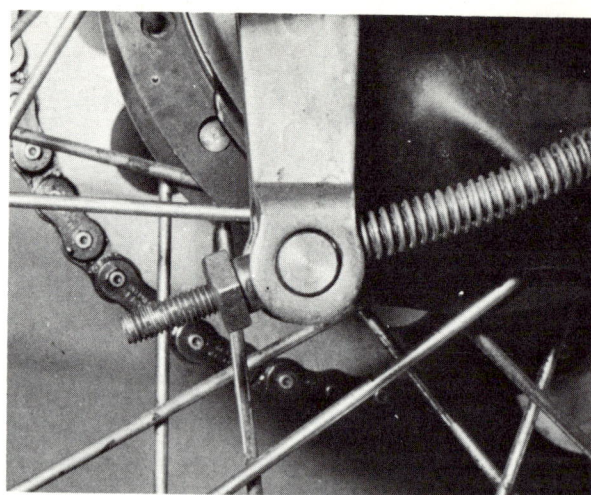

Rear brake adjustment is by nut on threaded brake rod

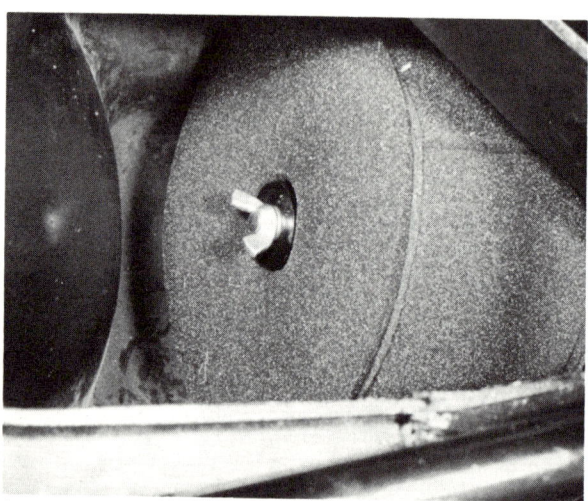

Air filter element held by a butterfly nut (RM400)

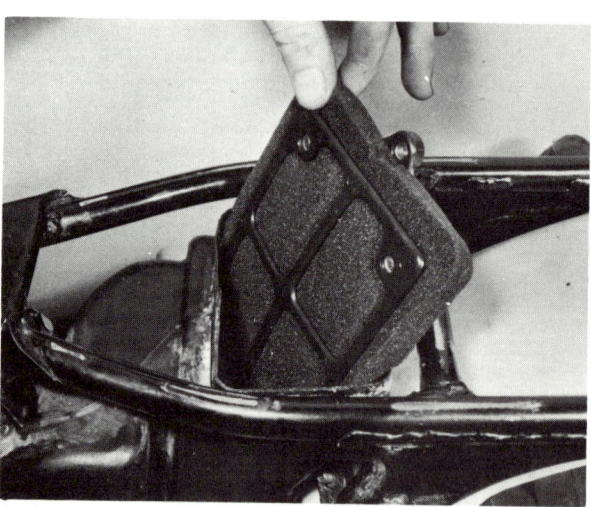

Air filter element supported on flat frame (RM80)

Maintenance check 2: after each event

The following operations should be carried out after each event, and in addition to the operations listed under Maintenance check 1. This work should be undertaken before the machine is put away for storage, and it is intended to leave the machine in a ready-to-race condition.

1   Cleaning

Ensure that the engine unit has cooled down, then hose the machine down thoroughly to soften and remove accumulated mud. If available, a high pressure spray will greatly ease this operation, and will dislodge most of the dirt without any need for brushing. Pay particular attention to the front forks, the front and underside of the engine unit, the swinging arm, the wheels and the undersides of the mudguards.

2   Damage check

Check the machine carefully for signs of damage, particularly after the machine has been dropped or involved in a collision. If any unusual handling tendencies or noises were noticed, check particularly carefully, and rectify the cause of the problem before the next event. Check all control levers, pedals, footrests and cables for wear or damage.

3   Front forks

Release the dust seals or gaiters from the lower legs and check around the fork seals for signs of oil leakage. If present, refer to Chapter 4 for details of seal renewal. Clean out any dirt or water from around the seal, because this can quickly cause damage to the seal faces and the fork stanchion. If the forks are of the ungaitered type, it is strongly recommended that full gaiters are fitted to prevent expensive wear or damage to the forks. See Chapter 4 for details.

4   Brakes and wheel bearings

Remove each wheel in turn and dismantle the brake plate components. Clean out any dirt or water which may have entered the brake during the last event. Before reassembling the brake, grease the operating cam.

The wheel bearings are of the sealed type and should last a long time. Water *can* enter the bearings, however, and their demise will follow shortly after this. Check the bearings for any signs of roughness when turned. On floating brake plate models, check the needle roller outrigger bearing as well.

See Chapter 5 for further details on brake and bearing maintenance and renewal.

Removal of brake plate allows inspection of brake linings and wheel bearings

5   Controls and pivots

The various control levers and pedals, and any moving parts such as the prop stand pivot (where fitted) and footrest pivots should be cleaned and lubricated. Check for damage at the same time. Pedals and footrests can often be straightened out if bent in a collision (see Chapter 4).

The swinging arm is not equipped with a grease nipple, so regular greasing is not a practical proposition. Periodically, throughout the season, withdraw the swinging arm pivot and check the bushes or bearings for wear and water contamination. If the latter problem is discovered, dismantle the swinging arm completely as described in Chapter 4, and clean out the bearings before regreasing them. If water has found its way in, remove all traces of it or rusting and pitting will rapidly develop. Renew the end cap seals to prevent further problems. Note that the swinging arm should not normally require frequent attention, but a lot of work and expense may be avoided if it is checked occasionally.

6   Control cables

Remove all control cables and clean carefully. The cables cannot be dismantled for cleaning, but normal unlined cables can be flushed through with petrol to remove dust and mud if necessary. Push one end of the cable through a plastic bag, and tape it to the outer cable. Pour a small quantity of petrol into the bag and allow it to run through the cable (Note that this should **not** be done to nylon lined cables, which should be left dry or lubricated with a suitable silicone-based lubricant).

Check the exposed portions of the inner cable for fraying or any obvious damage, and renew them if they are less than perfect. Check that the cable has not become kinked or crushed in use. If the outer cable has become snagged in use, it may have stretched. If this is the case, renew the cable, because it will always be slightly springy in use.

The cables can be lubricated by forming a 'funnel' at one end using a plastic bag, as described earlier for cleaning, or by making a plasticene funnel as shown in the accompanying diagram. Alternatively, an hydraulic cable oiler makes the job quicker, although they do tend to be a little messy in use. Engine oil will suffice as a lubricant, although a number of riders are now using Triflon, a PTFE-based lubricant which will make the cable extra smooth in operation, and which is unlikely to be washed out by water.

Refit the cables, ensuring that they take the least tortuous path between the operating lever and the business end. The throttle cable should, of course, exit parallel to, or slightly above, the level of the handlebar to prevent it catching on obstacles in use. The same applies to brake and clutch cables; always choose the least vulnerable path.

The control lever ends of the various cables, particularly the throttle cable should be gaitered or taped up to prevent the ingress of water or mud. Once the new lubricated cable is positioned, adjustment of the controls is largely a matter of personal choice, and each rider will develop his own preference for the amount of free play. As a guideline, leave about $\frac{1}{8}$ in free play in the throttle cable to allow for steering movement and any changes of the cable's position when racing. The clutch and brake cables should have about $\frac{1}{4}$ in clearance, but this can be increased so that the lever is in a convenient position when maximum leverage is required.

Remember to carry a spare set of cables to each meeting to allow for any unexpected breakage during a race. The manufacturer recommends that the cables should be renewed every 5 races or 300 miles (500 km)

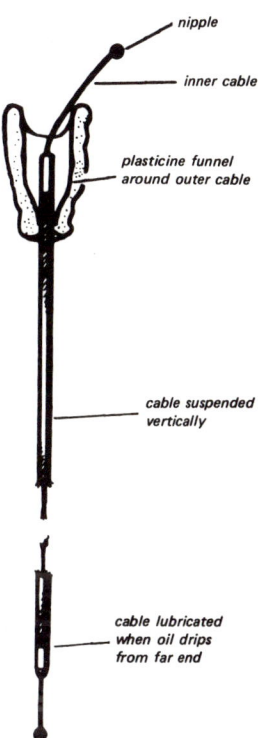

nipple

inner cable

plasticine funnel
around outer cable

cable suspended
vertically

cable lubricated
when oil drips
from far end

Oiling control cable

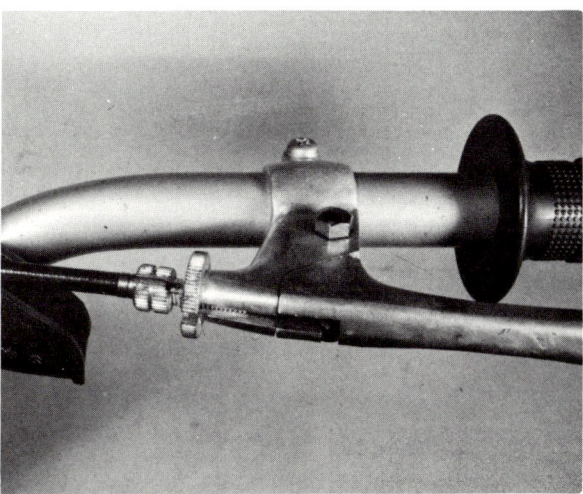

Front brake adjust at lever is protected by rubber shroud

7   Final drive chain

Remove the final drive chain and clean it by immersing it in paraffin (kerosene) or a cleaning solvent, and wire-brushing to remove mud. Rinse in clean petrol (gasoline) and allow the chain to dry off. If the chain is worn, it should be renewed to prevent damage to the sprockets or possible subsequent failure. The manufacturer recommends that it should be renewed every 3rd race or 180 miles (300 km), along with the guide roller.

The best method of lubrication is to immerse the chain in a molten graphite or molybdenum based chain grease. This will flow into the chain rollers and pins, setting hard when cold. A less effective method is to soak the chain in gear oil for a few hours, wiping off the excess before refitting. Again, the recently-introduced PTFE lubricant has been well received in Motocross circles, and promises to be a popular choice in the future.

8   Fuel system

Remove the petrol tap and float bowl and remove any water or dirt which may have entered the system. If water is discovered, drain and flush the fuel tank, ensuring that every trace of water is removed. One small globule of water can block a jet and lose a race.

9   Contact breakers and timing – RM50 only

All RM models, with the exception of the RM50, employ CDI ignition systems which can be ignored between overhauls. In the case of the RM50 however, the contact breaker gap and timing should be checked as described in Chapter 3.

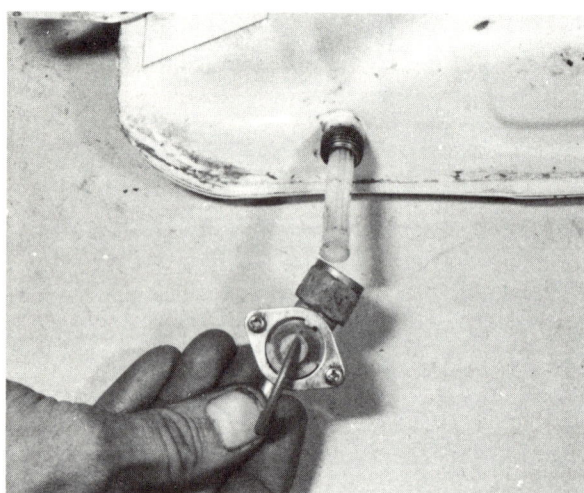

Withdraw petrol tap to allow inspection and cleaning of filter

Maintenance check 3: pre-race check

If the guidelines given in maintenance checks 1 and 2 are followed, there should be little need for pre-race maintenance, leaving the rider free to make any last-minute adjustments to suit the course, and to get on with the more important business of practice and racing.

Check that the fuel tank is filled with the correct mixture of petrol and oil. Bounce the machine to ensure that the suspension operates correctly. Ensure that the controls are correctly set up and fall within easy and convenient reach.

Last minute adjustments to tyre pressures and, where applicable, front fork air pressure should be made to suit the type of track and ambient conditions at each event.

Trackside repairs and overhauling

With careful preparation and maintenance, the frequency of trackside repairs will be minimised. However, problems will inevitably occur, and can only be dealt with on the spot if time and equipment permit.

A toolkit comprised of those tools most frequently used in the workshop should be considered a basic necessity. Any additional equipment is less essential but is useful if it can be carried to the event with reasonable ease.

Always carry a tyre pump, tyre levers and a puncture repair kit, and spare tyres and tubes if available. A supply of duct tape and/or PVC insulating tape can also be considered essential, as can RTV gasket compounds and sealants, a selection of hose clips, nuts, bolts and washers, and some pieces of electrical and locking wire. Do not omit some form of improvised stand, such as a stout wooden box or a crate. Experience will show what additional items will need to be carried, and this varies widely between different riders. It must be accepted that any major failure, such as a siezed engine, will mean abandoning that event, and returning the machine to the workshop for overhauling.

A full stripdown and overhaul should be undertaken at the end of the season, allowing the then battered and tired machine to be restored to competitive condition for the next season's events. With the machine stripped completely, the frame can be checked and repainted, and any radical modifications can be undertaken. The engine/gearbox unit should also be stripped right down and checked meticulously for damage or wear. This presents a good opportunity to repaint the engine casings with a heat-resistant matt black engine enamel.

Manufacturer's maintenance schedule

The following is a list of operations and service intervals recommended by Suzuki. Riders may find that in some instances, certain operations need to be carried out more or less frequently, depending on individual requirements and racing conditions.

1   Piston rings

RM50, RM60, RM80: Renew the piston rings every 5 races or 300 miles (500 km)

RM100, RM125, RM250, RM400: Renew the piston rings every 2 races or 120 miles (200 km)

2   Transmission oil

RM50, RM60, RM80: Change every 2 races or 120 miles (200 km)

RM100, RM125, RM250, RM400: Change every 3 races or 180 miles (300 km)

3   Gearbox sprocket

RM50, RM60, RM80: Renew every 10 races or 600 miles (1000 km)

RM100, RM125, RM250, RM400: Renew every 5 races or 300 miles (500 km)

4   Drive chain

RM50, RM60, RM80: Lubricate after each race or 60 miles (100 km). Renew after every 10 races or 600 miles (1000 km)

RM100, RM125, RM250, RM400: Lubricate after each race or 60 miles (100 km). Renew after 5 races or 300 miles (500 km)

5   Rear wheel sprocket

RM50, RM60, RM80: Renew after every 10 races or 600 miles (1000 km)

RM100, RM125, RM250, RM400: Renew after every 3 races or 180 miles (300 km)

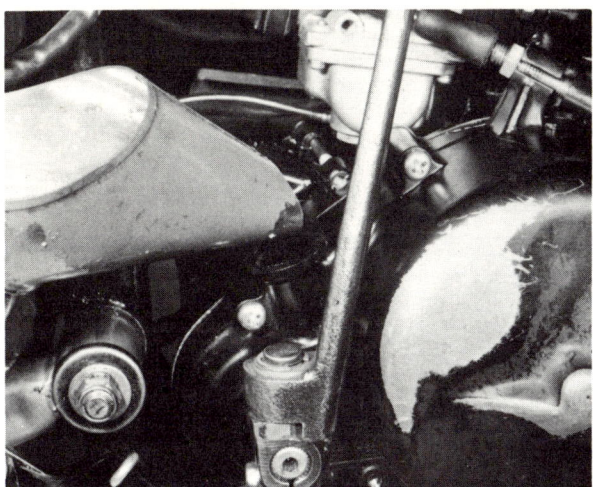
Replenish gearbox oil level with specified grade of oil until ...

... oil seeps from level hole in casing

6 Drive chain buffer
RM50, RM60, RM80: Renew after every 5 races or 300 miles (500 km)

RM100, RM125, RM250, RM400: Renew after every 3 races or 180 miles (300 km)

7 Drive chain guide roller
RM100, RM125, RM250, RM400 models only: Renew after every 3 races or 180 miles (300 km)

8 Spokes
All models: Check tension after every race or 30 miles (50 km). With newly-rebuilt wheel, check after every 5 miles (10 km) for the first 30 miles (50 km)

9 Air cleaner
All models: Clean after every race or 60 miles (100 km). Renew if badly clogged or damaged.

10 Kick start lever
All models: Lubricate after every race or 60 miles (100 km)

11 Control cables
RM50, RM60, RM80: Renew after every 10 races or 600 miles (1000 km)

RM100, RM125, RM250, RM400: Renew after every 5 races or 300 miles (500 km)

12 Nuts and bolts
All models: Check and tighten after every race or 60 miles (100 km)

13 Sparking plug
All models: Check and clean after every race or 60 miles (100 km)

14 Piston
RM100, RM125, RM250, RM400 models only: Renew after every 5 races of 300 miles (500 km)

15 Contact breaker points
RM50 only: check and adjust after every race or 60 miles (100 km)

16 Front fork oil
RM100, RM125, RM250, RM400 models only: Change after every 3 races or 300 miles (500 km)

Quick glance
maintenance adjustments and capacities

Engine oil

    Type . . . .   Shell Super M, Castrol R.30, Golden Spectro synthetic blend,
                                                                B.P. Racing, Bel-Ray MC1 or equivalent

The above lubricants should be pre-mixed with petrol (gasoline) at a ratio of 20:1 **Important Note**: Do not mix different brands and grades of oil without first flushing the entire fuel system with petrol. If mineral and vegetable-based oils are mixed, the resulting sludge will block the carburettor jets.

Gearbox/primary drive

Type   Any good quality SAE 20W/40 engine oil

Quantity

Model	cc	Oil changes			Dry (after overhaul)		
		US pint	Imp pint	cc	US pint	Imp pint
RM50N, T	650	1·38	1·14	700	1·48	1·24
RM60N, T	700	1·48	1·24	750	1·58	1·32
RM80N, T	700	1·48	1·24	750	1·58	1·32
RM100N, T	800	1·69	1·41	900	1·90	1·58
RM125N, T	800	1·69	1·41	900	1·90	1·58
RM250N, T	800	1·69	1·41	900	1·90	1·58
RM400N, T	1000	2·11	1·76	1100	2·32	1·94

Sparking plug gap

RM50N	0·6 − 0·7 mm (0·024 − 0·028 in)
RM60N	0·6 − 0·7 mm (0·024 − 0·028 in)
RM80N	0·6 − 0·7 mm (0·024 − 0·028 in)
RM50T	0·6 − 0·8 mm (0·024 − 0·031 in)
RM60T	0·6 − 0·8 mm (0·024 − 0·031 in)
RM80T	0·6 − 0·8 mm (0·024 − 0·031 in)
RM100N	0·5 − 0·6 mm (0·020 − 0·024 in)
RM100T	0·5 − 0·6 mm (0·020 − 0·024 in)
RM125N	0·5 − 0·6 mm (0·020 − 0·024 in)
RM125T	0·5 − 0·6 mm (0·020 − 0·024 in)
RM250N	0·5 − 0·6 mm (0·020 − 0·024 in)
RM250T	0·5 − 0·6 mm (0·020 − 0·024 in)
RM400N	0·5 − 0·6 mm (0·020 − 0·024 in)
RM400T	0·5 − 0·6 mm (0·020 − 0·024 in)

Contact breaker gap

RM50N	0·3 − 0·4 mm (0·012 − 0·016 in)
RM50T	0·3 − 0·4 mm (0·012 − 0·016 in)

(Note: remaining models have CDI ignition)

Front fork oil capacity

RM50N, T	65 cc (2·20/2·29 US/Imp fl oz)
RM60N, T	72 cc (2·43/2·58 US/Imp fl oz)
RM80N	150 cc (5·07/5·28 US/Imp fl oz)
RM80T	166 cc (5·61/5·84 US/Imp fl oz)
RM100N, T	270 cc (9·13/9·51 US/Imp fl oz)

All other models, refer to Chapter 4, Section 2

Tyre pressures

    The tyre pressures listed below are intended as a guide to the rider. Pressures can be varied to suit individual preference or particular track conditions. All pressures are measured with the tyre cold.

RM50N, T	11 − 16 psi (0·8 − 1·1 kg cm^2/80 − 100 kPa)
RM60N, T	11 − 16 psi (0·8 − 1·1 kg cm^2/80 − 100 kPa)
RM80N, T	10 − 14 psi (0·7 − 1·0 kg cm^2/70 − 100 kPa)
RM125N, ...	10 − 14 psi (0·7 − 1·0 kg cm^2/70 − 100 kPa)
RM250N, T	10 − 14 psi (0·7 − 1·0 kg cm^2/70 − 100 kPa)
RM400T	10 − 14 psi (0·7 − 1·0 kg cm^2/70 − 100 kPa)
RM100N, T	10 psi (0·7 kg cm^2/70 kPa)
RM125T	10 psi (0·7 kg cm^2/70 kPa)
RM400N	10 psi (0·7 kg cm^2/70 kPa)

Recommended lubricants

Engine . . . . (petroil mixture)
Shell Super M
Castrol R30
Golden Spectro synthetic blend
B.P. Racing
Bel-Ray MC-1
or equivalent

Note: Drain and flush fuel system before changing oil brands or grades.

Gearbox . . . . SAE 20W/50 engine oil

Front forks . . . . SAE 5W/20 or Automatic Transmission Fluid (ATF)

Rear damper units (RM125, 250 and 400T) . . . . Bel-Ray LT100 or equivalent SAE 5 damper oil

Steering head bearings . . . . High melting point grease

Wheel bearings . . . . High melting point grease

Swinging arm pivot . . . . High melting point grease

Brake pivots . . . . High melting point grease

Cables, control pivots, etc . . . . Engine oil or Teflon-based lubricant

Electrical contacts . . . . WD40 aerosol, or equivalent

Chain . . . . Hot immersion lubricant, plus aerosol chain lubricant

Tightening torques

The torque settings given below are of particular importance when dealing with motocross machines. The various nuts and fittings are far more prone to loosening in service than they would be on a road-going motorcycle, due to the extremes of terrain and the consequent vibration and shock loadings. Although the most skilled mechanics can often tighten bolts by feel alone, a torque wrench should be considered essential by most riders. Nuts and bolts should be checked for tightness after each race or event, and the specified torque settings should be adhered to when the machine is overhauled.

Torque settings – engine/gearbox unit

Component/model	lbf ft	kgf cm
Cylinder head nuts:		
RM50N, T	13·0 – 16·0	180 – 220
RM60N, T	13·0 – 16·0	180 – 220
All other models	16·5 – 19·5	230 – 270
Flywheel rotor nut:		
RM80T	14·5 – 18·0	200 – 250
All other models	21·5 – 29·0	300 – 400
Gearbox sprocket nut:		
RM50N, T	21·5 – 36·0	300 – 500
RM60N, T	21·5 – 36·0	300 – 500
RM80N, T	21·5 – 36·0	300 – 500
All other models	29·0 – 43·0	400 – 600
Clutch centre nut:		
RM50N, T	21·5 – 36·0	300 – 500
RM60N, T	21·5 – 36·0	300 – 500
RM80N, T	21·5 – 36·0	300 – 500
RM100N, T	21·5 – 36·0	300 – 500
RM125N	21·5 – 36·0	300 – 500
All other models	29·0 – 43·0	400 – 600
Crankshaft pinion nut:		
RM50N, T	29·0 – 43·0	400 – 600
RM60N, T	29·0 – 43·0	400 – 600
RM80N, T	29·0 – 43·0	400 – 600
RM100N, T	58·0 – 72·0	800 – 1000
RM125N	58·0 – 72·0	800 – 1000
RM125T	65·0 – 72·0	900 – 1000
RM250N, T	36·0 – 50·5	500 – 700
RM400N, T	36·0 – 50·5	500 – 700

Torque settings – frame, forks and wheels

Component/model	lbf ft	kgf cm
Handlebar clamp bolts:		
All models	8·5 – 14·5	120 – 200
Upper yoke pinch bolts:		
RM50N	11·0 – 21·5	150 – 300
RM50T	8·5 – 14·5	120 – 200
RM60N, T	8·5 – 14·5	120 – 200
RM80N, T	8·5 – 14·5	120 – 200
RM100N, T	11·0 – 18·0	150 – 250
All other models	14·5 – 21·5	200 – 300
Lower yoke pinch bolts:		
RM50N, T	14·5 – 21·5	200 – 300
RM60N, T	14·5 – 21·5	200 – 300
RM80N, T	14·5 – 21·5	200 – 300
RM100N, T	18·0 – 21·5	250 – 300
All other models	11·0 – 18·0	150 – 250
Steering stem clamp bolt:*		
All models	11·0 – 18·0	150 – 250
*Not fitted to RM50N, T RM60N, T or RM80N, T.		
Front fork cap bolt:		
RM80N, T	8·5 – 14·5	120 – 200
RM100N, T	25·5 – 36·0	350 – 500
All other models	11·0 – 21·5	150 – 300
Steering stem top bolt:		
RM50N, T	25·5 – 40·0	350 – 550
RM60N, T	25·5 – 40·0	350 – 550
RM80N, T	25·5 – 40·0	350 – 550
All other models	25·5 – 36·0	350 – 500
Front brake arm pinch bolt:		
RM80N	3·0 – 5·0	40 – 70
All other models	3·5 – 6·0	50 – 80

Component/model	lbf ft	kgf cm
Front wheel spindle nut:		
RM50N, T	19·5 – 31·0	270 – 430
RM60N, T	19·5 – 31·0	270 – 430
RM80N, T	19·5 – 31·0	270 – 430
All other models	26·0 – 37·5	360 – 520
Swinging arm pivot:		
RM50N, T	18·0 – 29·0	250 – 400
RM60N, T	18·0 – 29·0	250 – 400
RM80N	18·0 – 29·0	250 – 400
RM80T	32·5 – 50·5	450 – 700
RM100N, T	32·5 – 50·5	450 – 700
RM125N, T	32·5 – 50·5	450 – 700
RM250N, T	36·0 – 58·0	500 – 800
RM400N, T	36·0 – 58·0	500 – 800
Rear suspension mounting (upper):		
RM50N, T	14·5 – 21·5	200 – 300
RM80N	14·5 – 21·5	200 – 300
RM80T	4·5 – 7·0	60 – 100
RM100N, T	7·5 – 11·0	100 – 150
RM125N, T	7·5 – 11·0	100 – 150
RM250N, T	7·5 – 11·0	100 – 150
RM400N, T	7·5 – 11·0	100 – 150
Note: figures for RM60N, T not available		
Rear suspension mounting (lower):		
RM50N, T	14·5 – 21·5	200 – 300
RM60N, T	14·5 – 21·5	200 – 300
RM80N	14·5 – 21·5	200 – 300
RM80T	7·0 – 11·0	100 – 150
RM100N, T	14·5 – 21·5	200 – 300
All other models	7·0 – 11·0	100 – 150
Rear brake torque arm (front):		
RM80N	6·5 – 10·0	90 – 140
All other models	7·5 – 11·0	100 – 150
Rear brake torque arm (rear):		
RM50N, T	7·5 – 11·0	100 – 150
RM60N, T	7·5 – 11·0	100 – 150
RM80N	7·0 – 10·0	90 – 140
RM80T	7·5 – 11·0	100 – 150
All other models	14·5 – 21·5	200 – 300
Rear wheel spindle nut:		
RM50N, T	26·0 – 37·5	360 – 520
RM60N, T	26·0 – 37·5	360 – 520
RM80N, T	26·0 – 37·5	360 – 520
RM100N, T	26·0 – 37·5	360 – 520
All other models	36·0 – 58·0	500 – 800
Rear brake arm pinch bolt:		
RM80N	3·0 – 5·0	40 – 70
All other models	3·5 – 6·0	50 – 80

Additional torque setting information

For nuts and bolts not covered by the main torque settings table above, refer to the table below for bolt diameters and appropriate torque settings

Unmarked bolts, or bolts with "4" marked on head

Bolt diameter (mm)	lbf ft	kgf cm
5	1·5 – 3·0	20 – 40
6	3·0 – 5·0	40 – 70
8	6·5 – 10·0	90 – 140
10	13·0 – 20·0	180 – 280

Bolts marked with Suzuki "S" or number 7

Bolt diameter (mm)	lbf ft	kgf cm
5	2·0 – 4·5	30 – 60
6	5·0 – 7·5	70 – 100
8	14·5 – 18·0	200 – 250
10	25·5 – 29·0	350 – 400

Note: When using a torque wrench calibrated in Newton-metres (N-m) the correct values can be found by dividing the kgf cm figure by a factor of 10. Thus 350 – 400 kgf cm is equal to 35.0 – 40.0 N-m.

Working conditions and tools

When a major overhaul is contemplated, it is important that a clean, well-lit working space is available, equipped with a workbench and vice, and with space for laying out or storing the dismantled assemblies in an orderly manner where they are unlikely to be disturbed. The use of a good workshop will give the satisfaction of work done in comfort and without haste, where there is little chance of the machine being dismantled and reassembled in anything other than clean surroundings. Unfortunately, these ideal working conditions are not always practicable and under these latter circumstances when improvisation is called for, extra care and time will be needed.

The other essential requirement is a comprehensive set of good quality tools. Quality is of prime importance since cheap tools will prove expensive in the long run if they slip or break and damage the components to which they are applied. A good quality tool will last a long time, and more than justify the cost. The basis of any tool kit is a set of open-ended spanners, which can be used on almost any part of the machine to which there is reasonable access. A set of ring spanners makes a useful addition, since they can be used on nuts that are very tight or where access is restricted. Where the cost has to be kept within reasonable bounds, a compromise can be effected with a set of combination spanners — open-ended at one end and having a ring of the same size on the other end. Socket spanners may also be considered a good investment, a basic $\frac{3}{8}$ in or $\frac{1}{2}$ in drive kit comprising a ratchet handle and a small number of socket heads, if money is limited. Additional sockets can be purchased, as and when they are required. Provided they are slim in profile, sockets will reach nuts or bolts that are deeply recessed. When purchasing spanners of any kind, make sure the correct size standard is purchased. Almost all machines manufactured outside the UK and the USA have metric nuts and bolts, whilst those produced in Britain have BSF or BSW sizes. The standard used in the USA is AF, which is also found on some of the later British machines. Other tools that should be included in the kit are a range of crosshead screwdrivers, a pair of pliers and a hammer.

When considering the purchase of tools, it should be remembered that by carrying out the work oneself, a large proportion of the normal repair cost, made up by labour charges, will be saved. The economy made on even a minor overhaul will go a long way towards the improvement of a tool kit.

In addition to the basic tool kit, certain additional tools can prove invaluable when they are close to hand, to help speed up a multitude of repetitive jobs. For example, an impact screwdriver will ease the removal of screws that have been tightened by a similar tool during assembly, without risk of damaging the screw heads. And, of course, it can be used again to retighten the screws, to ensure an oil or airtight seal results. Circlip pliers have their uses too, since gear pinions, shafts and similar components are frequently retained by circlips that are not too easily displaced by a screwdriver. There are two types of circlip pliers, one for internal and one for external circlips. They may also have straight or right-angled jaws.

One of the most useful of all tools is the torque wrench, a form of spanner that can be adjusted to slip when a measured amount of force is applied to any bolt or nut. Torque wrench settings are given in almost every modern workshop or service manual, where the extent is given to which a complex component, such as a cylinder head, can be tightened without fear of distortion or leakage. The tightening of bearing caps is yet another example. Overtightening will stretch or even break bolts, necessitating extra work to extract the broken portions.

As may be expected, the more sophisticated the machine, the greater is the number of tools likely to be required if it is to be kept in first class condition by the home mechanic. Unfortunately there are certain jobs which cannot be accomplished successfully without the correct equipment and although there is invariably a specialist who will undertake the work for a fee, the home mechanic will have to dig more deeply in his pocket for the purchase of similar equipment if he does not wish to employ the services of others. Here a word of caution is necessary, since some of these jobs are best left to the expert. Although an electrical multimeter of the AVO type will prove helpful in tracing electrical faults, in inexperienced hands it may irrevocably damage some of the electrical components if a test current is passed through them in the wrong direction. This can apply to the synchronisation of twin or multiple carburettors too, where a certain amount of expertise is needed when setting them up with vacuum gauges. These are, however, exceptions. Some instruments, such as a strobe lamp, are virtually essential when checking the timing of a machine powered by a CDI ignition system. In short, do not purchase any of these special items unless you have the experience to use them correctly.

Although this manual shows how components can be removed and replaced without the use of special service tools (unless absolutely essential), it is worthwhile giving consideration to the purchase of the more commonly used tools if the machine is regarded as a long term purchase. Whilst the alternative methods suggested will remove and replace parts without risk of damage, the use of the special tools recommended and sold by the manufacturer will invariably save time.

Chapter 1 Engine, clutch and gearbox

Contents

Specifications

Engine

Type	Single cylinder air-cooled two-stroke
Bore:	
RM50N,T	41.0 mm (1.614 in)
RM60N,T	42.0 mm (1.654 in)
RM80N,T	49.0 mm (1.929 in)
RM100N,T	50.0 mm (1.969 in)
RM125N,T	54.0 mm (2.126 in)
RM250N,T	67.0 mm (2.640 in)
RM400N,T	80.0 mm (3.150 in)
Stroke:	
RM50N,T	37.8 mm (1.488 in)
RM60N,T	42.0 mm (1.654 in)
RM80N,T	42.0 mm (1.654 in)
RM100N,T	50.0 mm (1.969 in)
RM125N,T	54.0 mm (2.126 in)
RM250N,T	70.0 mm (2.760 in)
RM400N,T	83.0 mm (3.268 in)

Displacement:
RM50N,T . . . .   49 cc (3.0 cu in)
RM60N,T . . . .   58 cc (3.5 cu in)
RM80N,T . . . .   79 cc (4.8 cu in)
RM100N,T . . . .   98 cc (6.0 cu in)
RM125N,T . . . .   123 cc (7.5 cu in)
RM250N,T . . . .   246 cc (15.0 cu in)
RM400N,T . . . .   417 cc (25.4 cu in)

Compression ratio:
RM50N,T 7.4:1
RM60N 7.4:1
RM60T 7.9:1
RM80N 8.2:1
RM80T 8.1:1
RM100N,T 8.5:1
RM125N 8.0:1
RM125T 8.1:1
RM250N 7.7:1
RM250T 7.9:1
RM400N 7.3:1
RM400T 6.9:1

Pistons and rings

Piston to cylinder bore clearance
RM50N,T . . . .   0.065 – 0.075 mm (0.0026 – 0.0030 in)
RM400N,T . . . .   0.070 – 0.080 mm (0.0028 – 0.0031 in)
All other models . . . .   0.060 – 0.070 mm (0.0024 – 0.0028 in)

Piston ring end gap (ring installed in bore) – nominal
RM50N,T . . . .   0.10 – 0.25 mm (0.004 – 0.010 in)
RM60N,T . . . .   0.10 – 0.30 mm (0.004 – 0.012 in)
RM80N . . . .   0.10 – 0.25 mm (0.004 – 0.010 in)
RM100N,T . . . .   0.15 – 0.35 mm (0.006 – 0.014 in)
RM125N,T . . . .   0.15 – 0.35 mm (0.006 – 0.014 in)
RM250N,T . . . .   0.20 – 0.40 mm (0.008 – 0.016 in)
RM400N,T . . . .   0.20 – 0.40 mm (0.008 – 0.016 in)

Piston ring end gap (ring installed in bore) – wear limit
RM50N,T . . . .   0.75 mm (0.030 in)
RM60N,T . . . .   0.75 mm (0.030 in)
RM80N . . . .   0.75 mm (0.030 in)
RM80T . . . .   2.00 mm (0.080 in)
RM100N,T . . . .   0.80 mm (0.031 in)
RM125N,T . . . .   0.80 mm (0.031 in)
RM250N,T . . . .   0.85 mm (0.033 in)
RM400N,T . . . .   0.85 mm (0.033 in)

Note: no nominal figure available for RM80T

Clutch

Type . . . .   Wet, multiplate (all models)

No of plates:	Plain	Friction
RM50N,T	2	3
RM60N,T	4	5
RM80N,T	4	5
RM100N,T	5	6
RM125N,T	5	6
RM250N,T	4	5
RM400N,T	5	6

Friction plate thickness:	nominal	wear limit
All models	2.9 – 3.1 mm (0.114–0.123 in)	2.6 mm (0.10 in)

Plain plate thickness:	nominal	wear limit
RM50N,T	1.6 mm (0.063 in)	1.5 mm (0.060 in)
RM60N,T	1.6 mm (0.063 in)	1.5 mm (0.060 in)
RM80N,T	1.6 mm (0.063 in)	1.5 mm (0.060 in)
RM100N,T	1.6 mm (0.063 in)	1.5 mm (0.060 in)
RM125N,T	1.5–1.7 mm (0.059 – 0.067)	N/A
RM250N,T	2.0 mm (0.079 in)	N/A
RM400N,T	1.9–2.1 mm (0.075–0.083 in)	N/A

Plain plate maximum warpage:
All models . . . .   0.1 mm (0.004 in)

Primary drive

Type	Gear – all models

Primary reduction ratio:

RM50N,T	3.842:1 (73/19)
RM60N,T	3.842:1 (73/19)
RM80N,T	3.842:1 (73/19)
RM100N,T	3.444:1 (62/18)
RM125N,T	3.157:1 (60/90)
RM250N,T	2.727:1 (60/22)
RM400N	2.384:1 (62.26)

Gearbox

	RM50N,T	RM60 and 80 N,T	RM100 and 125 N,T	RM250N,T	RM400N,T
Type		Constant mesh, all models			
No. of gears	5-speed	6-speed	6-speed	5-speed	5-speed

Ratios: (Pinion tooth ratios shown in brackets):

	RM50N,T	RM60 and 80 N,T	RM100 and 125 N,T	RM250N,T	RM400N,T
1st gear	2.333:1 (35/15)	2.571:1 (36/14)	2.333:1 (28/12)	2.076:1 (27/13)	2.000:1 (28/14)
2nd gear	1.684:1 (32/19)	1.889:1 (34/18)	1.750:1 (28/16)	1.750:1 (28.16)	1.625:1 (26/16)
3rd gear	1.318:1 (29/22)	1.500:1 (30/20)	1.411:1 (24/17)	1.352:1 (23/17)	1.263:1 (24/19)
4th gear	1.083:1 (26/24)	1.250:1 (25/20)	1.190:1 (25/21)	1.105:1 (21/19)	1.000:1 (21/21)
5th gear	0.923:1 (24/26)	1.083:1 (26/24)	1.045:1 (23/22)	0.913:1 (21/23)	0.869:1 (20/23)
6th gear	–	0.961:1 (25/26)	0.956:1 (22/23)	–	–

Final reduction ratio

50N,T	3.500:1
60N	3.666:1
60T	3.500:1
80N,T	3.425:1
100N	4.692:1
100T	4.769:1
125N	4.538:1
125T	4.250:1
250N	3.571:1
250T	3.500:1
400N,T	3.500:1

Selector fork to groove clearances:	RM50N,T	RM60 and 80N,T	RM100 and 125N,T	RM250 and 400N,T
3rd (mainshaft)	0.10 – 0.30 mm (0.004 – 0.012 in)	N/A	0.05 – 0.25 mm (0.002 – 0.010 in)	0.20 – 0.40 mm (0.008 – 0.016 in)
Wear limit	0.50 mm (0.020 in)		0.45 mm (0.018 in)	0.6 mm (0.024 in)
3rd/4th (mainshaft)	N/A	0.10 – 0.30 mm (0.004 – 0.012 in)	N/A	N/A
Wear limit		0.50 mm (0.020 in)		
4th (layshaft)	0.10 – 0.30 mm (0.004 – 0.012 in)	N/A	N/A	0.40 – 0.60 mm (0.016 – 0.024 in)
Wear limit	0.50 mm (0.020 in)			0.8 mm (0.031 in)
5th (layshaft)	0.10 – 0.30 mm (0.004 – 0.012 in)	0.10 – 0.30 mm (0.004 – 0.012 in)	0.05 to 0.25 mm (0.002 – 0.010 in)	0.20 – 0.40 mm (0.008 – 0.016 in)
Wear limit	0.50 mm (0.020 in)	0.50 mm (0.020 in)	0.45 mm (0.018 in)	0.6 mm (0.024 in)
6th layshaft	N/A	0.10 – 0.30 mm (0.004 – 0.012 in)	0.05 – 0.25 mm (0.002 – 0.010 in)	N/A
Wear limit		0.50 mm (0.020 in)	0.45 mm (0.018 in)	

Note: N/A indicates not applicable to this model

Mainshaft cluster assembly length	76 mm (2.992 in)	87.5 mm (3.445 in)	N/A	N/A

1 General description

The seven Suzuki RM models each employ a simple single-cylinder air-cooled two-stroke engine. The various units share a common basic layout, although there are sufficient detail differences between them to preclude parts interchangeability. Each engine is of unit construction, the gearbox components being housed in a separate chamber integral with the crankcase castings.

The crankshaft assembly is supported on a caged ball main bearing at each end, and consists of two full flywheels. The big-end and small-end bearings are of the caged needle roller type.

The cylinder barrel carries a reed valve assembly which is used as a supplementary means of controlling the induction timing, in addition to the conventional piston-porting method.

All models employ a conventional multi-plate clutch, running in an oil bath behind the right-hand engine casing. The clutch outer drum incorporates a large helical gear, forming part of the primary drive train. Drive from the crankshaft is transmitted to the clutch outer drum, and thence through the clutch to the gearbox mainshaft.

The gearbox is of the conventional constant mesh type running in an oil bath. The RM50, RM250 and RM400 models employ a five-speed arrangement, whilst the RM60, RM80, RM100 and RM125 each utilise a six-speed gearbox.

2   Operations with the engine in the frame

It is not necessary to remove the engine unit from the frame unless attention to the crankshaft assembly or gearbox internals require attention. Most other operations are easily accomplished with the engine in place, such as:

1   Removal and replacement of the cylinder head
2   Removal and replacement of the cylinder barrel and piston
3   Removal and replacement of the flywheel rotor
4   Removal and replacement of the clutch assembly
5   Removal and replacement of the gearbox selector shaft

Where a number of operations are to be undertaken simultaneously, as in the case of a full engine overhaul, it is advantageous to remove the engine unit to permit full dismantling on the workbench.

3   Removing the engine/gearbox unit

1   Before any dismantling work is undertaken, the machine should be thoroughly cleaned and any accumulation of mud removed from the underside of the frame and crankcase. It will be necessary to construct some sort of stand for the machine, and this can range from a stout wooden or plastic crate beneath the lower frame tubes, to a properly constructed tubular steel stand. A reasonable compromise would be a pair of car axle stands supporting a length of timber positioned beneath the frame. Make sure that the arrangement is secure and that the machine cannot topple whilst it is being worked on, and that the stand does not obscure any engine mounting or drain bolts. It is useful, but not essential, to raise the machine to a convenient working height by placing it on a low bench or table.
2   The seat and fuel tank should be removed to permit better access to the engine unit. The seat is retained by two bolts which pass through lugs into the frame. The bolts should be removed and the seat lifted away. Check that the fuel tap is off, then prise off the fuel pipe at the carburettor. Slacken the single bolt or release the strap which secures the rear of the tank to the frame. On RM50, RM60 and RM80 models, the tank is retained by two rubber blocks at the front, and can be removed by lifting the rear of the tank and pulling it back to disengage it from the mounting blocks.
3   In the case of the larger models, a more secure and complicated arrangement is used, in which the tank is located by two L-shaped brackets and rubber mounting washers. It is best to remove the brackets along with the tank, because this will permit better working access, and entails less work. Each bracket is secured by a single bolt which passes through a rubber block and metal spacer. Remove the bolts noting the order in which the various parts are fitted. The fuel tank can now be lifted clear of the frame and placed to one side.
4   The plastic side panels are engaged with the frame tubes by means of small lugs, and are secured by screws. Release the screws and disengage the side panels from the machine. Unhook the springs which retain the exhaust pipe to the cylinder barrel. These springs are fairly strong and may require the use of a self-locking wrench to dislodge them. The manufacturer's tool for this job consists of a stiff wire hook with a T-handle, which can easily be made up in the workshop if required. Remove the silencer retaining bolt, and release the springs or clamp which secures the end of the silencer to the spark arrester. The latter can be left attached to the frame, and the silencer/exhaust pipe unit disengaged from the frame.
5   Unscrew the carburettor mixing chamber top, and withdraw the throttle valve assembly. It is not necessary to disconnect the cable from the throttle valve unless specific attention is required, and it can be conveniently lodged around the top frame tube, clear of the engine. Slacken the two hose clips which secure the carburettor to the intake adaptor and air cleaner hoses. The carburettor may prove reluctant to come free

of the hoses, and a certain amount of force may need to be exerted to disengage it. If necessary, remove the air cleaner element and displace the connecting hose inwards to aid carburettor removal. On machines with remote reservoir rear suspension units, slacken the reservoir mounting clamps and swivel them clear of the carburettor to provide adequate clearance.
6   On RM50, RM60 and RM80 machines, remove the gear change pedal, then release the four screws which secure the left-hand engine casing. The casing can be lifted away to expose the gearbox sprocket. On the larger models, release the three screws which secure the sprocket cover to the crankcase. Before the drive chain is disconnected, it should be noted that it is convenient to slacken the sprocket retaining nut if it is considered likely that this will require attention at a later stage. Knock back the tab washer, then apply the rear brake to prevent the sprocket from moving whilst the nut is slackened.
7   Turn the wheel until the drive chain joining link is located. Use a pair of pliers to displace the spring clip, then remove the side plate and slide the joining link apart. The joining link should be reassembled on one end of the chain to prevent its subsequent loss. The chain may now be run off the sprockets and placed to one side.
8   Slacken off the clutch cable adjuster, and disconnect the cable at the engine end. This can be achieved by releasing the pinch bolt which secures the operating arm to its splined shaft. The arm can then be pulled off together with the clutch cable. Trace the ignition system wiring from the engine unit, separating it at the connector block.
9   The engine unit on RM50, RM60 and RM80 models is secured by three bolts. At the front, a single bolt passes through a lug welded to the frame, whilst at the rear of the unit, an upper and lower bolt are used. The RM100 and RM125 models employ separate engine plates at the front of the unit, secured by a total of four bolts. The engine plates must be removed to allow engine removal. In the case of the RM250 and RM400 models, the arrangement is similar to the latter models, with an additional bolt which passes through a central lug on the underside of the unit, making a total of six bolts on the RM250, which has a three-bolt front engine plate, and seven bolts in the case of the RM400.
10   Slacken and remove the engine mounting nuts and bolts, dismantling the front engine plates where fitted. The engine unit will now rest on the frame cradle, and can be lifted out by one person without undue difficulty. Before any further dismantling takes place, clean off any remaining caked mud before cleaning the unit as described in the next Section. If the right-hand casing is to be removed, slacken and remove the gearbox drain plug from the underside of the engine unit. Allow the oil to drain completely, then refit the drain plug to exclude any dirt.

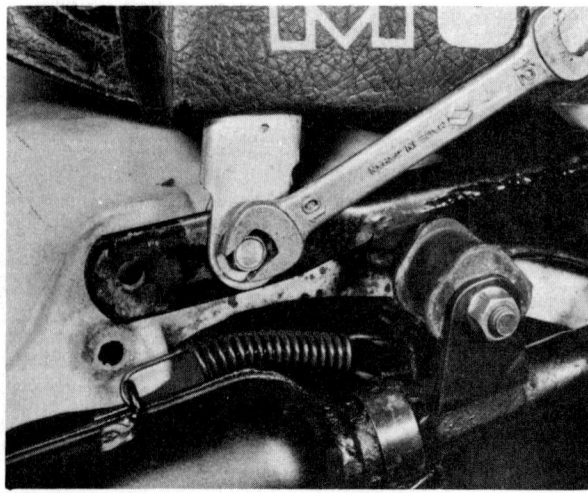

3.2a Seat is secured by bolts at rear (RM80)

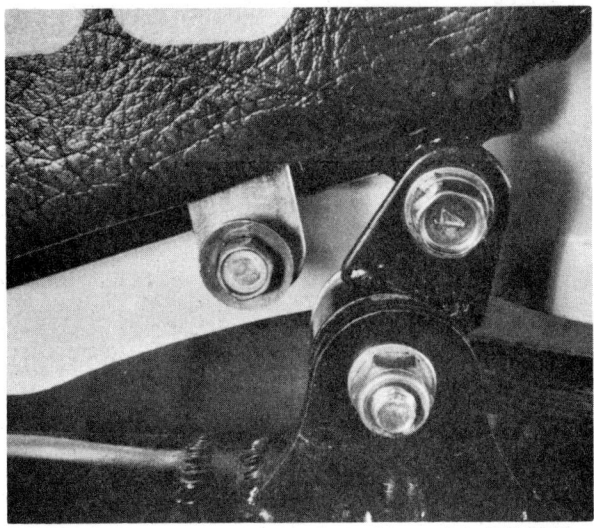
3.2b Similar arrangements is used on other models (RM100)

3.2c Hook engages on frame brace tube (RM400)

3.2d Rear of tank is held by bolt (RM80) ...

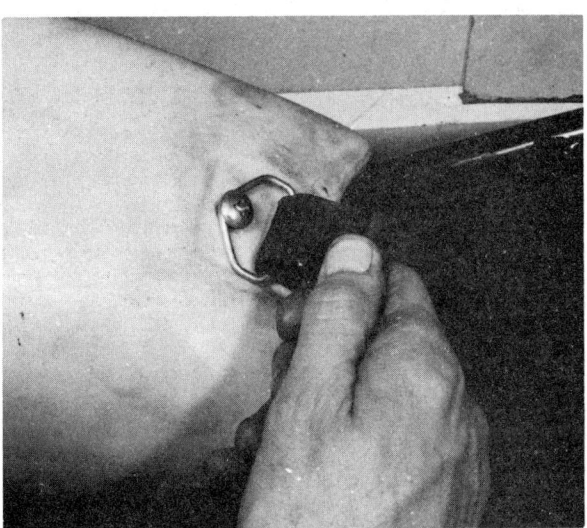
3.2e ... or by rubber strap (RM400)

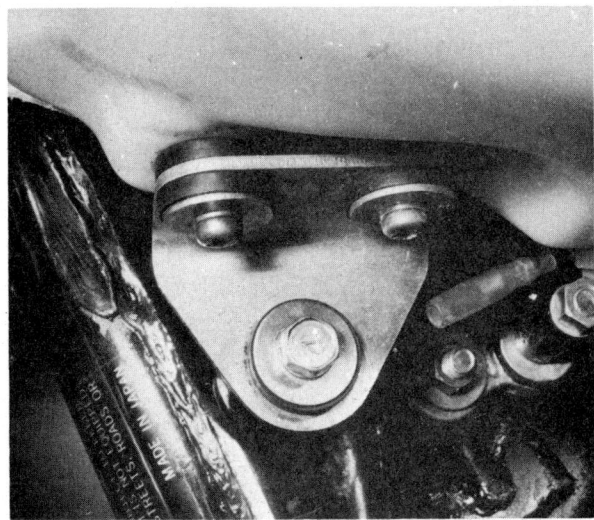
3.3 Release retaining bolts at front of tank (RM400)

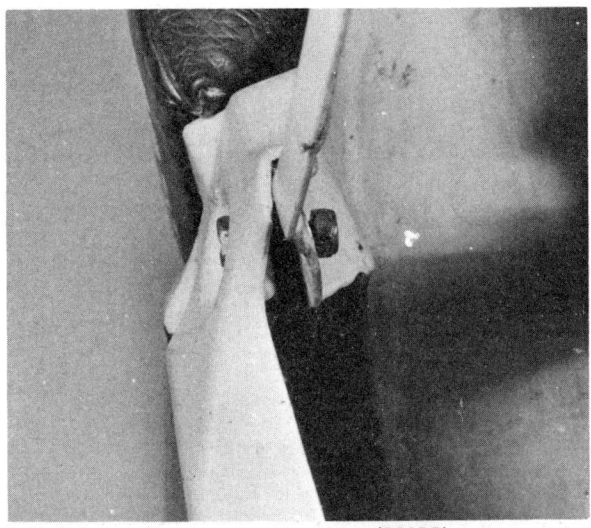
3.4a Side panels are retained by screws (RM80)

3.4b Exhaust pipe is retained by springs (RM80)

3.4c Similar arrangement is used on other models (RM400)

3.4d Link secures exhaust system to frame (RM100)

3.4e Springs hold spark arrester to exhaust (RM400)

3.5a Remove mixing chamber top and withdraw valve (RM400)

3.5b Disengage carburettor from mounting stubs (RM400)

3.8a Slacken clutch cable adjuster and release cable (RM400)

3.8b Unscrew lower adjuster from crankcase (RM400)

3.8c Release cable and arm after slackening bolt (RM400)

3.8d Other models use similar arrangement (RM80)

3.9a Front of engine is secured as shown (RM80)

3.9b Engine upper rear mounting bolt (RM80)

3.9c Engine lower mounting bolt (RM80)

3.9d Engine front mounting plates (RM100)

3.9e Engine upper rear mounting bolt (RM400)

3.9f RM400 engine front mounting plates

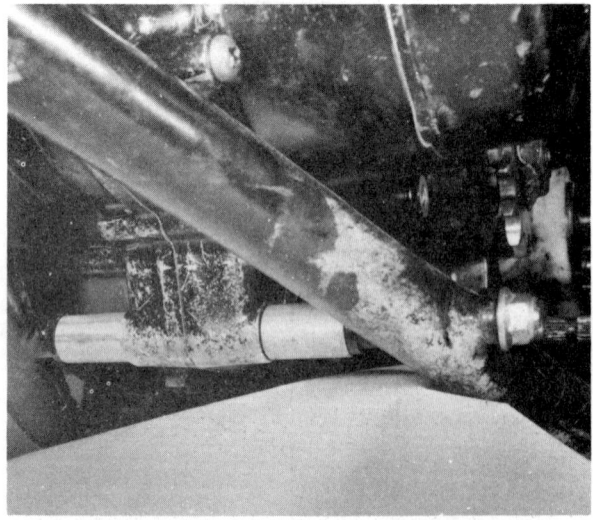

3.9g Note spacers on lower mounting bolt (RM400)

3.10 Engine is now ready for removal (RM80)

4 Dismantling the engine and gearbox: general

1 Before commencing work on the engine unit, the external surfaces should be cleaned thoroughly. A motorcycle engine has very little protection from grit and other foreign matter, which will find its way into the dismantled engine if this simple precaution is not taken. One of the proprietary cleaning compounds such as Gunk or Jizer can be used to good effect, particularly if the compound is permitted to work into the film of oil and grease before it is washed away. Special care is necessary when washing down to prevent water from entering the now exposed parts of the engine unit.

2 Never use undue force to remove any stubborn part unless specific mention is made of this requirement. There is invariably good reason why a part is difficult to remove often because the dismantling operation has been tackled in the wrong sequence. Dismantling will be made easier if a simple engine stand is constructed to correspond with the engine mounting points. This arrangement will permit the complete engine unit to be clamped rigidly to the workbench, leaving both hands free.

5 Dismantling the engine unit: removing the cylinder head, barrel and piston

1 The procedure for removing the cylinder head is the same for each model, with the exception that the RM50, RM60 and RM80 models employ four holding studs, whilst the remainder are fitted with six. The cylinder head nuts should be slackened progressively in a diagonal sequence to avoid any possibility of warping the cylinder head jointing face. The cylinder head can now be lifted away.

2 It will be noted that on RM50, RM60 and RM80 models, the cylinder barrel is retained by a total of six studs, four of which are also used to retain the cylinder head. The two remaining studs are located at the rear of the cylinder barrel, and the retaining nuts should be slackened and removed to allow the cylinder barrel to be lifted clear. On the remaining models, separate cylinder head and cylinder barrel studs are used, and in consequence, six securing nuts arranged around the cylinder base must be removed before the barrel can be lifted clear.

3 Lift the barrel upwards, taking care to support the piston as it emerges from the cylinder bore. It is recommended that some rag is packed into the crankcase mouth to prevent any debris or pieces of broken ring from dropping into the crankcase. When the cylinder barrel has been lifted clear, place it upside down to prevent accidental damage to the reed valve unit which is attached to the underside of the base flange.

4 Using a small screwdriver in the slot provided, prise out the circlips at each end of the gudgeon pin bore. The gudgeon pin

can often be pushed out of position by hand, but if it proves to be a tight fit, resist the temptation to drift it out as this can easily damage the connecting rod if not supported correctly. A simple drawbolt arrangement can be made up using a long bolt and nut, a spacer with an internal diameter larger than the gudgeon pin, and a few washers. This can then be used to draw the pin free without risk of damage to the connecting rod or bearings. With the piston removed, the small end needle roller bearing can be displaced.

6 Dismantling the engine unit: removing the flywheel magneto – RM50

1 The RM50 remains the only model in the range to retain the use of a flywheel magneto/contact breaker system for ignition purposes. It should be noted before work commences, that a puller of some sort will be required to effect the removal of the rotor. Because this will be required on a number of occasions during the machine's life, it is recommended that a suitable tool is purchased. The manufacturer's service tool takes the form of a slide hammer and an adaptor to fit the rotor boss, but its purchase price will make it an unrealistic buy for home use. A suitable legged puller will do almost as well, and these are easily obtained from tool stockists and accessory shops. Make sure that the puller legs will engage in the slots in the outer face of the rotor, as many proprietary pullers will be too large for this.

2 Remove the left-hand casing by releasing its four securing screws, if this has not been done already. Before the rotor nut is slackened, it will be necessary to devise some means of preventing the crankshaft from rotating. If the engine is still in the frame, select top gear and apply the rear brake, thus locking the crankshaft via the drive train. With the engine partly dismantled on the workbench, a round bar can be passed through the connecting rod eye, and arranged to rest on wooden blocks placed on either side of the crankcase mouth.

3 Slacken the rotor nut until the top of the nut is flush with the end of the crankshaft. Assemble the puller, ensuring that the puller legs are in no danger of fouling or breaking any of the stator components. Gradually tighten the puller bolt to place the rotor under tension. If the rotor does not draw off easily, try tapping the centre bolt to jar the taper free. It should not be necessary to use excessive force during this operation, and care must be taken not to damage the crankshaft end. Once the taper joint has broken, remove the securing nut completely and lift the rotor away.

4 The stator assembly is retained by a total of three screws arranged around its periphery. Slacken these screws, and lift the stator away from the crankcase. The leads from the stator pass through a rubber grommet at the top of the casing and should be disengaged as the stator is lifted away.

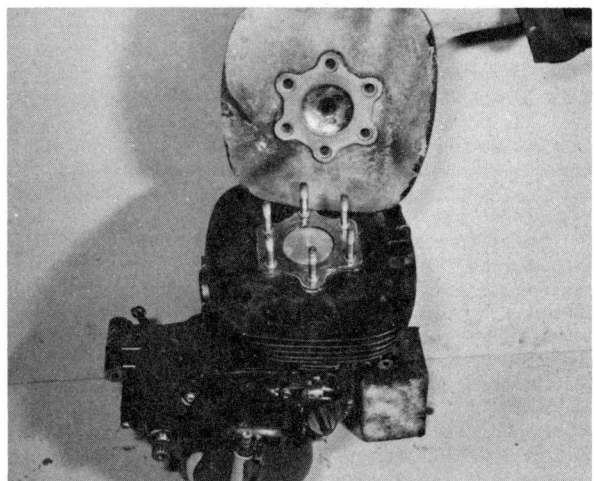

5.1 Cylinder head is retained by four or six studs (RM100)

5.2 Slacken cylinder flange nuts and remove barrel (RM100)

5.4 Displace gudgeon pin to free piston (RM400)

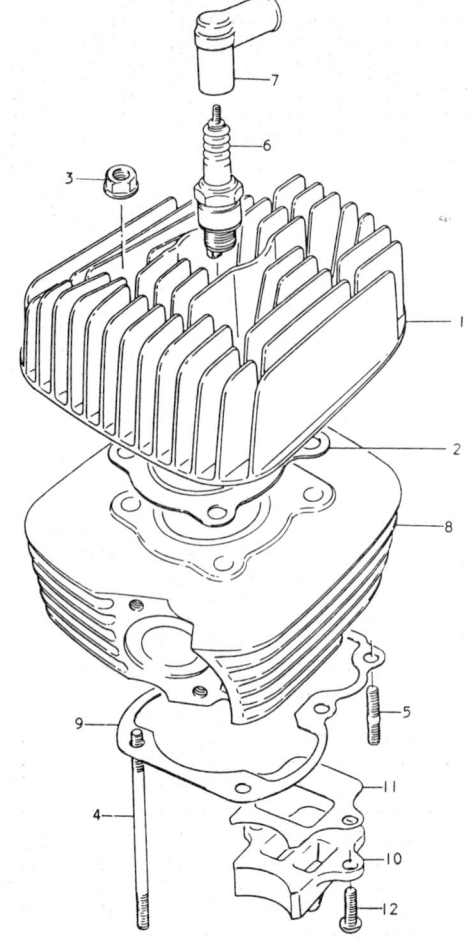

Fig. 1.2 Cylinder head and barrel – RM50 model

1   Cylinder head   7   Suppressor cap
2   Cylinder head gasket   8   Cylinder barrel
3   Nut – 6 off   9   Cylinder base gasket
4   Stud bolt – 4 off   10   Reed valve assembly
5   Stud bolt – 2 off   11   Reed valve assembly gasket
6   Sparking plug   12   Screw – 2 off

7   Dismantling the engine unit: removing the CDI stator and rotor – all models except RM50

1   As mentioned in the previous Section, all models except the RM50 make use of CDI ignition systems. The CDI stator and rotor are housed beneath the left-hand outer cover, which should be removed to gain access.

2   Slacken and remove the stator securing screws and lift the stator assembly clear. The ignition coil leads pass through a grommet in the casing, and this should be displaced as the stator is withdrawn.

3   Immobilise the crankshaft by one of the methods described in paragraph 2 of the preceding Section, then slacken and remove the rotor securing nut. The manufacturer's tool for removing the rotor consists of a slide hammer with an adaptor which fits the two or three threaded holes in the outer face of the rotor. In the absence of this, a conventional legged puller may be used, or a simple extractor made up in the following manner.

4   Obtain a piece of stout steel plate about $\frac{1}{4}$ in thick, and drill two or three holes, as appropriate, to correspond with those in the rotor. Fit suitable bolts through the holes and check that they will retain the plate when screwed into the rotor. Mark and

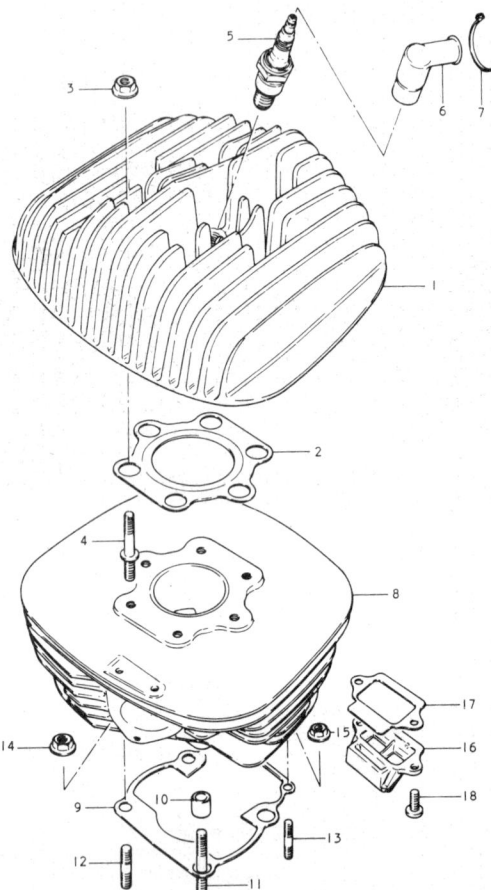

Fig. 1.1 Cylinder head and barrel – RM125 model

1   Cylinder head   10   Dowel pin – 2 off
2   Cylinder head gasket   11   Stud – 2 off
3   Nut – 6 off   12   Stud – 2 off
4   Stud – 6 off   13   Stud – 2 off
5   Sparking plug   14   Nut – 4 off
6   Suppressor cap   15   Nut – 2 off
7   Cable tie   16   Reed valve assembly
8   Cylinder barrel   17   Gasket
9   Cylinder base gasket   18   Screw – 2 off

drill a larger central hole to suit an extractor bolt. Find a suitably sized bolt and nut, grinding a taper on the bolt end to locate it in the machined centre of the crankshaft., To finish the job off, tack weld the nut to the plate. See the accompanying sketch for details.

5 Arrange the puller on the rotor, and screw down the central bolt to draw the rotor off its taper. If it refuses to draw off easily, apply pressure with the centre bolt, then tap is lightly to jar the rotor free. Grasp the Woodruff key with pliers and pull it out of its keyway, placing it with the rotor for safe keeping.

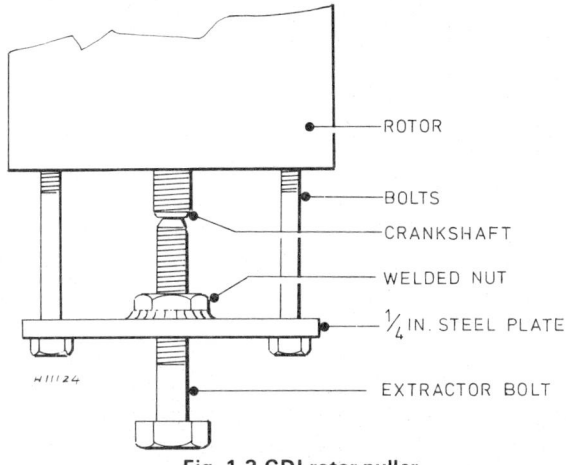

Fig. 1.3 CDI rotor puller

8 Dismantling the engine unit: removing the gearbox sprocket

1 If the dismantling work is being carried out as a precursor to crankcase separation, the gearbox sprocket should be removed at this juncture. With the engine in position in the frame, it is easiest to release the sprocket retaining nut with the chain in place and the rear brake applied, as described in Section 3.6 of this Chapter.

2 With the engine on the workbench, the sprocket can be prevented from rotating by locking the crankshaft with a bar passed through the connecting rod eye, and selecting top gear. Alternatively, loop the drive chain around the sprocket and clamp the ends with a self-locking wrench. Knock back the locking tab, and slacken and remove the securing nut, washer and spacer.

7.3 Rotor may be restrained as shown (RM100)

8.2a Slacken nut to release sprocket (RM50)

8.2b Seal can be renewed after spacer has been withdrawn (RM100)

9 Dismantling the engine unit: removing the clutch and crankshaft pinion

1 Slacken the retaining screws which secure the right-hand outer cover to the crankcase, having first disconnected the clutch arm if this is still in position. The cover may now be lifted away. Note that some residual transmission oil may be released, and some provision must be made to catch this.

2 If it is necessary to remove the crankshaft pinion whilst the engine is still in the frame, this operation should be attended to before the clutch is removed. Knock back the tab washer which locks the crankshaft nut. If the drive chain and sprocket are still in position, select top gear and apply the rear brake. This will effectively immobilise the gearbox and primary drive, allowing the nut to be removed. An alternative method, which is less satisfactory, is to wedge some rag between the primary gear teeth, effectively jamming the primary drive. If this method is unavoidable, take care not to strain any of the components concerned. If a full stripdown is being undertaken, the nut can be slackened after locking the crankshaft with a bar passed through the connecting rod eye, as described earlier in this Chapter.

3 The clutches employed on the various models differ in detail. The unit fitted to the RM50, RM60 and RM80 and that

of the RM250 and RM400 have conventional compression springs, the cover being secured by five screws in the case of the two smaller models, and six on the larger machines. In the case of the RM100 and RM125, tension springs are used, these being anchored by pins at the clutch cover, or pressure plate.

4   To remove the clutch cover, release the retaining bolts in a diagonal sequence, then remove the springs and lift the cover away. On RM100 and RM125 machines, the springs should be pulled upwards to allow the anchor pins to be pulled out, using pointed nose pliers. The manufacturer produces a tool for this purpose, consisting of a stiff wire hook with a T-handle. This is a useful addition to the toolkit, and is easily fabricated in the workshop.

5   With the clutch cover released, remove the clutch friction and plain plates as an assembly, and place them to one side. To hold the clutch centre whilst the retaining nut is slackened, the manufacturer produces an elaborate holding tool which will usually be unavailable to most owners. In its absence, a simple but effective device can be made up using an L-shaped steel strip secured to the clutch centre by means of a large worm drive hose clip, as shown in the accompanying diagram.

6   Slacken and remove the clutch centre nut, then lift away the clutch centre. Note the thrustwasher which is fitted between the clutch centre and the outer drum, taking care not to lose it. Remove the clutch outer drum, and place it to one side along with the rest of the clutch components.

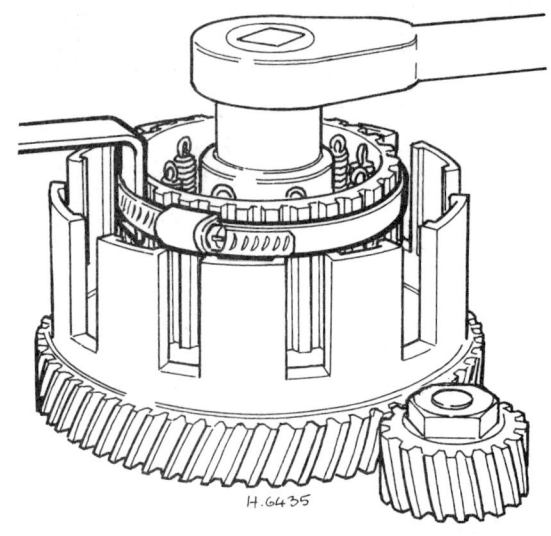

Fig. 1.4 Clutch centre holding arrangement

9.1 Release screws and lift outer cover away (RM80)

9.3a Clutch cover is retained by screws ... (RM80)

9.3b ... or by tension springs and pins (RM100)

9.4 Use wire hook to release tension on pins (RM100)

9.5a Clutch plates should be removed as shown (RM100)

9.5b Slacken clutch centre nut and remove centre (RM80)

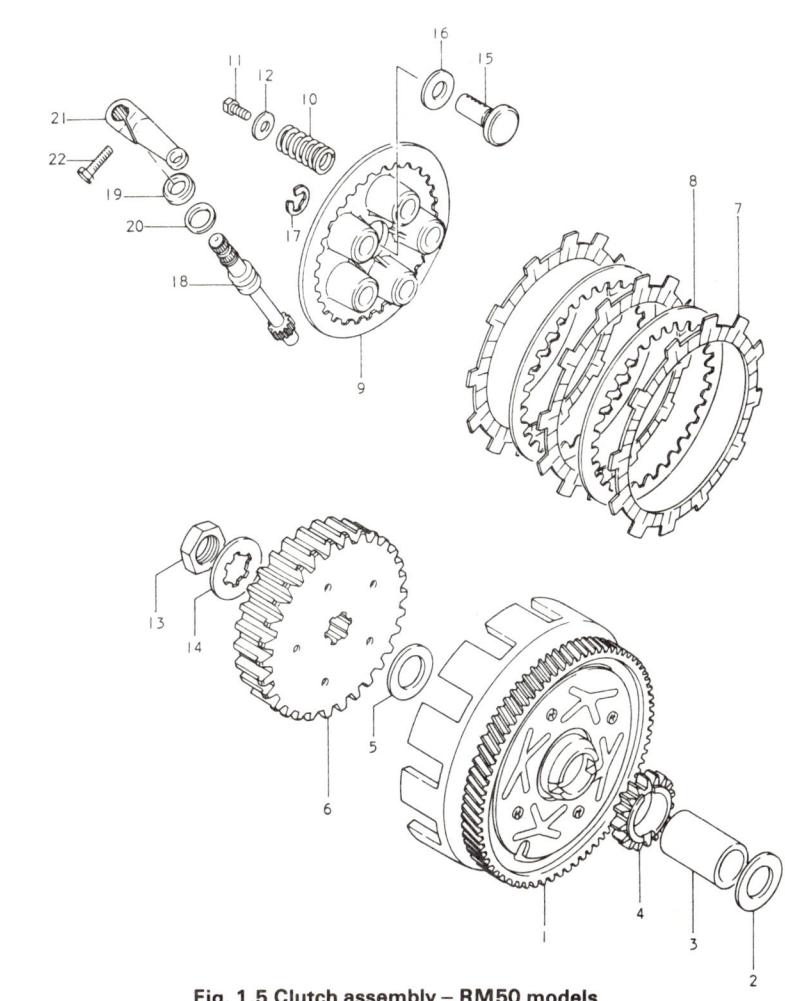

Fig. 1.5 Clutch assembly – RM50 models

1	Primary driven gear	7	Clutch plate – friction (3 off)	13	Nut	18	Clutch release shaft
2	Thrust washer	8	Clutch plate – plain (2 off)	14	Tab washer	19	Oil seal
3	Spacer	9	Clutch pressure plate	15	Clutch release piece	20	Washer
4	Kickstarter drive gear	10	Spring – 5 off	16	Thrust bearing	21	Clutch operating arm
5	Thrust washer	11	Bolt – 5 off	17	Circlip	22	Pinch bolt
6	Clutch centre	12	Washer – 5 off				

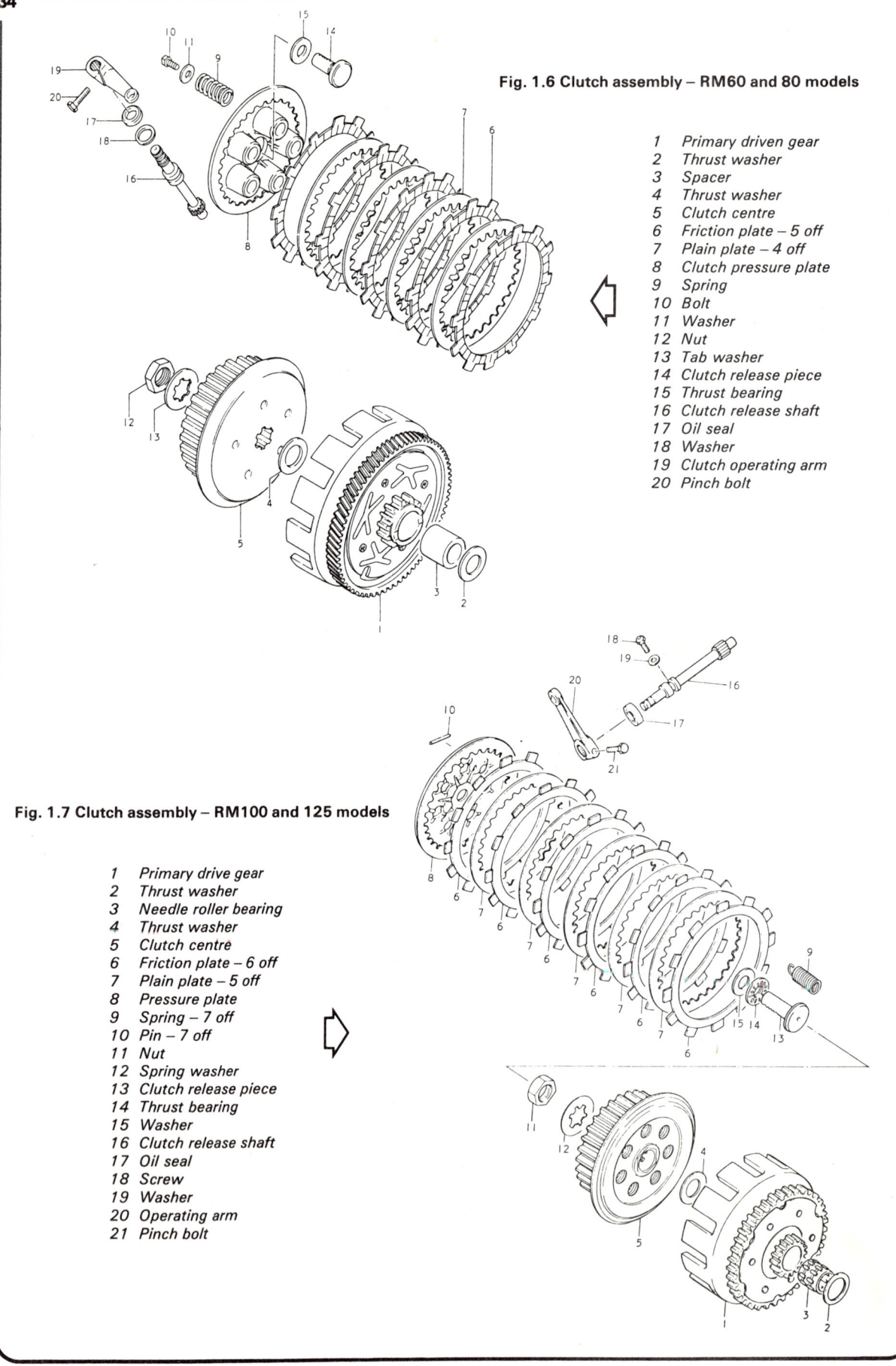

Fig. 1.6 Clutch assembly – RM60 and 80 models

1   Primary driven gear
2   Thrust washer
3   Spacer
4   Thrust washer
5   Clutch centre
6   Friction plate – 5 off
7   Plain plate – 4 off
8   Clutch pressure plate
9   Spring
10 Bolt
11 Washer
12 Nut
13 Tab washer
14 Clutch release piece
15 Thrust bearing
16 Clutch release shaft
17 Oil seal
18 Washer
19 Clutch operating arm
20 Pinch bolt

Fig. 1.7 Clutch assembly – RM100 and 125 models

1   Primary drive gear
2   Thrust washer
3   Needle roller bearing
4   Thrust washer
5   Clutch centre
6   Friction plate – 6 off
7   Plain plate – 5 off
8   Pressure plate
9   Spring – 7 off
10 Pin – 7 off
11 Nut
12 Spring washer
13 Clutch release piece
14 Thrust bearing
15 Washer
16 Clutch release shaft
17 Oil seal
18 Screw
19 Washer
20 Operating arm
21 Pinch bolt

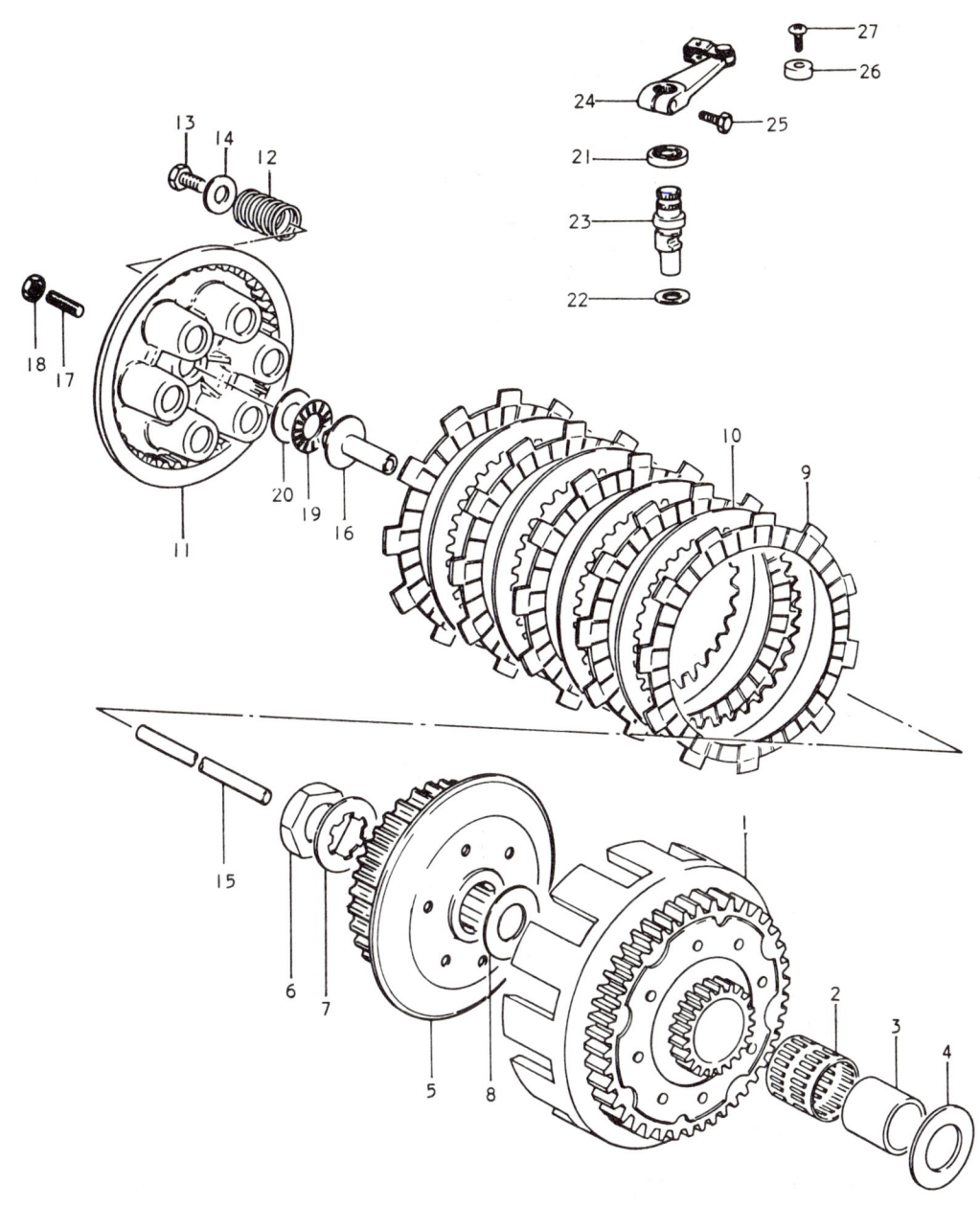

Fig. 1.8 Clutch assembly – RM250 and 400 models

1	Primary driven gear	10	Plain plate – 4 off	19	Thrust bearing
2	Needle roller bearing	11	Pressure plate	20	Thrust washer
3	Spacer	12	Spring – 6 off	21	Oil seal
4	Thrust washer	13	Bolt – 6 off	22	Washer
5	Clutch centre	14	Washer – 6 off	23	Releasing cam
6	Nut	15	Push rod	24	Clutch operating lever
7	Tab washer	16	Push rod end piece	25	Pinch bolt
8	Thrust washer	17	Adjusting screw	26	Washer
9	Friction plate – 5 off	18	Locknut	27	Screw

10 Dismantling the engine unit: removing the gear selector and kickstart mechanisms – RM50, RM60 and RM80

1   If the spacer and kickstart driven pinion remained in position when the clutch assembly was removed, these should be slid off the gearbox mainshaft. Using circlip pliers, release the circlip and plain washer which retain the kickstart idler pinion, and remove the pinion from the end of the layshaft. The kickstart pinion can now be removed by turning it clockwise. The kickstart shaft and spring cannot be removed until the crankcase halves have been separated.

2   Prise off the E-clip which secures the gear selector claw to its pivot. The claw can now be disengaged from the pins in the selector drum, and lifted clear. Remove the shouldered bolt which retains the neutral detent and stopper arms, allowing them to be disengaged together with their return springs.

3   Remove the single cross-head screw which secures the end plate to the selector drum, then remove the selector pins using a pair of pointed-nose pliers. Release the selector drum guide plate after removing its two retaining screws. Withdraw the selector shaft assembly from its bore in the casing.

10.1 Remove kickstart and idler pinion (RM80)

10.2a Selector claw is secured by E-clip (RM80)

10.2b Detent and stopper arms are held by bolt (RM80)

10.3 Remove selector shaft and drum end plate (RM80)

11 Dismantling the engine unit: removing the gear selector mechanism and kickstart idler pinion – RM100, RM125, RM250 and RM400

1   Withdraw the selector shaft assembly from the casing. As it is pulled from position, the centring spring will disengage and will remain attached to the quadrant at the end of the shaft. Remove the screws which retain the ratchet guide plate and the retainer plate. The ratchet can now be removed from the end of the selector drum, taking care not to allow the pawls, pins or springs to become lost.

2   Release the circlip which retains the kickstart idler pinion to the end of the gearbox layshaft. The pinion can now be removed, together with the washer which is fitted between it and the circlip. It should be noted that the remainder of the kickstart mechanism can only be removed after the crankcase halves have been separated.

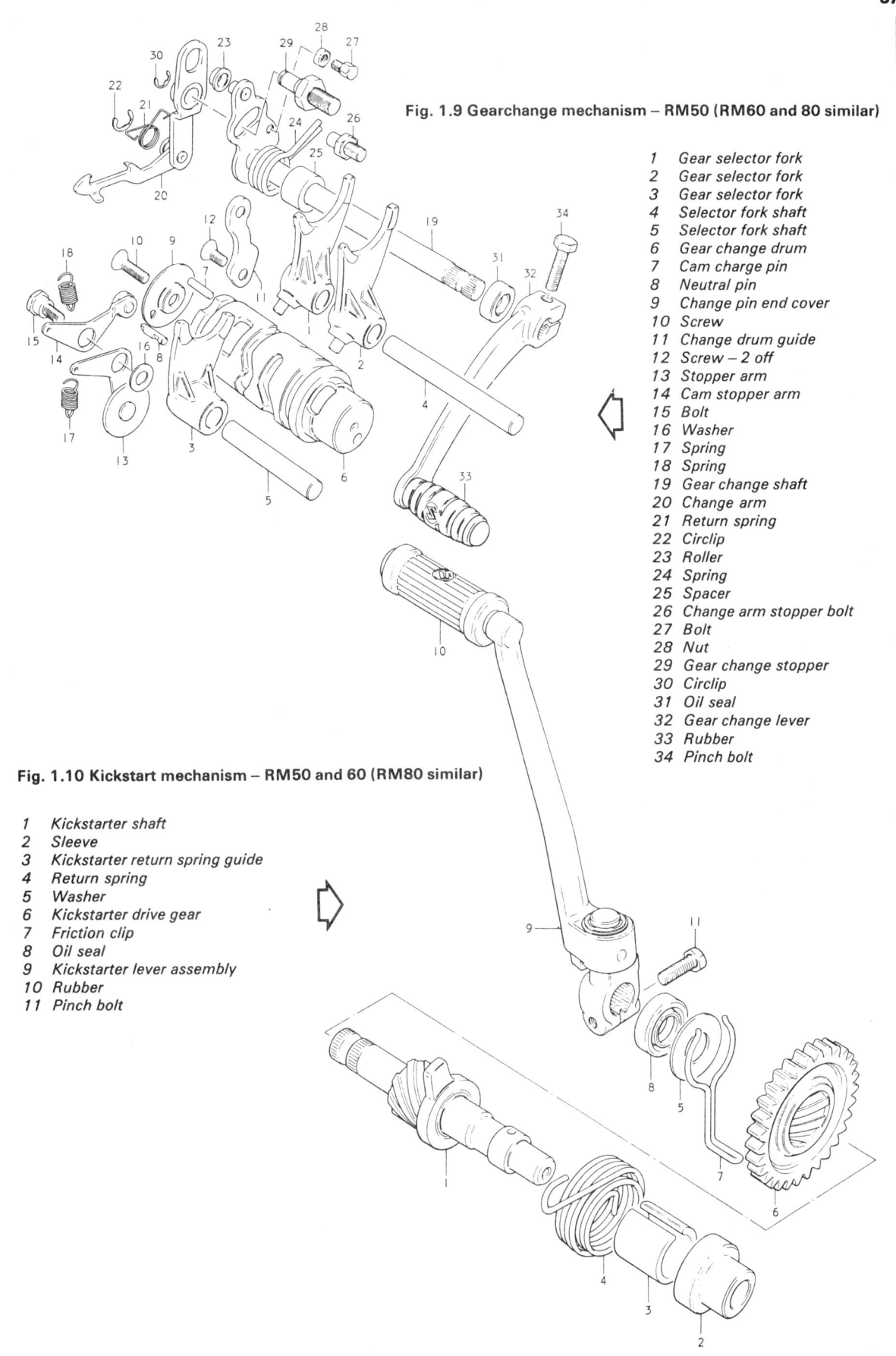

Fig. 1.9 Gearchange mechanism – RM50 (RM60 and 80 similar)

1   Gear selector fork
2   Gear selector fork
3   Gear selector fork
4   Selector fork shaft
5   Selector fork shaft
6   Gear change drum
7   Cam charge pin
8   Neutral pin
9   Change pin end cover
10 Screw
11 Change drum guide
12 Screw – 2 off
13 Stopper arm
14 Cam stopper arm
15 Bolt
16 Washer
17 Spring
18 Spring
19 Gear change shaft
20 Change arm
21 Return spring
22 Circlip
23 Roller
24 Spring
25 Spacer
26 Change arm stopper bolt
27 Bolt
28 Nut
29 Gear change stopper
30 Circlip
31 Oil seal
32 Gear change lever
33 Rubber
34 Pinch bolt

Fig. 1.10 Kickstart mechanism – RM50 and 60 (RM80 similar)

1   Kickstarter shaft
2   Sleeve
3   Kickstarter return spring guide
4   Return spring
5   Washer
6   Kickstarter drive gear
7   Friction clip
8   Oil seal
9   Kickstarter lever assembly
10 Rubber
11 Pinch bolt

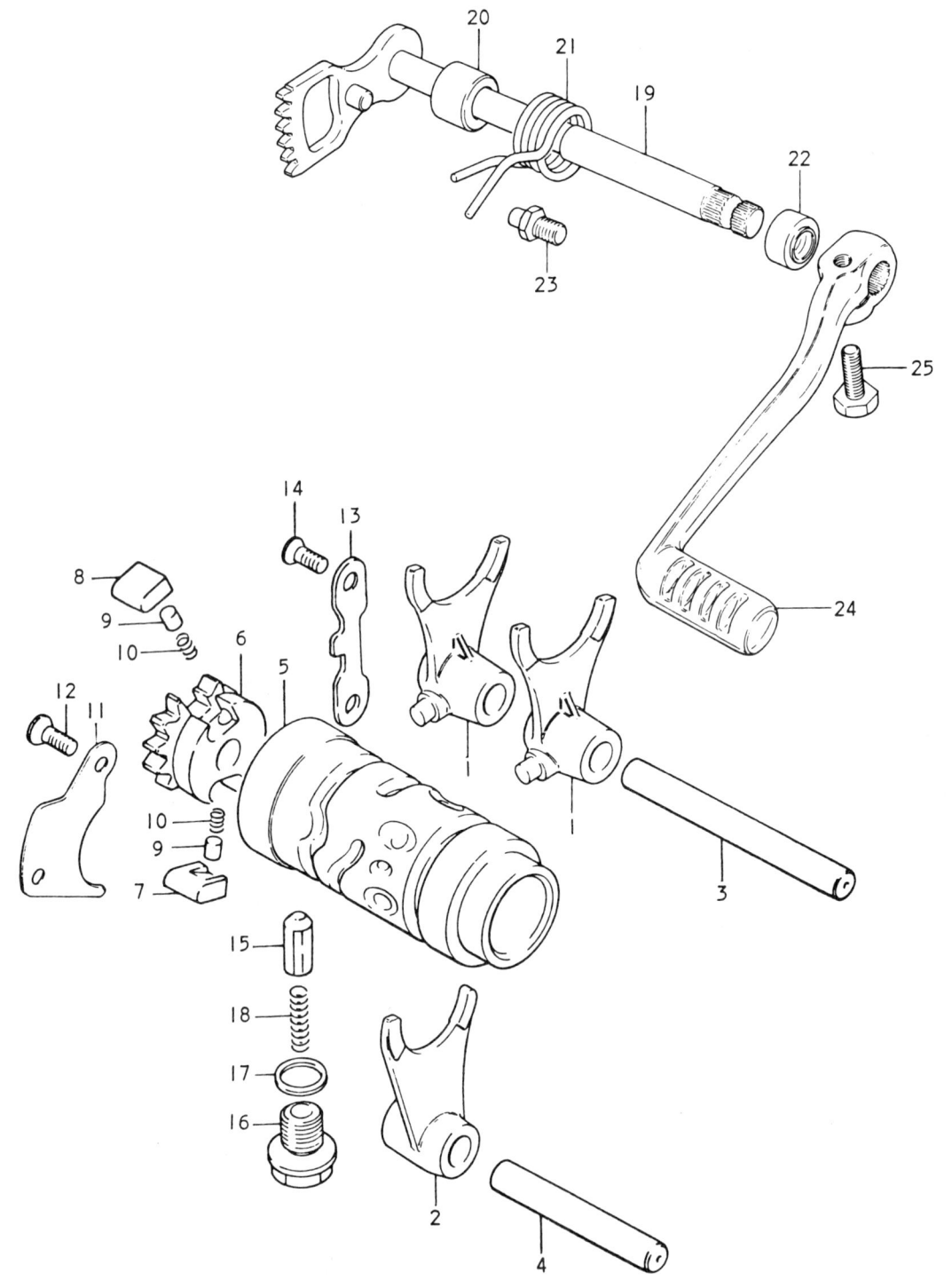

Fig. 1.11 Gearchange mechanism – RM100 and 125 models

1	Gear selector fork – 2 off	10	Spring – 2 off	18	Detent spring
2	Gear selector fork	11	Pawl lifter	19	Gear change shaft
3	Selector fork shaft No. 1	12	Screw – 2 off	20	Spacer
4	Selector fork shaft No. 2	13	Change cam guide	21	Centraliser spring
5	Gear change cam	14	Screw – 2 off	22	Oil seal
6	Cam drive gear	15	Detent plunger	23	Change arm stopper
7	Gear change pawl No. 1	16	Detent spring bolt	24	Gear change lever
8	Gear change pawl No. 2	17	Gasket	25	Pinch bolt
9	Plunger – 2 off				

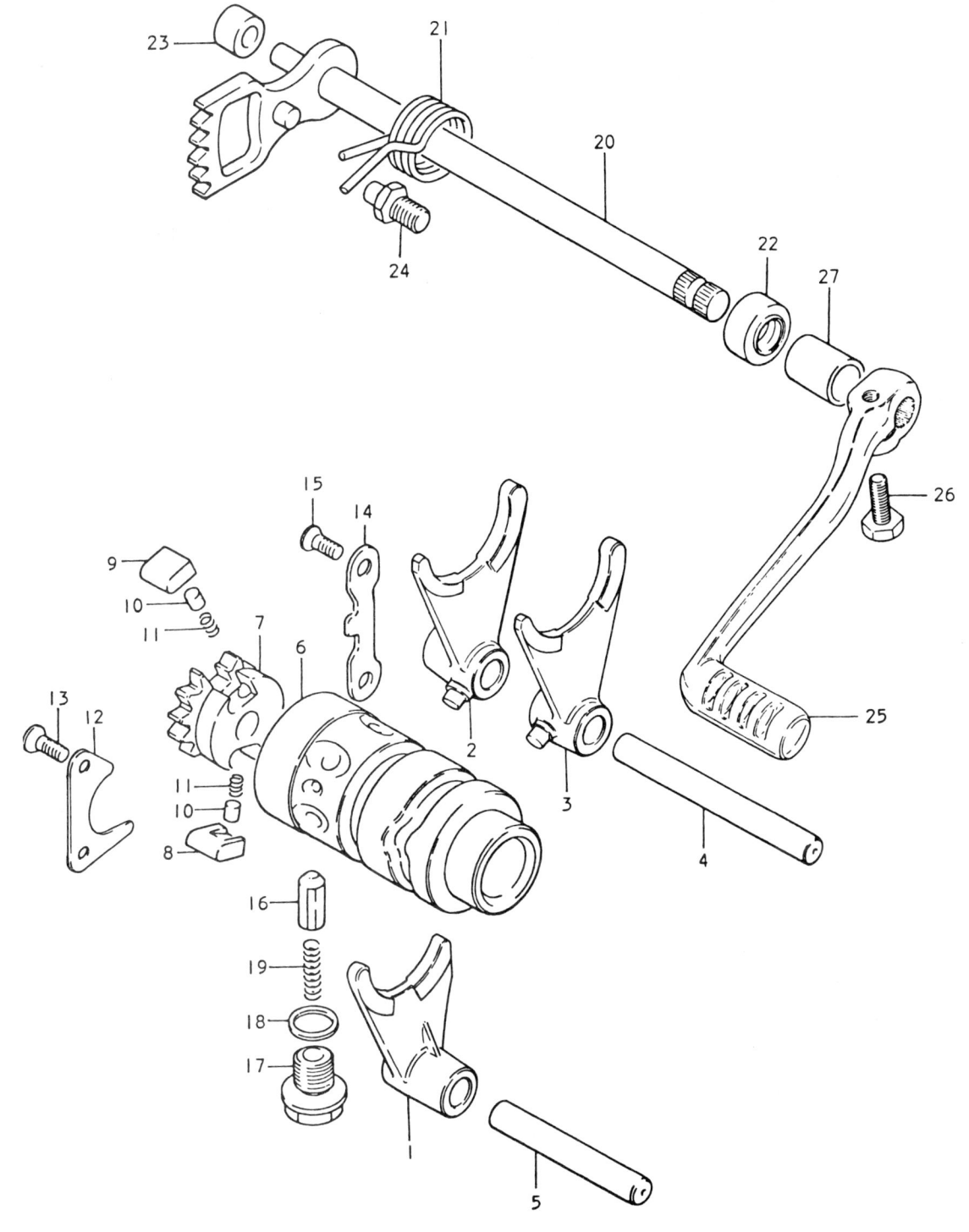

Fig. 1.12 Gearchange mechanism – RM250 (RM400 similar)

1	Selector fork	10	Plunger – 2 off	19	Spring
2	Selector fork	11	Spring – 2 off	20	Gear change shaft
3	Selector fork	12	Pawl lifter	21	Centraliser spring
4	Selector fork shaft	13	Screw – 2 off	22	Oil seal
5	Selector fork shaft	14	Change cam guide	23	Spacer
6	Gear change cam	15	Screw – 2 off	24	Change arm stopper
7	Cam driven gear	16	Detent plunger	25	Gear change lever
8	Gear change pawl A	17	Detent bolt	26	Pinch bolt
9	Gear change pawl B	18	Sealing washer	27	Cushion

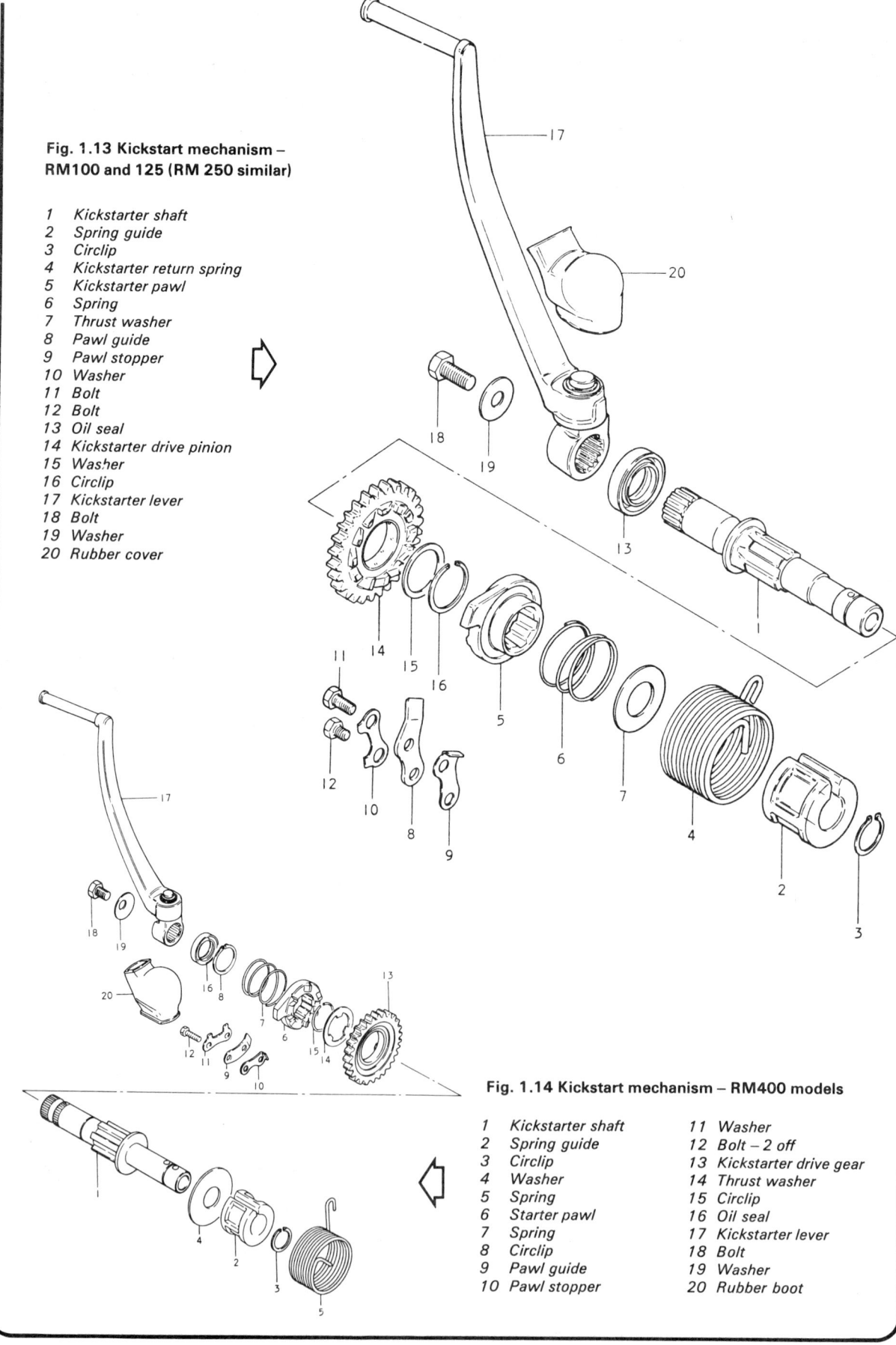

**Fig. 1.13 Kickstart mechanism –
RM100 and 125 (RM 250 similar)**

1 Kickstarter shaft
2 Spring guide
3 Circlip
4 Kickstarter return spring
5 Kickstarter pawl
6 Spring
7 Thrust washer
8 Pawl guide
9 Pawl stopper
10 Washer
11 Bolt
12 Bolt
13 Oil seal
14 Kickstarter drive pinion
15 Washer
16 Circlip
17 Kickstarter lever
18 Bolt
19 Washer
20 Rubber cover

Fig. 1.14 Kickstart mechanism – RM400 models

1 Kickstarter shaft
2 Spring guide
3 Circlip
4 Washer
5 Spring
6 Starter pawl
7 Spring
8 Circlip
9 Pawl guide
10 Pawl stopper
11 Washer
12 Bolt – 2 off
13 Kickstarter drive gear
14 Thrust washer
15 Circlip
16 Oil seal
17 Kickstarter lever
18 Bolt
19 Washer
20 Rubber boot

12 Dismantling the engine unit: separating the crankcase halves

1   The crankcase halves are secured by a total of eleven screws on RM50, RM60 and RM80 models. The RM100, RM125 and RM400 have thirteen screws, whilst the RM250 is held by twelve. These screws are almost invariably very tight, and attempts to dislodge them with a conventional screwdriver will usually result in damaged but unmoved screws. An impact driver should be considered essential, unless the original screws are rejected in favour of a set of more robust Allen screws. It should be noted that an extended impact driver bit may be required for the more inaccessible screws.

2   Slacken and remove the securing screws, placing them to one side. It is helpful, but not essential, to keep the screws in order by pushing them through them through a sheet of corrugated cardboard in their correct relative positions. This will speed up reassembly. The manufacturer recommends the use of a crankcase separation tool. Whilst this is of great value in a large workshop, its price and infrequent use make it an unreasonable proposition for the private owner. No problems were found in separating the crankcases by conventional methods.

3   Using a rubber or hide-faced mallet, tap around the jointing face to assist in breaking the crankcase seal. If necessary, place a hardwood block against the crankcase mouth and use this in conjunction with the hide mallet to drive the cases apart. This technique can be applied at other points around the casing, but take care not to damage the more fragile areas, bearing in mind that the crankcases are expensive to renew. Once the joint begins to separate, the shaft ends can be tapped to continue separation, but on no account should the use of levers be resorted to, as these will damage the sealing faces. Once the seal has been broken and the locating dowels are clear, the two halves are easily pulled apart.

13 Dismantling the engine unit: removing the crankshaft, kickstart shaft and gearbox components

1   When the crankcase halves are separated, the gearbox components and crankshaft will remain in the left-hand crankcase. Withdraw the selector fork support shaft to permit the removal of the forks. Reassemble the forks in their correct relative positions on the shaft, as an aid to reassembly. The selector drum may now be lifted out of the casing and placed to one side.

2   The gearbox mainshaft and layshaft clusters can be removed as a single unit. If the gearbox components require no further attention, assemble the two clusters, the selector forks and drum, and retain them by wrapping some stout elastic bands around the assembly. This will ensure that none of the components are mislaid or fitted incorrectly. If further dismantling is required, the above should be ignored.

3   On RM50 and RM60 machines, remove the kickstart shaft support piece. Slide the plastic spring guide out from the centre of the kickstart return spring. The spring end should now be grasped with a pair of pointed-nose pliers and disengaged from its drilling in the shaft. Allow the spring to unwind slowly and remove it from the casing. The kickstart shaft can now be tapped out of the casing.

4   On RM80, RM100, RM125 and RM250 models, no support piece is fitted, but a circlip is used to retain the spring guide. Apart from this, the assembly is removed as described above. On the RM400, the procedure differs in that the shaft assembly is removed inwards. In consequence, a circlip is fitted round the shaft on the **outside** of the crankcase, and this must be removed to allow the shaft to be withdrawn.

5   The crankshaft assembly can now be removed from the left-hand crankcase half. In many cases, the crankshaft can be simply pulled free, but where necessary, a hide mallet may be used to tap the crankshaft clear of the main bearing.

12.1 Recessed screws will require extended bit (RM80)

13.1a Withdraw selector fork pins ... (RM400)

13.1b ... to release selector forks (RM100)

13.1c Remove selector drum and forks (RM80)

13.2a Gearbox cluster removal (RM400)

13.2b Gearbox cluster removal (RM80)

13.4 Kickstart spring and shaft arrangement (except RM400)

13.5 Crankshaft assembly can be lifted out of casing (RM80)

14 Examination and renovation: general

1   Before examining the component parts of the dismantled engine/gear unit for wear, it is essential that they should be cleaned thoroughly. Use a paraffin/petrol mix to remove all traces of oil and sludge which may have accumulated within the engine.

2   Examine the crankcase castings for cracks or other signs of damage. If a crack is discovered, it will require professional attention, or in an extreme case, renewal of the casting.

3   Examine carefully each part to determine the extent ot wear. If in doubt, check with the tolerance figures whenever they are quoted in the text. The following sections will indicate what type of wear can be expected, and in many cases, the acceptable wear limits. General wear limits and tolerances can be found in the Specifications section at the beginning of this Chapter.

15 Engine casings, bearings and oil seals: examination and renovation

1   The aluminium alloy casings and covers are unlikely to suffer damage through ordinary use. However, damage can

occur if the machine is dropped, or if sudden mechanical breakages occur, such as the rear chain breaking.

2   Small cracks or holes may be repaired with an epoxy resin adhesive, such as Araldite, as a temporary expedient. Permanent repairs can only be effected by argon-arc welding, and a specialist in this process is in a position to advise on the viability of proposed repair. Often it may be cheaper to buy a new replacement. Some of the outer covers are made from an alloy containing a proportion of magnesium. This makes for a strong, lightweight casing, but does pose problems if a breakage occurs, because magnesium alloys will burn in a fairly dramatic manner if sufficient heat is applied to them. As a general rule, repairs should be confined to the use of an epoxy adhesive. If severely damaged, the cover should be renewed.

3   Damaged threads can be economically reclaimed by using a diamond section wire insert, of the Helicoil type, which is easily fitted after drilling and re-tapping the affected thread. The process is quick and inexpensive, and does not require as much preparation and work as the older method of fitting brass, or similar inserts. Most motorcycle dealers and small engineering firms offer a service of this kind.

4   Sheared studs or screws can usually be removed with screw extractors, which consist of tapered, left-hand thread screws, of very hard steel. These are inserted by screwing anti-clockwise, into a pre-drilled hole in the stud, and usually suceed in dislodging the most stubborn stud or screw. The only alternative to this is spark erosion, but as this is a very limited, specialised facility, it will probably be unavailable to most owners. It is wise, however, to consult a professional engineering firm before condemning an otherwise sound casing. Many of these firms advertise regularly in the motorcycle papers.

5   The crankshaft main bearings and gearbox bearings should be examined for wear and roughness when turned, and if suspect, should be renewed. Remove the bearing oil seal retainer and prise out the old seal, where appropriate. The bearings can easily be removed by applying heat to the casing, causing the aluminium alloy to expand at a faster rate than that of the steel bearing, allowing the bearing to become loose. The safest way of doing this is to place the casing in an oven, heating it to about 80° – 100°C. The casing can then be banged on a wooden bench or board, face down, to jar the bearing free. The new bearings can be tapped into position using a large diameter socket as a drift. Care should always be exercised when heating alloy casings as excessive or localised heat can easily cause warpage. Seek specialist advice if you are not familiar with this task.

6   Main bearing failure will immediately be obvious when the bearings are inspected, after the old oil has been washed out. If any play is evident or if the bearings do not run freely, renewal is essential. Warning of main bearing failure is usually given by a characteristic rumble that can readily be heard when the engine is running. Some vibration will also be felt, which is transmitted via the footrests.

7   Oil seal failure is a common occurrence in two-stroke engines that have seen a reasonable amount of service. When the oil seals begin to wear, air is admitted to the crankcase which will dilute the incoming mixture. This in turn causes uneven running and difficulty in starting.

8   Examine the seals carefully, paying particular attention to the thin lip of each seal. This area performs the sealing function, and the seal should be renewed without question if it is scored or marked in any way. In view of the important part these seals play, it is considered good practice to renew them as a matter of course whilst the engine is stripped for rebuilding. A worn seal can be prised out of position without having to remove the relevant bearing. When fitting a new seal, take great care not to damage or distort it. Tap the seal gently into place, using a large socket or similar to ensure that it is fitted squarely.

9   Bushes may be dealt with in a similar manner to that described for ball bearings. Check the fit of the relevant shaft end in the bush. It should be a light fit, without any discernible free play.

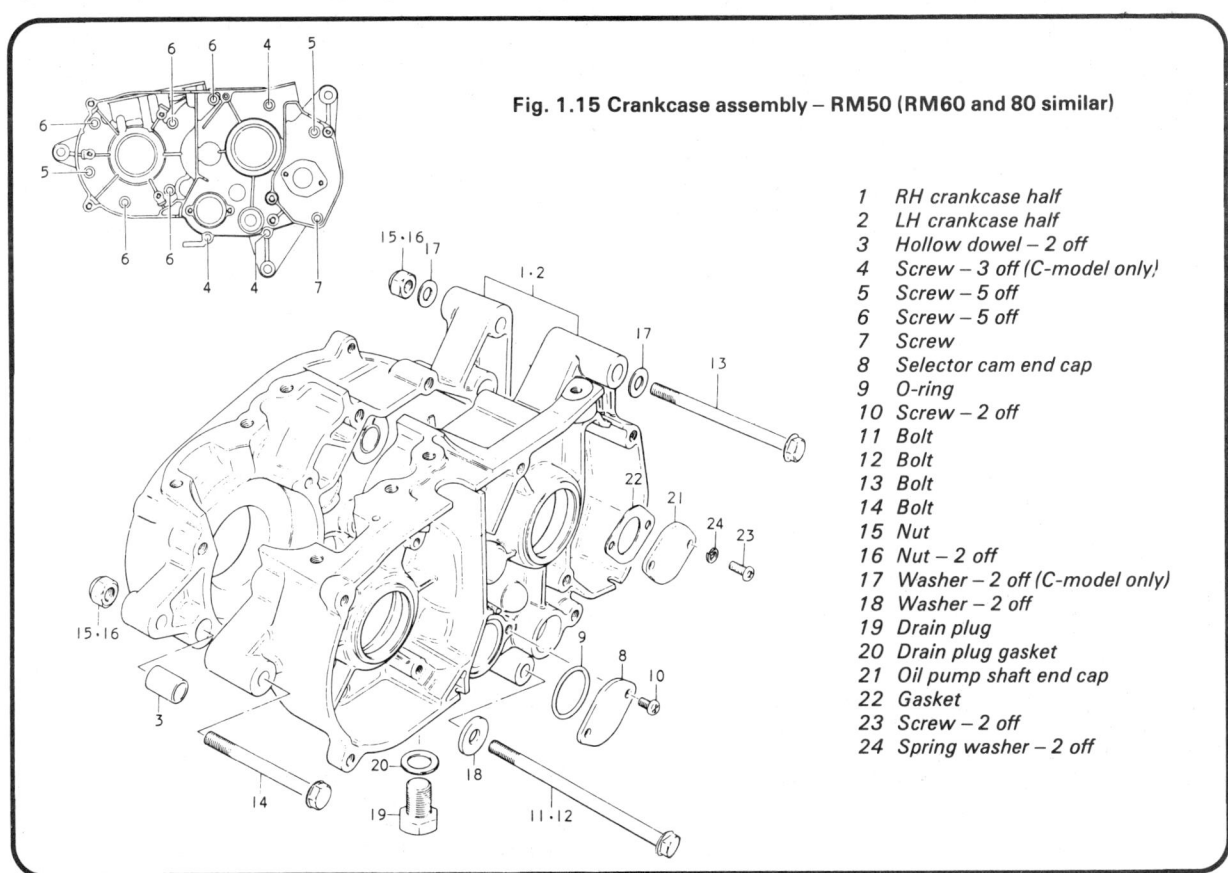

Fig. 1.15 Crankcase assembly – RM50 (RM60 and 80 similar)

1   RH crankcase half
2   LH crankcase half
3   Hollow dowel – 2 off
4   Screw – 3 off (C-model only)
5   Screw – 5 off
6   Screw – 5 off
7   Screw
8   Selector cam end cap
9   O-ring
10   Screw – 2 off
11   Bolt
12   Bolt
13   Bolt
14   Bolt
15   Nut
16   Nut – 2 off
17   Washer – 2 off (C-model only)
18   Washer – 2 off
19   Drain plug
20   Drain plug gasket
21   Oil pump shaft end cap
22   Gasket
23   Screw – 2 off
24   Spring washer – 2 off

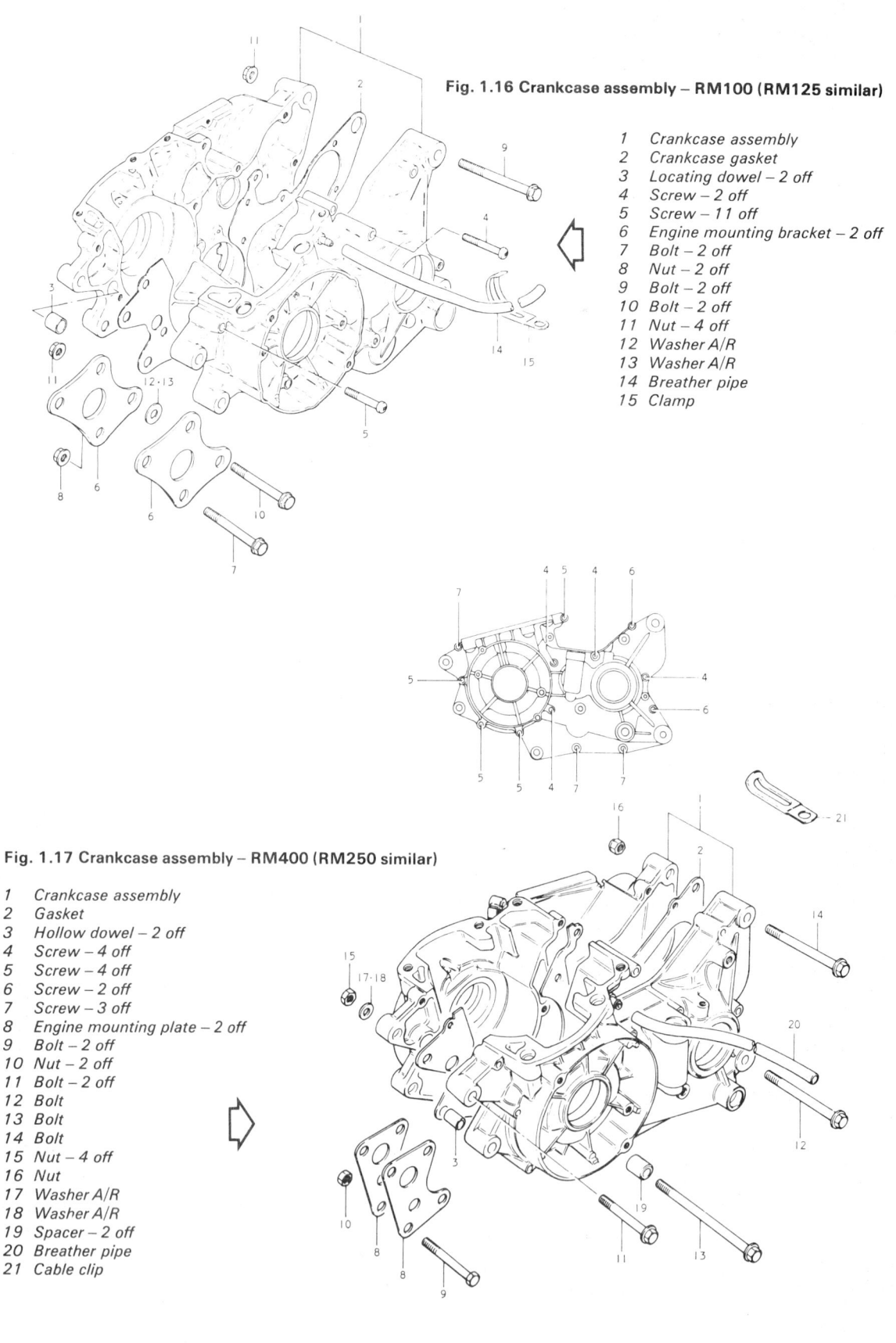

Fig. 1.16 Crankcase assembly – RM100 (RM125 similar)

1	Crankcase assembly
2	Crankcase gasket
3	Locating dowel – 2 off
4	Screw – 2 off
5	Screw – 11 off
6	Engine mounting bracket – 2 off
7	Bolt – 2 off
8	Nut – 2 off
9	Bolt – 2 off
10	Bolt – 2 off
11	Nut – 4 off
12	Washer A/R
13	Washer A/R
14	Breather pipe
15	Clamp

Fig. 1.17 Crankcase assembly – RM400 (RM250 similar)

1	Crankcase assembly
2	Gasket
3	Hollow dowel – 2 off
4	Screw – 4 off
5	Screw – 4 off
6	Screw – 2 off
7	Screw – 3 off
8	Engine mounting plate – 2 off
9	Bolt – 2 off
10	Nut – 2 off
11	Bolt – 2 off
12	Bolt
13	Bolt
14	Bolt
15	Nut – 4 off
16	Nut
17	Washer A/R
18	Washer A/R
19	Spacer – 2 off
20	Breather pipe
21	Cable clip

15.5a Bearings are retained by lip or plate (RM100)

15.5b Warm casing to release grip on bearing (RM100)

15.5c Note locating circlip (RM80)

15.5d Gearbox bearing has locating pin (RM400)

15.6a Check main bearings for roughness (RM100)

15.6b Heat the crankcase to allow bearing removal (RM400)

15.8a Main bearing seals may be external (RM400)

15.8b ... or internal as shown here (RM80)

16 Crankshaft assembly: examination and renovation

1   The crankshaft assembly comprises two full flywheels, two mainshafts, a crankpin and big end bearing, a connecting rod and a caged needle roller small end bearing. The general condition of the big end bearing may be established with the assembly removed from the engine, or with just the cylinder head and barrel removed, as would be the case during a normal decoke. In this way it is possible to decide whether big end renewal is necessary, without a great deal of exploratory dismantling.

2   Big end failure is characterised by a pronounced knock which will be most noticeable when the engine is worked hard. The usual causes of failure are normal wear, or a failure of the lubrication supply. In the case of the latter, big end wear will become apparent very suddenly, and will rapidly worsen. Check for wear with the crankshaft set in the TDC (top dead centre) position, by pushing and pulling the connecting rod. No discernible movement will be evident in an unworn bearing, but care must be taken not to confuse end float, which is normal, with bearing wear.

3   If play is found or suspected, it is recommended that the complete crankshaft assembly is taken to a Suzuki Service Agent who will be able to confirm the worst, and supply a new or service-exchange assembly. The task of dismantling and reconditioning the big end assembly is a specialist task, and is considered to be beyond the scope and facilities of the average owner.

4   The small end bearing is of the caged needle roller type, and will seldom give trouble unless a lubrication failure has occurred. The gudgeon pin should be a good sliding fit in the bearing without any play. The bearing must be tested whilst it is in place in the small end eye. If play develops, a noticeable rattle will be heard when the engine is running, indicative of the need for bearing renewal.

5   No problem is encountered when replacing the caged needle roller bearing as it is a light push fit in the eye of the connecting rod. New small end bearings are normally supplied whenever the crankshaft assembly is renewed or service-exchanged.

17 Decarbonising

1   Decarbonising must take place as part of any major overhaul, in addition to being a normal routine maintenance function. In the case of the latter, the operation can be undertaken with minimal dismantling, namely removal of the cylinder head. Carbon build up in a two-stroke engine is more rapid than that of its four-stroke counterpart, due to the oily nature of the combustion mixture. It is however, rather softer and is therefore more easily removed.

2   The object of the exercise is to remove all traces of carbon whilst avoiding the removal of the metal surface on which it is deposited. It follows that care must be taken when dealing with the relatively soft alloy cylinder head and piston. Never use a steel scraper or screwdriver for carbon removal. A hardwood, brass or aluminium scraper is the ideal tool as these are harder than the carbon, but no harder that the underlying metal. Once the bulk of the carbon has been removed, a brass wire brush of the type used to clean suede shoes can be used to good effect.

3   The whole of the combustion chamber should be cleaned, as should the piston crown. It is recommended that as smooth a finish as possible is obtained, as this will slow the subsequent build up of carbon. If desired metal polish can be used to obtain a smooth surface. The exhaust port must also be cleaned out, as a build up of carbon in this area will restrict the flow of exhaust gases from the cylinder. Take care to remove all traces of debris from the cylinder and ports, prior to reassembly.

18 Cylinder head: examination and renovation

1   Using a wire brush, clean out any road dirt or other debris from the cylinder head fins, to prevent any possibility of overheating.

2   Check the condition of the thread in the sparking plug hole. If it is damaged an effective repair can be made using Helicoil thread insert. This service is available from most Suzuki Service Agents. The cause of a damaged thread can usually be traced to overtightening of the plug or using a plug of too long a reach. Always use the correct plug and do not overtighten.

3   Check the cylinder head for warpage (usually caused by uneven tightening and/or overtightening), with a straight edge across several places on the gasket face; or preferably, with engineers' blue on a surface plate (a sheet of plate glass can be used as a substitute for a surface plate). If the cylinder head is warped, grind it down on a surface plate with emery paper. Start with 200 grade paper and finish with 400 grade and oil.

4   If it is necessary to remove a substantial amount of metal before the cylinder head will seat correctly, a new cylinder head should be obtained.

16.2 Check big end bearing for free play (RM400)

16.4 Small end bearing is of caged needle type (RM80)

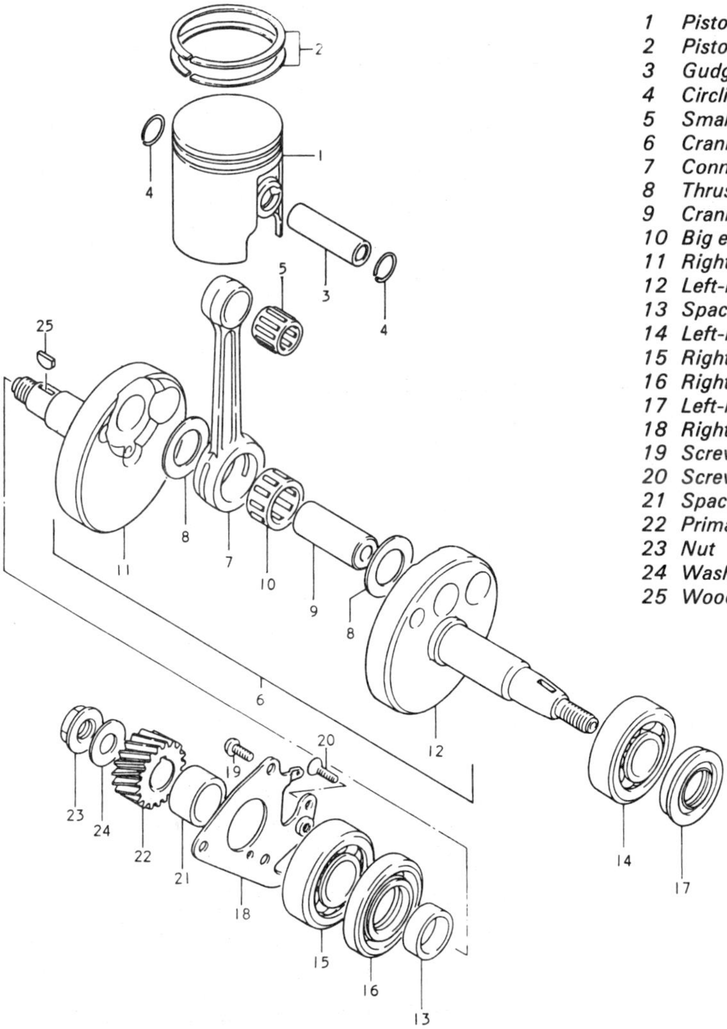

1   Piston
2   Piston ring set
3   Gudgeon pin
4   Circlip – 2 off
5   Small end bearing
6   Crankshaft assembly
7   Connecting rod
8   Thrust washer – 2 off
9   Crank pin
10   Big end bearing
11   Right-hand crankshaft/flywheel
12   Left-hand crankshaft/flywheel
13   Spacer
14   Left-hand main bearing
15   Right-hand main bearing
16   Right-hand oil seal
17   Left-hand oil seal
18   Right-hand bearing retainer
19   Screw – 2 off
20   Screw – 2 off
21   Spacer
22   Primary drive pinion
23   Nut
24   Washer
25   Woodruff key

Fig. 1.18 Crankshaft assembly – RM80 (RM50 and 60 similar)

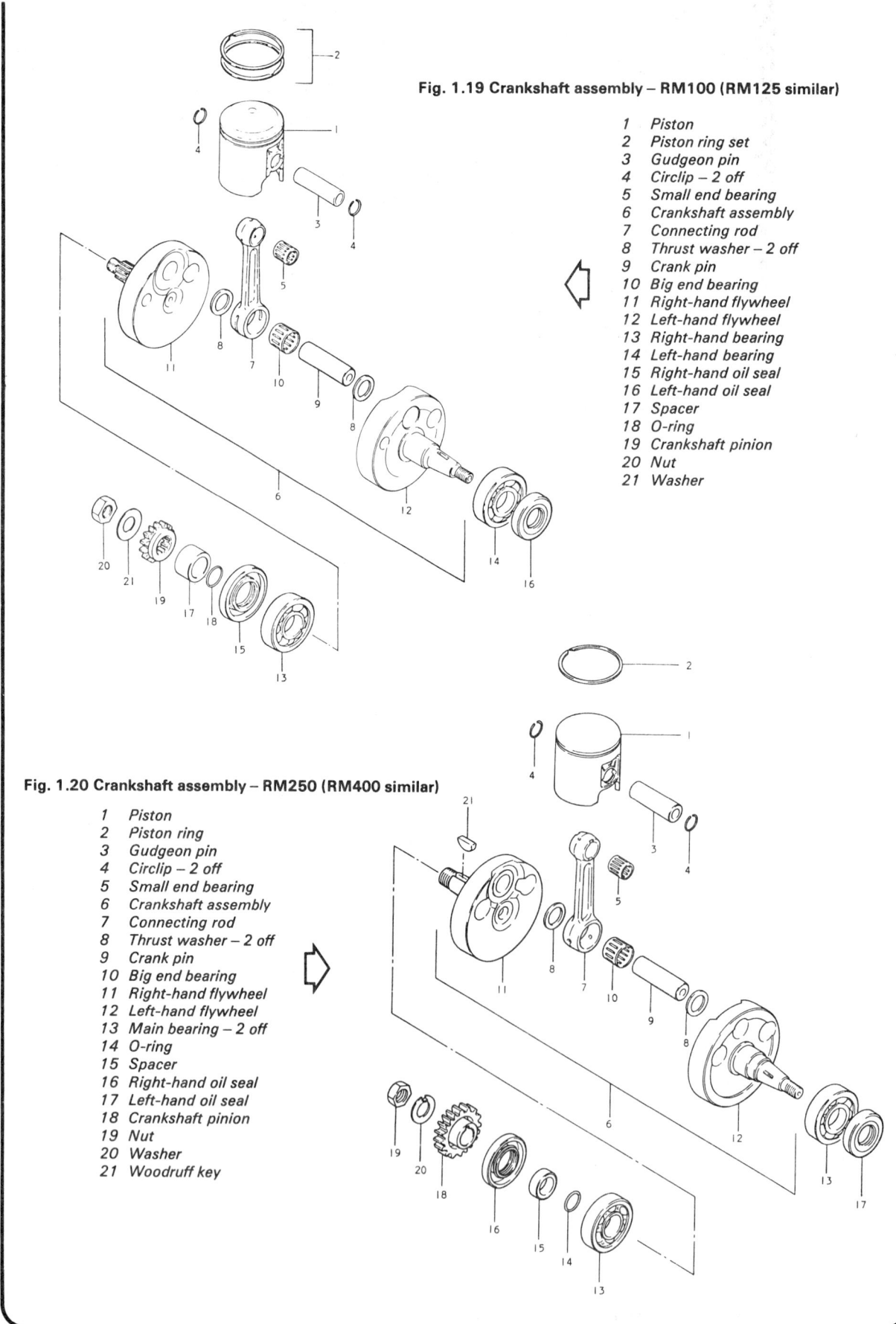

Fig. 1.19 Crankshaft assembly – RM100 (RM125 similar)

1   Piston
2   Piston ring set
3   Gudgeon pin
4   Circlip – 2 off
5   Small end bearing
6   Crankshaft assembly
7   Connecting rod
8   Thrust washer – 2 off
9   Crank pin
10 Big end bearing
11 Right-hand flywheel
12 Left-hand flywheel
13 Right-hand bearing
14 Left-hand bearing
15 Right-hand oil seal
16 Left-hand oil seal
17 Spacer
18 O-ring
19 Crankshaft pinion
20 Nut
21 Washer

Fig. 1.20 Crankshaft assembly – RM250 (RM400 similar)

1   Piston
2   Piston ring
3   Gudgeon pin
4   Circlip – 2 off
5   Small end bearing
6   Crankshaft assembly
7   Connecting rod
8   Thrust washer – 2 off
9   Crank pin
10 Big end bearing
11 Right-hand flywheel
12 Left-hand flywheel
13 Main bearing – 2 off
14 O-ring
15 Spacer
16 Right-hand oil seal
17 Left-hand oil seal
18 Crankshaft pinion
19 Nut
20 Washer
21 Woodruff key

19 Cylinder barrel and bore: examination and renovation

1　Clean the outside of the cylinder barrel, taking care to remove any accumulation of dirt from between the cooling fins. Carefully remove the ring of carbon from the mouth of the bore, so that an accurate assessment of bore wear can be made.

2　A close visual examination of the bore surface must be made, to check for scoring or any other damage, particularly if broken piston rings were encountered during the stripdown. Any damage of this nature will necessitate reboring and a new piston, as it is impossible to obtain a satisfactory seal if the bore is not perfectly finished.

3　There will probably be a lip at the uppermost end of the cylinder bore which marks the limit of travel of the top of the piston ring. The depth of the lip will give some indication of the amount of bore wear that has taken place even though the amount of wear is not evenly distributed.

4　The best way of measuring bore wear is by the use of a cylinder bore DTI (Dial Test Indicator) or a bore micrometer. However, it is most unlikely that the average owner will have this type of equipment at his disposal. A slightly less accurate, but more practical method is to insert the piston into the cylinder bore, and measure the gap between the piston skirt and bore using feeler gauges. The measurement should be taken at various positions and the average clearance assessed. It should be noted that the curvature of the gap precludes accurate measurement by this method, but it should be possible to gain a good indication of whether a rebore is necessary by comparing the measurements taken at an unworn and worn areas of the bore surface.

5　If the amount of wear exceeds the limits given in the Specifications section, it will be necessary to have the cylinder barrel rebored to the next oversize, and the appropriate oversize piston fitted. Care must be exercised if the bore proves to be part-worn and new rings are required, as a ridge will be present at the top of the bore, and the new top ring may strike the ridge, causing it to fracture. It is suggested that the advice of a Suzuki Service Agent be sought if this likelihood arises. Note that bore wear must always be assessed in conjunction with piston and piston ring conditions as described in the following Section.

6　If the barrel is to be rebored, the appropriate oversized piston should be obtained first. These are available in various sizes, and this factor is dependent upon the model concerned. RM50 machines have 0.5 mm and 1.0 mm oversize pistons available. The RM80 can be fitted with 0.5 mm, 1.0 mm and 1.5 mm oversize pistons. The remaining models in the range have two oversizes, namely 0.25 mm and 0.5 mm.

7　The reboring work should be carried out by an authorised Suzuki Agent, or entrusted to a reputable engineering company. The new piston should be sent with the barrel, because the reboring should be carried out to suit the new component. After reboring, the port windows must be lightly chamfered to avoid any risk of the rings catching and breaking.

20 Piston and rings: examination and replacement

1　Attention to the piston and rings can be overlooked if a rebore is necessary as a new piston and rings will be fitted under these circumstances.

2　If a rebore is not considered necessary, the piston should be examined closely. Reject the piston if it is badly scored or discoloured as the result of the exhaust gases by-passing the rings. Check the gudgeon pin bosses to ensure that they are not enlarged or that the grooves retaining each circlip are not damaged.

3　Remove all carbon deposits from the piston crown and use metal polish to finish off, so that a high polish is obtained. Carbon will adhere much less readily to a polished surface. Examination of the piston crown will show whether the engine has been rebored previously, since the amount of rebore is always stamped on the piston crown.

4　The grooves in which the piston rings locate can become enlarged in use. The clearance between the edge of each piston ring and the groove in which it is fitted should be just enough for the ring to be able to move smoothly. If the grooves become worn, gas will be allowed past the ring, and the piston will become scorched down its skirt. This sort of wear is unusual unless very high mileages have been covered, and if found will probably indicate that a rebore is long overdue. If the engine is otherwise sound, the piston alone can be renewed, but check first that no wear ridge is present at the top of the cylinder bore.

5　Remove the piston rings by pushing the ends apart with the thumbs whilst gently easing the ring from its groove. Great care is necessary throughout this operation because the rings are brittle and will break easily if overstressed. If the rings are gummed in their grooves, three strips of tin can be used to ease them free, as shown in the accompanying illustration.

6　Piston ring wear can be checked by inserting the rings one at a time in the cylinder bore from the top and pushing them down about $1\frac{1}{2}$ inches with the base of the piston so that they rest square in the bore. Make sure that the end gap is away from any of the ports. If the piston ring end gap is within the correct range then the rings are suitable for further service. Refer to the Specifications section at the beginning of this Chapter for the piston ring end gap figures for each model.

7　Examine the working surface of each piston ring. If discoloured areas are evident, the ring should be renewed because these areas indicate the blow-by of gas. Check that there is not a build-up of carbon on the back of the ring or in the piston ring groove, which may cause an increase in the radial pressure. A portion of broken ring affords the best means of cleaning out the piston ring grooves.

8　Check that the piston ring pegs are firmly embedded in each piston ring groove. It is imperative that these retainers should not work loose, otherwise the rings will be free to rotate and there is danger of the ends being trapped in the ports.

9　Examine the piston skirt for scoring. If this is discovered, and the engine is otherwise undamaged, it may be removed by carefully rubbing down the scored area with 400 grit sandpaper. Take care not to remove more metal than is absolutely necessary.

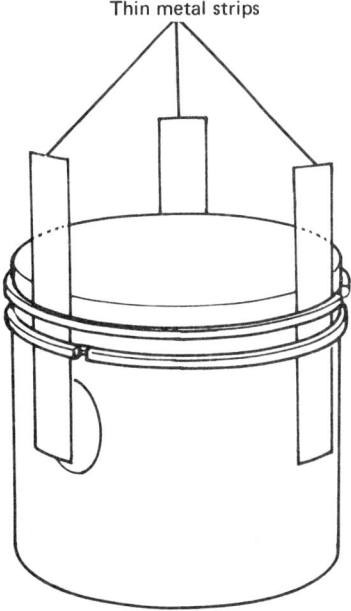

Fig. 1.21 Freeing and removing gummed piston rings

20.2a RM400 piston has single ring only

20.2b Complete piston assembly for RM100

20.3 Arrow must face forward when piston is fitted (RM100)

10 It cannot be over-emphasised that the condition of the piston and piston rings is of prime importance because they control the opening and closing of the ports by providing an effective moving seal. A two-stroke engine has only three working parts, of which the piston is one. It follows that the efficiency of the engine is very dependent on the condition of the piston and the parts with which it is closely associated.

21 Gearbox components: examination and renovation

1 Examine each of the gear pinions to ensure that there are no chipped or broken teeth and that the dogs on the end of the pinions are not rounded. Gear pinions with any of these defects should be removed from their shafts and replaced by new gears. On all models the gear pinions are secured by a series of circlips and washers which may be displaced using suitable circlip pliers. The position of these components can be seen in the accompanying illustrations of the gearbox components. On RM 60 and 80 models the mainshaft 2nd gear pinion is a tight press fit on the mainshaft and this must be drawn or pressed from

position before the remainder of the gear pinions can be removed. A similar situation exists with the 5th gear pinion on the RM50 models. Ideally a hydraulic press should be used to remove the pinion but failing this a heavy three-legged puller may be employed.

2 The gearbox bearings must be free from play and show no signs of roughness or jamming when rotated. Once again it is necessary to make sure any old oil is removed from the bearings before they are inspected. The gearbox incorporates both caged needle roller and journal ball bearings which can be tapped out for renewal once the oil seals have been prised out of place.

3 It is advisable to renew the gearbox oil seals irrespective of their condition. Should a re-used oil seal fail at a later date, a considerable amount of dismantling is necessary to gain access and renew it.

4 Check the gear selector rods for straightness by rolling them on a sheet of plate glass. A bent rod will cause difficulty in selecting gears and will make the gearchange action particularly heavy. The remaining circlips on the fork shafts must be removed in order to test them. Replace the circlips once the test is complete.

5 The selector forks should be examined closely, to ensure that they are not bent or badly worn. Wear is unlikely to occur unless the gearbox has been run for a period with a particularly low oil content. Place each selector fork in engagement with the groove in its associated gearbox pinion. The clearance between the two can be measured using feeler gauges, comparing the clearance found with that given in the Specifications for each model.

6 The tracks in the gear selector drum, with which the selector forks engage, should not show any undue signs of wear unless neglect has led to underlubrication of the gearbox. Check that the plunger spring bearing on the cam plate plunger has not lost its action and that the springs of the gearchange lever pawl assembly have good tension. Any damage to, or weakness of, the gearchange lever return spring will be self-evident.

7 If the kickstarter has shown a tendency to slip, it will be necessary to examine the kickstarter gear and shaft. The kickstarter assembly can be inspected without dismantling, the most likely cause of failure being a broken kickstarter spring clip. If the kickstart ratchet teeth are found to be rounded off or damaged, the relevant components must be renewed. A slipping kickstart is far from desirable when racing, and any suspect parts should be renewed now to avoid lengthy dismantling in the future.

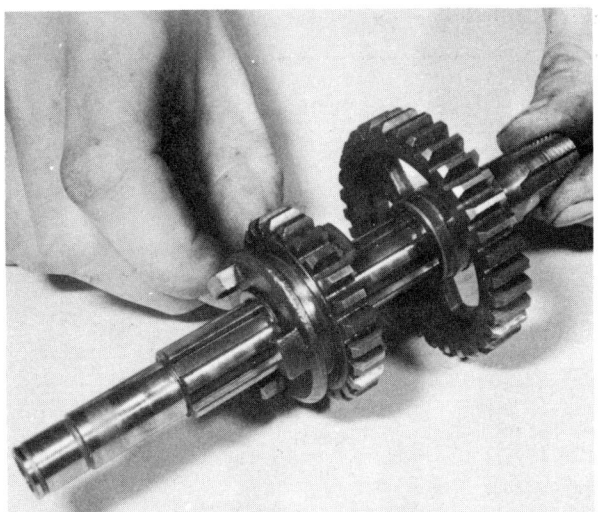

21.1a Fit layshaft 2nd gear pinion, circlip and 6th gear pinion ... (RM80)

21.1b ... followed by circlip and thrustwasher (RM80)

21.1c Fit 3rd gear pinion, ... (RM80)

21.1d ... 4th gear pinion ... (RM80)

21.1e ... and secure with washer and circlip (RM80)

21.1f Fit the 5th gear layshaft pinion, ... (RM80)

21.1g ... 1st gear pinion and plain washer (RM80)

21.1h Note O-ring fitted to sprocket end (RM80)

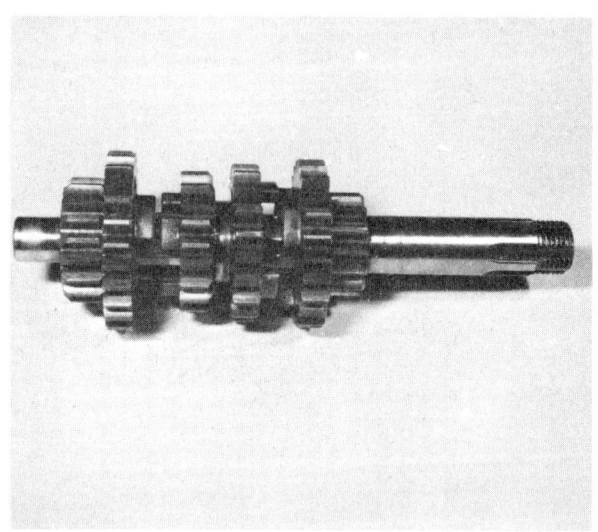

21.1i Mainshaft assembly is a pressed-up unit (RM80)

21.1j Gearbox cluster ready for installation (RM80)

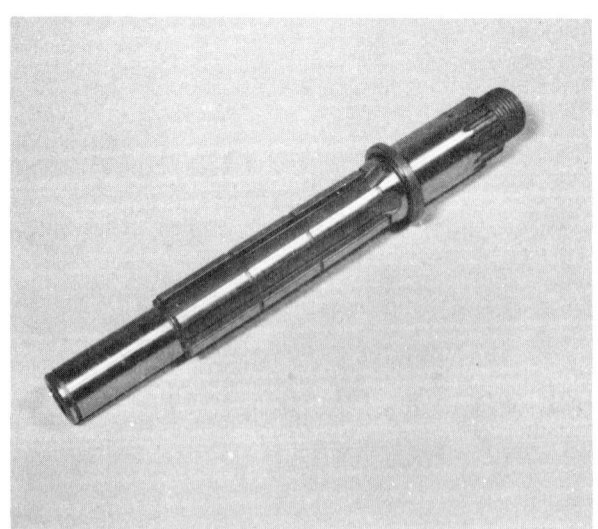

21.2a Bare layshaft – RM100 and 125 (RM100)

21.2b Fit 2nd gear layshaft pinion ... (RM100)

21.2c ... and secure with circlip (RM100)

21.2d Fit 6th gear layshaft pinion ... (RM100)

21.2e ... followed by circlip and washer (RM100)

21.2f Fit 3rd gear layshaft pinion, ... (RM100)

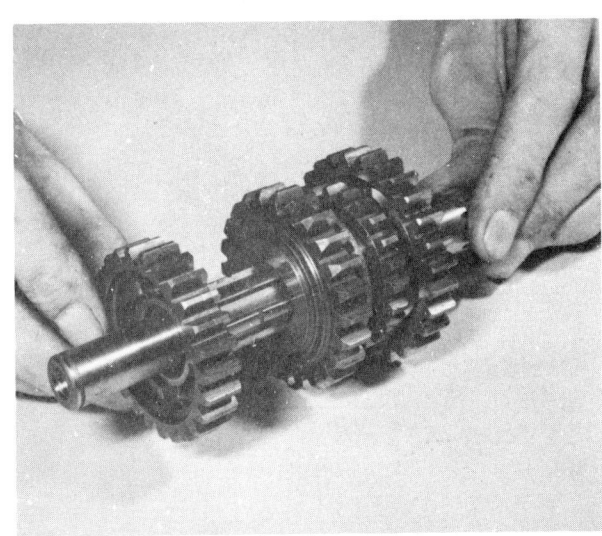

21.2g ... 4th gear layshaft pinion ... (RM100)

21.2h ... and secure with washer and circlip (RM100)

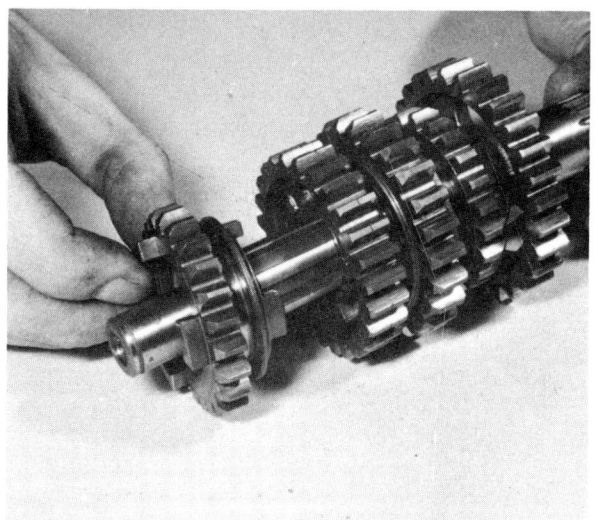

21.2i Fit 5th gear pinion as shown ... (RM100)

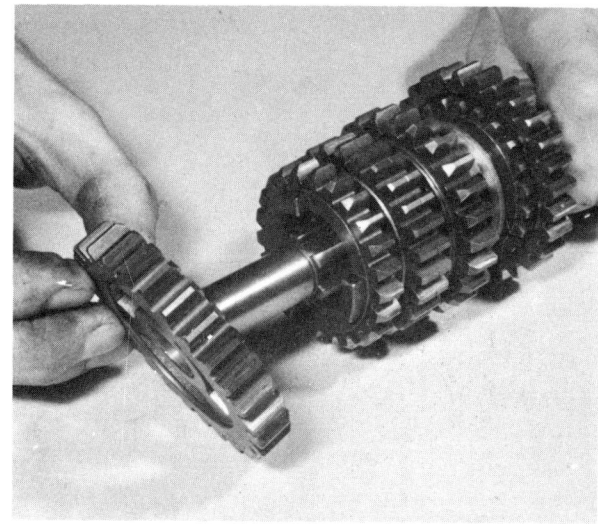

21.2j ... followed by 1st gear pinion ... (RM100)

21.2k ... and plain washer (RM100)

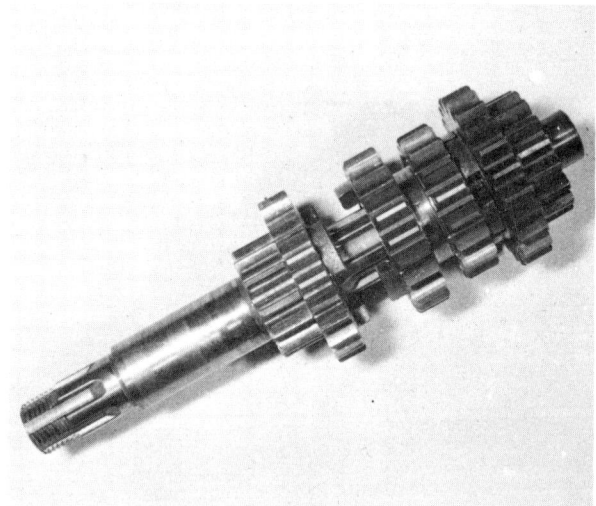

21.2l Mainshaft assembly is a pressed-up unit (RM100)

21.2m Gearbox cluster ready for installation (RM100)

21.3a Fit mainshaft 5th gear pinion, washer, circlip and 3rd gear pinion (RM400)

21.3b Place circlip and washer as shown ... (RM400)

21.3c ... to permit fitting of final circlip (RM400)

21.3d Fit 4th gear pinion and 2nd gear pinion (RM400)

21.3e Position final circlip, then slide pinions and 3rd gear circlip and washer into place (RM400)

21.3f 4th and 2nd gear pinions in final position (RM400)

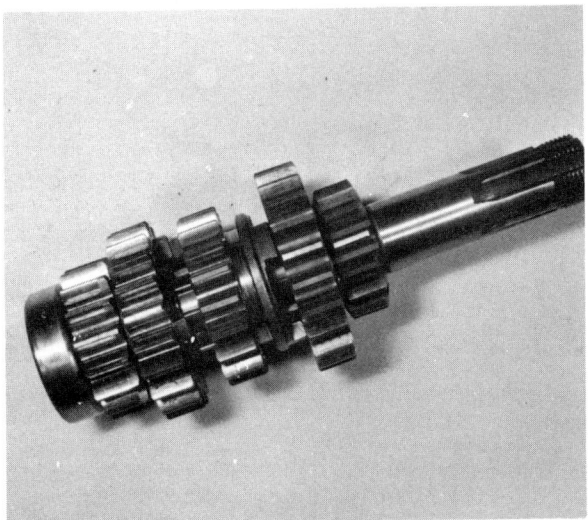

21.3g Assembled complete with bearing (RM400)

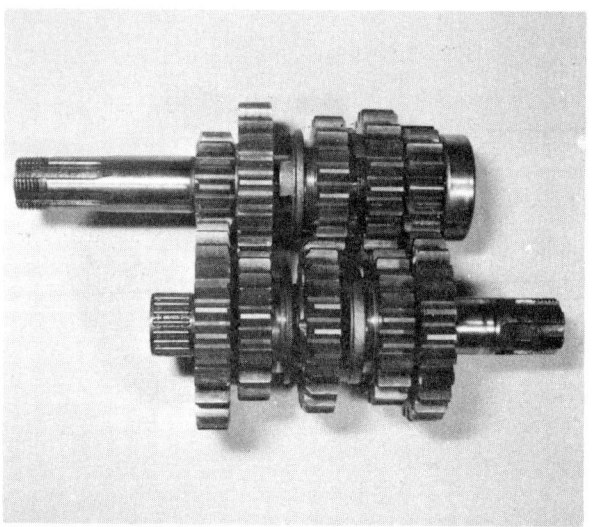

21.3h Completed gearbox cluster ready for installation (RM400)

21.3i Assemble 2nd, 4th and 3rd gear pinions ... (RM400)

21.3j ... securing with washer and circlip

21.3k Fit 5th gear layshaft pinion

21.3l Fit thrustwasher and small needle roller bearing ... (RM400)

21.3m ... followed by 1st gear layshaft pinion (RM400)

21.3n Fit thrustwasher and large needle roller bearing (RM400)

21.3o Completed layshaft assembly (RM400)

21.4a Examine selector shaft for wear or damage (RM400)

21.4b Check selector pawls for wear (RM100)

21.7a Kickstart gears are unlikely to wear (RM80)

21.7b Ratchet teeth must be unworn as shown (RM400)

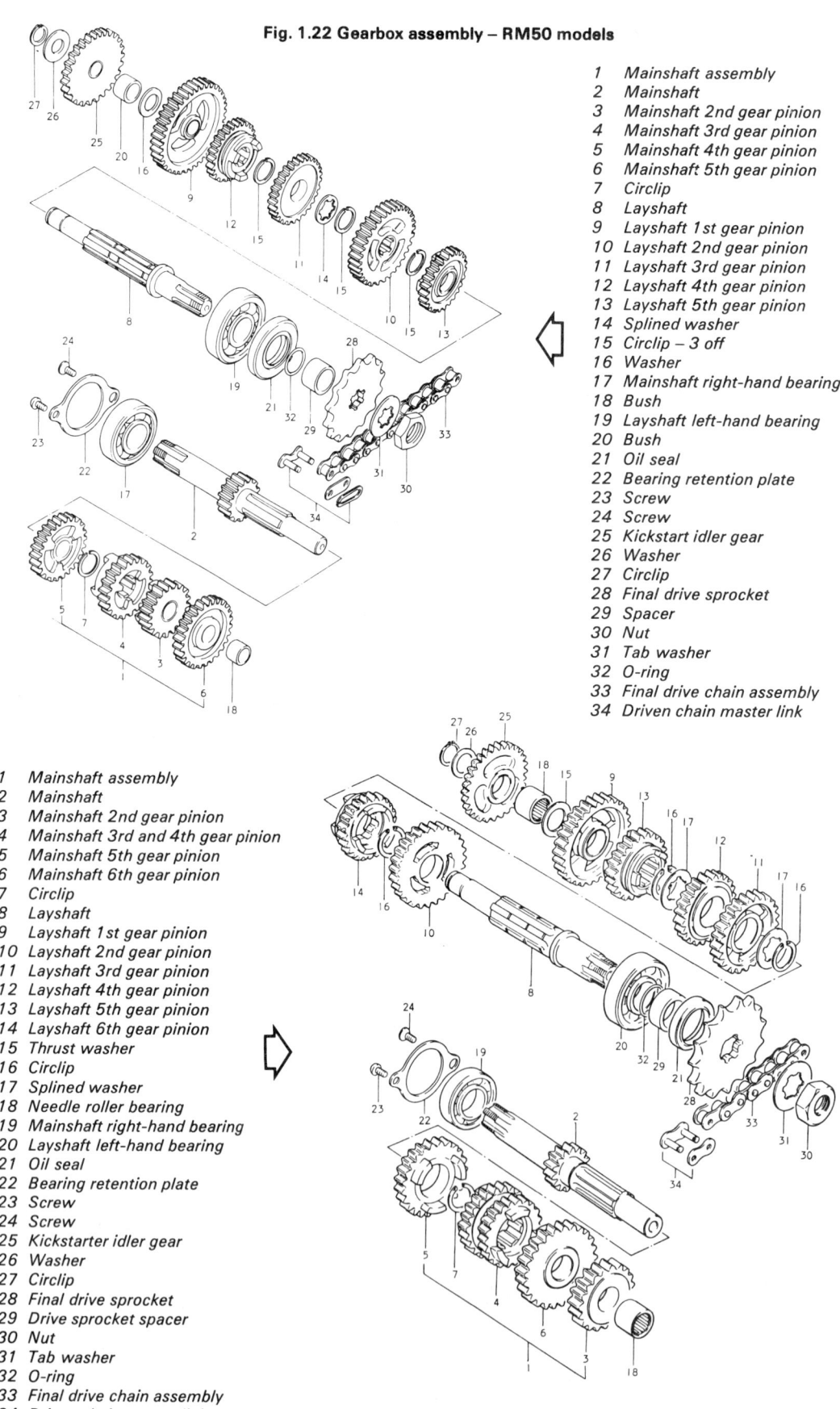

Fig. 1.22 Gearbox assembly – RM50 models

1 Mainshaft assembly
2 Mainshaft
3 Mainshaft 2nd gear pinion
4 Mainshaft 3rd gear pinion
5 Mainshaft 4th gear pinion
6 Mainshaft 5th gear pinion
7 Circlip
8 Layshaft
9 Layshaft 1st gear pinion
10 Layshaft 2nd gear pinion
11 Layshaft 3rd gear pinion
12 Layshaft 4th gear pinion
13 Layshaft 5th gear pinion
14 Splined washer
15 Circlip – 3 off
16 Washer
17 Mainshaft right-hand bearing
18 Bush
19 Layshaft left-hand bearing
20 Bush
21 Oil seal
22 Bearing retention plate
23 Screw
24 Screw
25 Kickstart idler gear
26 Washer
27 Circlip
28 Final drive sprocket
29 Spacer
30 Nut
31 Tab washer
32 O-ring
33 Final drive chain assembly
34 Driven chain master link

1 Mainshaft assembly
2 Mainshaft
3 Mainshaft 2nd gear pinion
4 Mainshaft 3rd and 4th gear pinion
5 Mainshaft 5th gear pinion
6 Mainshaft 6th gear pinion
7 Circlip
8 Layshaft
9 Layshaft 1st gear pinion
10 Layshaft 2nd gear pinion
11 Layshaft 3rd gear pinion
12 Layshaft 4th gear pinion
13 Layshaft 5th gear pinion
14 Layshaft 6th gear pinion
15 Thrust washer
16 Circlip
17 Splined washer
18 Needle roller bearing
19 Mainshaft right-hand bearing
20 Layshaft left-hand bearing
21 Oil seal
22 Bearing retention plate
23 Screw
24 Screw
25 Kickstarter idler gear
26 Washer
27 Circlip
28 Final drive sprocket
29 Drive sprocket spacer
30 Nut
31 Tab washer
32 O-ring
33 Final drive chain assembly
34 Driven chain master link

Fig. 1.23 Gearbox assembly – RM80 (RM60 similar)

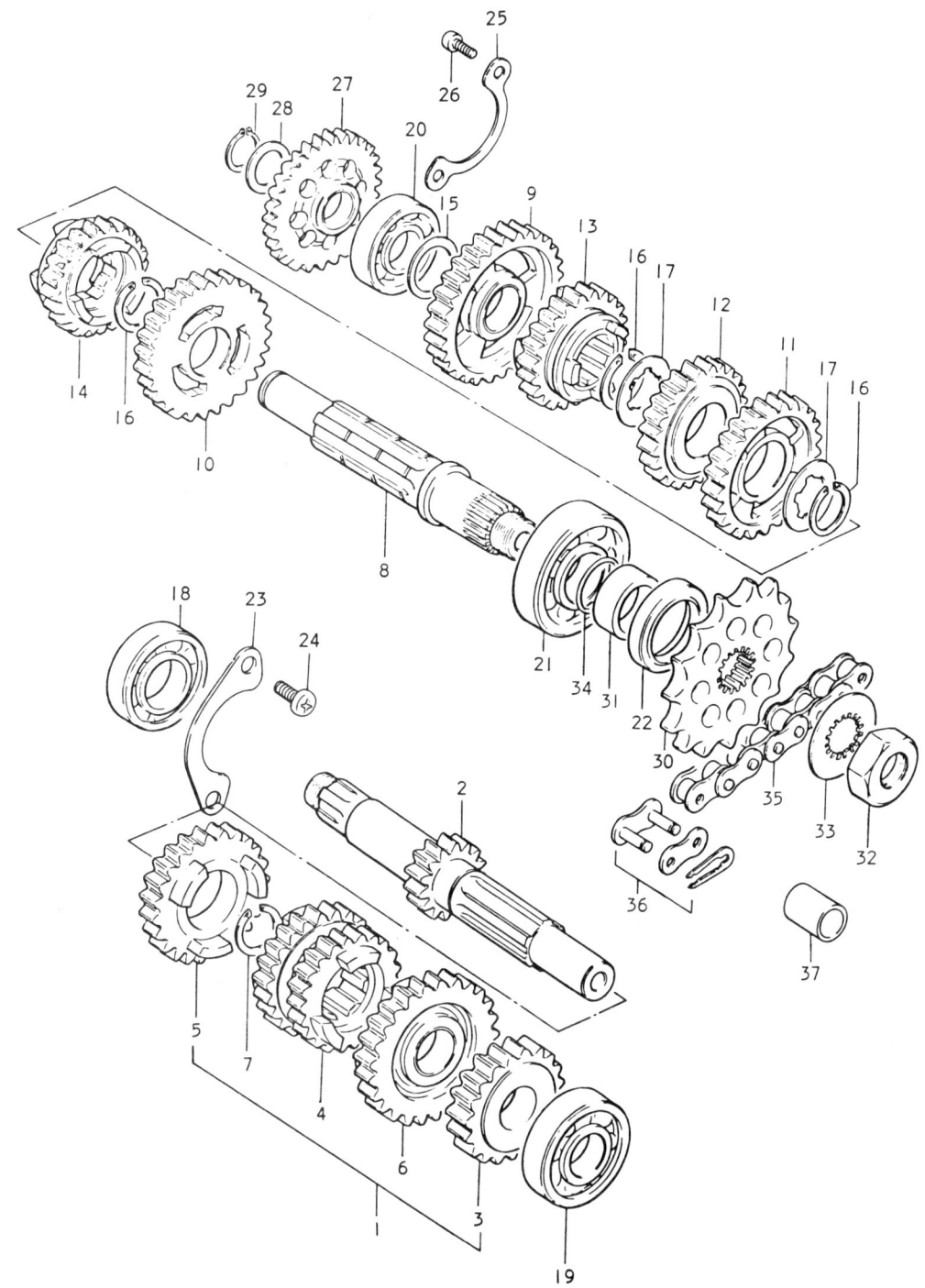

Fig. 1.24 Gearbox assembly – RM100 (RM125 similar)

1 Mainshaft assembly	14 Layshaft 6th gear pinion	26 Screw – 2 off
2 Mainshaft	15 Washer	27 Kickstarter idler gear
3 Mainshaft 2nd gear pinion	16 Circlip – 3 off	28 Thrust washer
4 Mainshaft 3rd gear pinion	17 Spline washer – 2 off	29 Circlip
5 Mainshaft 5th gear pinion	18 Mainshaft right-hand bearing	30 Final drive sprocket
6 Mainshaft 6th gear pinion	19 Mainshaft left-hand bearing	31 Spacer
7 Circlip	20 Layshaft right-hand bearing	32 Nut
8 Layshaft	21 Layshaft left-hand bearing	33 Tab washer
9 Layshaft 1st gear pinion	22 Oil seal	34 O-ring
10 Layshaft 2nd gear pinion	23 Mainshaft right-hand bearing retainer	35 Final drive chain
11 Layshaft 3rd gear pinion	24 Screw – 2 off	36 Chain master link
12 Layshaft 4th gear pinion	25 Layshaft right-hand bearing retainer	37 Drive chain cushion
13 Layshaft 5th gear pinion		

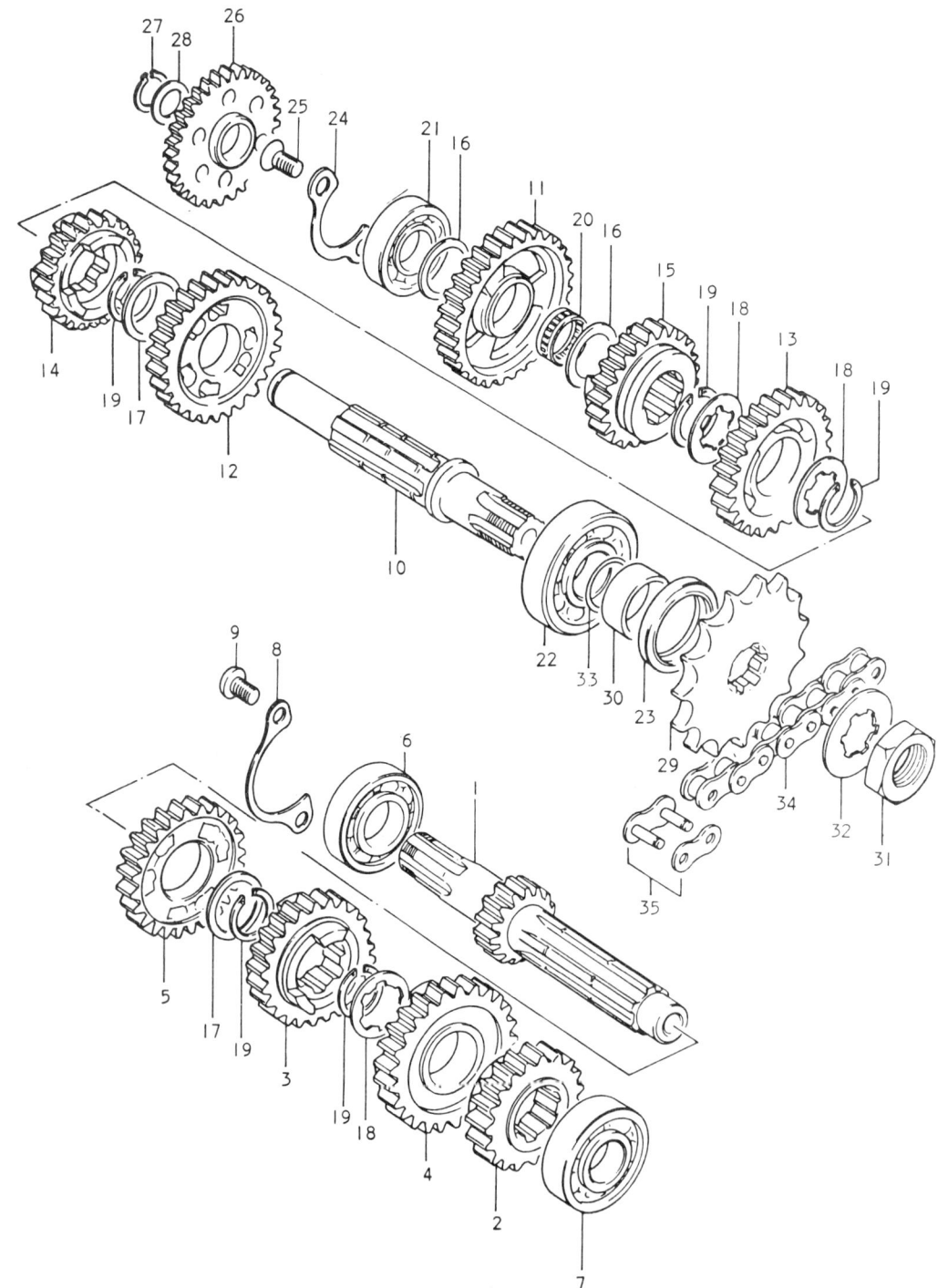

Fig. 1.25 Gearbox assembly – RM250 model

1	Mainshaft	13	Layshaft 3rd gear pinion	25	Screw
2	Mainshaft 2nd gear pinion	14	Layshaft 4th gear pinion	26	Kickstart idler gear
3	Mainshaft 3rd gear pinion	15	Layshaft 5th gear pinion	27	Circlip
4	Mainshaft 4th gear pinion	16	Thrust washer – 2 off	28	Thrust washer
5	Mainshaft 5th gear pinion	17	Washer – 2 off	29	Final drive sprocket
6	Mainshaft right-hand bearing	18	Thrust washer – 3 off	30	Spacer
7	Mainshaft left-hand bearing	19	Circlip – 5 off	31	Nut
8	Right-hand bearing retainer	20	Layshaft 1st gear pinion bearing	32	Tab washer
9	Screw – 2 off	21	Layshaft right-hand bearing	33	O-ring
10	Layshaft	22	Layshaft left-hand bearing	34	Final drive chain
11	Layshaft 1st gear pinion	23	Layshaft oil seal	35	Chain master link
12	Layshaft 2nd gear pinion	24	Layshaft right-hand bearing retainer		

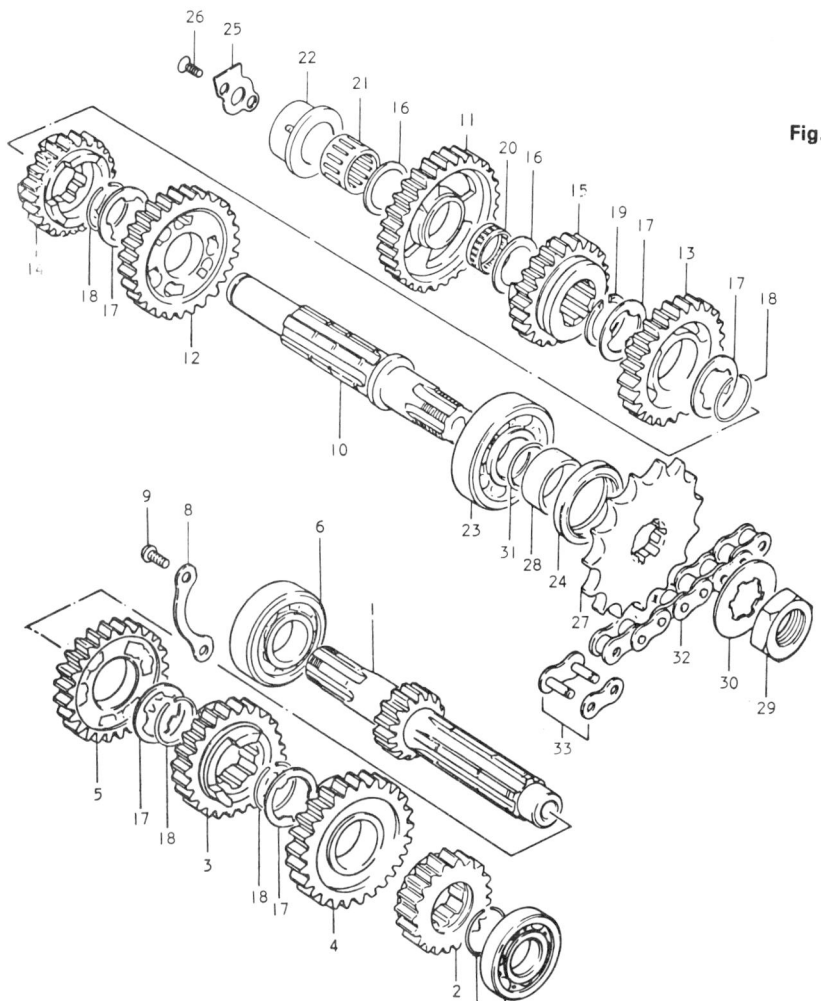

Fig. 1.26 Gearbox assembly – RM400 models

1 Mainshaft
2 Mainshaft 2nd gear pinion
3 Mainshaft 3rd gear pinion
4 Mainshaft 4th gear pinion
5 Mainshaft 5th gear pinion
6 Mainshaft right-hand bearing
7 Mainshaft left-hand bearing
8 Mainshaft right-hand bearing retainer
9 Screw – 2 off
10 Layshaft
11 Layshaft 1st gear pinion
12 Layshaft 2nd gear pinion
13 Layshaft 3rd gear pinion
14 Layshaft 4th gear pinion
15 Layshaft 5th gear pinion
16 Thrust washer – 2 off
17 Washer – 5 off
18 Circlip – 5 off
19 Circlip
20 Layshaft 1st gear pinion bearing
21 Layshaft right-hand bearing
22 Shouldered bush
23 Layshaft left-hand bearing
24 Oil seal
25 Layshaft right-hand bearing retainer
26 Screw – 2 off
27 Final drive sprocket
28 Spacer
29 Nut
30 Tab washer
31 O-ring
32 Final drive chain
33 Chain master link

22 Clutch assembly: examination and renovation

1   After an extended period of use the clutch linings will wear and promote clutch slip. The clutch plates should be measured with a vernier gauge or pair of calipers to ascertain the extent of wear. The measurements of thickness for the inserted plates and the maximum wear limits will be found in the Specifications section. If the friction plates are found to fall below the latter figure, they must be renewed.

2   The plain clutch plates should not show any evidence of overheating (blueing). If they do, check them for overall flatness by placing each plate on a flat surface. In the event of the plates being buckled they should be renewed.

3   The clutch springs may be of the compression or extension type, depending upon the model. After a long period of use, they will tend to weaken somewhat, and may eventually allow clutch slip, even with sound plates. If this condition is suspected, take one of the springs to a Suzuki Agent, and compare its free length with that of a new component. If wear is evident, renew the springs as a set. On machines with extension springs, these are 'screwed' into the clutch centre. When fitting new springs, the ends must be just flush with the inner face of the clutch centre.

4   A worn clutch spacer is often responsible for clutch noise and should be renewed if the fit within the clutch centre is particularly slack. Check the inner and outer surfaces for scratches; these will impair clutch action if not smoothed away.

The clutch release bearing can also cause noisy running if the clutch has been left incorrectly adjusted for long enough to allow the bearing to wear.

5   Check the condition of the slots in the outer surface of the clutch centre and the inner surfaces of the outer drum. In an extreme case, clutch chatter may have caused the tongues of the inserted plates to make indentations in the slots of the outer drum, or the tongues of the plain plates to indent the slots of the clutch centre. These indentations will trap the clutch plates as they are freed and impair clutch action. If the damage is only slight the indentations can be removed by careful work with a file and the burrs removed from the tongues of the clutch plates in similar fashion. More extensive damage will necessitate renewal of the parts concerned.

6   The clutch release mechanism employed on the RM250 and 400 models consists of a rack and pinion arrangement, the rack segment bearing upon a pushrod which conveys the movement to the inner face of the clutch cover, or pressure plate. In the case of the remaining models, the operating spindle and pinion is arranged on the right-hand outer casing, the pinion engaging a headed rack which is in effect a 'pullrod'. In both systems, a radial caged needle roller bearing is employed between the clutch cover and its operating piece. The two arrangements are commendably robust and are unlikely to give rise to problems during the normal life of the machine. If damage does occur, its cause will be readily apparent. It is worth greasing the moving parts during overhauls, but no other regular maintenance should be required.

22.3 Check that spring ends are flush with centre (RM100)

22.4 Renew thrust bearing if noisy in use (RM80)

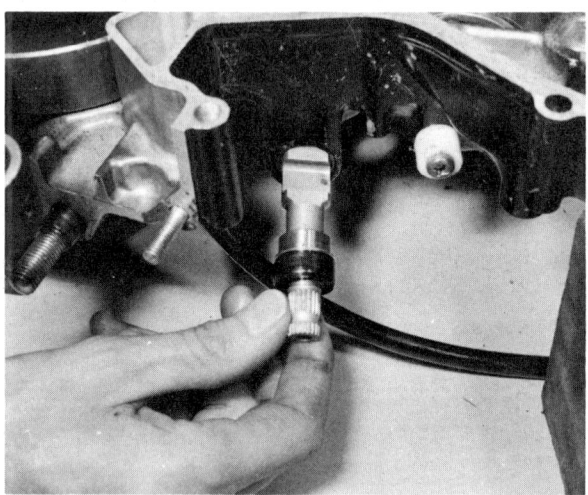

22.6a Operating shaft fits as shown – RM250, 400 (RM400)

22.6b Mechanism operates through shaft aperture (RM400)

22.6c All other models use rack and pinion system (RM100)

23 Engine reassembly: general

1   Before reassembly of the engine/gear unit is commenced, the various component parts should be cleaned thoroughly and placed on a sheet of clean paper, close to the working area.

2   Make sure all traces of old gaskets have been removed and that the mating surfaces are clean and undamaged. One of the best ways to remove old gasket cement is to apply a rag soaked in methylated spirit. This acts as a solvent and will ensure that the cement is removed without resort to scraping and the consequent risk of damage.

3   Gather together all the necessary tools and have available an oil can filled with clean engine oil. Make sure that all new gaskets and oil seals are to hand, also all replacement parts required. Nothing is more frustrating that having to stop in the middle of a reassembly sequence because a vital gasket or replacement has been overlooked.

4   Make sure that the reassembly area is clean and that there is adequate working space. Refer to the torque and clearance settings whenever they are given (a comprehensive list of torque settings is also given after the Routine Maintenance Section). Many of the smaller bolts are easily sheared if overtightened. Always use the correct size screwdriver bit for the

screws and never a punch. If the existing screws show evidence of maltreatment in the past, it is advisable to renew them as a complete set.

24 Engine reassembly: fitting the crankshaft assembly

1 Arrange the left-hand crankcase half on the workbench, placing wooden blocks beneath it so that room is allowed for the crankshaft to protrude when fitted. Check both crankcase halves to ensure that all seals and bearings have been fitted. All seal lips should be greased to avoid any risk of damage during installation.

2 All retainer plates should be fitted at this stage. The securing screws should be retained with a thread locking fluid to preclude their loosening in use. As with the other casing screws, they should be securely tightened using an impact driver.

3 Lubricate the crankshaft ends to ease fitting, then offer up the crankshaft assembly. The crankshaft should be a good sliding fit in the internal bore of the main bearing, and may need to be tapped into position usinggng a hide or plastic-faced mallet. The connecting rod should be supported during this operation, so that it enters the crankcase mouth squarely.

24.1 Seals should be fitted and greased (RM100)

24.2a Fit any new bearing into casing (RM100)

24.2b Use locking compound on retainer screws (RM400)

24.3 Fit crankshaft, with main bearing if appropriate (RM100)

25 Engine reassembly: refitting the gearbox components

1 The two gearbox shaft/cluster assemblies must be fitted simultaneously and as complete assemblies. If, therefore, removal of the pinions from the shafts has been carried out for inspection or renewal the assemblies must be rebuilt before proceeding further. Refer to the accompanying illustrations and photographs for the correct relative positions of the pinions and various washers and circlips. Great care must be taken to ensure that the assemblies are built-up correctly or the selection and engagement of one or more gears will prove impossible.

2 On RM50, 60 and 80 models the final pinion to be fitted on the mainshaft is a press fit. To ensure security, the bore of this pinion and the surface of the shaft over which it fits should be coated with thread locking fluid. Suzuki recommend the use of Suzuki thread lock 1333B (No 103K). The precise position of the pinion on the shaft must be adjusted so that the distance from its outside face to the outer face of the 1st gear pinion is as follows.

    RM50   *76 mm (2.992 in)*
    RM60, 80   *87.5 mm (3.445 in)*

Use a vernier gauge to take measurements and so ensure accuracy of the final positioning. Take care that the thread locking fluid does not prevent rotation of the adjacent gears.

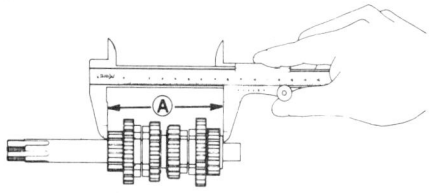

Fig. 1.27 Checking assembled length of gearbox mainshaft

3   Offer up the clusters simultaneously as an assembly, ensuring that both enter the casing squarely. Check that the pinions mesh correctly and turn freely.

4   Place the selector forks in position, ensuring that they are arranged so that the locating pins face in towards the selector drum bore. Place the selector drum in position, fitting it so that the selector fork pins engage in the drum tracks when they are swung round to their normal position. When the selector forks are located correctly, the support shafts should be inserted through their bosses and into the casing.

26 Engine reassembly: installing the kickstart shaft

1   The kickstart shaft and its internal components should now be refitted in the right-hand crankcase half. The arrangement differs between the various models, and the following points should be noted. On all models, slide the shaft into position in the casing. In the case of the RM400, the shaft is fitted from the **inside** of the crankcase half, whilst on all the other models, the shaft is fitted from the outside. On RM400 machines, do not omit to fit the retaining circlip at the outer face of the casing.

2   On RM50, RM60 , 80, 100, 125 and 250 machines, turn the kickstart to its fully returned position (clockwise when viewed from outside the casing half) until it touches its stop. Place the kickstart return spring over the shaft, and engage its hooked end with the casing lug. Grasp the free end of the spring with pliers, turning it clockwise by about 180° (about 90° in

25.1 Place gearbox shafts in left-hand casing (RM100)

25.2a Selector forks (RM80)

25.2b Selector forks (RM400)

25.2c Selector forks (RM100)

25.2d Fit selector drum and position forks (RM80)

25.2e Slide the support pins into fork and casing (RM80)

26.1a Kickstart gear is secured by circlip (RM100)

26.1b Check that index marks align as shown (RM100)

26.1c Fit ratchet spring and plain washer ... (RM100)

26.1d ... and install assembly in casing (RM100)

26.2a Turn shaft until it rests against stop ... (RM80)

26.2b ... and fit spring, guide and circlip (RM80)

26.2c RM100 return spring arrangment (RM100)

26.3a Fit kickstart gear and ratchet ...(RM400)

26.3b ... ensuring that marks align (RM400)

26.3c Fit spring and install from inside of casing (RM400)

26.3d Shaft is secured by a circlip ... (RM400)

26.3e Tension spring as shown ... (RM400)

26.3f ... then fit spring guide and circlip (RM400)

the case of the RM50, 60 and 80). The spring end may now be pushed into its hole in the shaft. Slide the plastic spring guide into position to prevent the spring from becoming disengaged. This is followed by a kickstart shaft support piece on RM50 and 60 models only. In the case of the remaining models, the spring guide is secured by a circlip.

3   On RM400 machines, fit the kickstart pinion and ratchet, if these were removed, noting that the index marks on the shaft and the ratchet should align. Place the ratchet spring in position, then slide the shaft assembly into the casing, retaining it with its circlip at the outer face. Fit the return spring, tensioning it by turning it through about 180° before engaging the spring end in the shaft. Note that the spring is preceded by a large plain washer. Fit the spring guide and retain it with a circlip.

27 Engine reassembly: joining the crankcase halves

1   Carefully clean both mating faces to remove any residual oil or dirt. Fit any locating dowels in their bores. Apply a thin coating of RTV jointing compound to the mating face of the right-hand crankcase half. This should be allowed to partially dry off as prescribed by the compound manufacturer, usually for about ten minutes.

2   Whilst waiting for the compound to dry, use an oil can to lubricate the various moving parts with clean engine oil. Offer up the right-hand crankcase half, ensuring that the various

shafts locate correctly in their bearings. If necessary, tap the casing down using a hide mallet, checking that it seats evenly.

3   Place one or two of the crankcase screws in position to retain the crankcase halves, then check that the gearbox shafts and crankshaft are free to rotate. If all is well, fit the remaining crankcase screws, tightening them evenly and in a diagonal sequence to prevent warpage. Note that a thread locking fluid should be used on each screw to prevent loosening in service. The number of securing screws varies between models and is as follows:

RM50, RM60, RM80	11 screws
RM100, RM125, RM400	13 screws
RM250	12 screws

4   The screws are of various lengths, and it is obviously important that they are fitted in the correct holes. If they were not pushed through some card during dismantling, the correct positions must be found by trial and error. With the screws just dropped into their holes in the casing, each screw head should stand proud by a similar amount. Final tightening is best done with an impact driver, unless Allen screws have been fitted.

28 Engine reassembly: refitting the kickstart and gear selector mechanisms – RM50, RM60 and RM80

1   If the right hand main bearing retainer plate was removed during dismantling, it should be refitted, using a thread locking fluid on its retaining screws. Note that the lower of the three screws has a countersunk head. The right-hand gearbox main bearing retainer should also be refitted, again using a locking fluid on the screw threads. The rear-most screw has a countersunk head.

2   Fit the neutral detent and stopper arms, retaining them with their common shouldered pivot bolt. The stopper arm, which has a large disc fitted at the end, is fitted nearest the casing and at the bottom of the casing. Both are tensioned by small extension springs, and these should be anchored to the lugs provided on the main bearing retainer so that they bear against the selector drum end.

3   Slide the gearchange shaft into its bore through the crankcase, ensuring that the limiter pin protrudes through the elongated slot in the plate at the right-hand end of the shaft. Fit the headed roller, followed by the selector claw assembly, this being retained by an E-clip at the end of the limiter pin. Place the selector pins in the end of the selector drum, then fit the end plate. This is retained by a single screw which should be treated with thread locking fluid prior to installation.

4   Temporarily refit the gearchange pedal, and check that the five gear positions (RM50) or six gear positions (RM60 and 80) can be selected. To facilitate engagement, the gearbox mainshaft should be rotated whilst the gearchange pedal is operated. Unless the adjuster pin has been disturbed or a new centring spring fitted, there should be no difficulty in selecting gears. If, however, it proves difficult to change up or down, the bias of the centring spring can be altered to adjust the rest position of the claw assembly. When set correctly, the two claw ends should be approximately equidistant from the nearest pins. Adjustment is made by means of the eccentric pin and locknut which bears upon the centring spring end. Move the pin only slightly, then tighten the locknut and recheck the selection.

5   Fit the kickstart pinion over the end of the kickstart shaft, turning it so that it engages its quick thread. Ensure that the friction clip seats in its recess in the casing, as shown in the accompanying photographs. Place the kickstart idler pinion over the end of the gearbox layshaft. Fit its plain washer and secure it with its circlip.

27.2a Fitting RH crankcase half (RM100)

27.2b Fitting RH crankcase half (RM400)

27.3 Fit and tighten securing screws (RM100)

28.1a Assemble the various retainer plates ... (RM100)

28.1b ... noting countersunk screws (arrowed) (RM80)

28.2a Fit cam drum retainer plate (RM80)

28.2b Connect stopper springs as shown (RM80)

28.3a Slide selector shaft into position (RM80)

28.3b Fit pins to selector drum end (RM80)

28.3c Place selector claw in position as shown ... (RM80)

28.3d ... and secure with E-clip (RM80)

28.5a Check position of starter gear and clip (RM80)

28.5b Idler gear is retained by washer and circlip (RM80)

29 Engine reassembly: refitting the kickstart and gear selector mechanisms – RM100, 125, 250 and 400

1   Assemble the selector drum ratchet mechanisms noting that the pawls have slots which are slightly offset. The slot should be nearest to the selector drum when the pawls are refitted. Check that the pawls, pins and springs move freely, then install the ratchet mechanism in the recess in the end of the selector drum.

2   The ratchet is fitted with a number of teeth arranged in two groups. Turn the ratchet so that the larger group of five teeth faces towards the selector shaft bore. Assemble the guide plate and retainer. Each is secured by two screws which should be treated with a thread locking fluid prior to final tightening. The gearbox layshaft bearing should also be refitted at this stage if it is not already in position.

3   Slide the selector shaft into place, ensuring that the centring spring locates on either side of its peg. The teeth on the selector shaft should engage evenly with those of the selector ratchet, as shown in the accompanying photographs. Fit the selector drum detent plunger assembly on the underside of the crankcase. The gearchange lever can be temporarily refitted to allow the selector mechanism to be checked. Check that each gear engages correctly, whilst turning the gearbox shafts to ease engagement. Note that the RM100 and RM125 models have six-speed gearboxes, whilst a five-speed gearbox is employed on the RM250 and RM400 machines.

4   On all models other than the RM400, fit the kickstart idler pinion, securing it to the layshaft end with its plain washer and circlip. In the case of the RM400, the entire kickstart mechanism is contained within the crankcases, and will have been assembled prior to the casing halves being joined.

30 Engine reassembly: refitting the clutch and crankshaft pinion

1   Before the clutch assembly is installed, it is essential to check that the gear selector mechanism and the various retainers have been fitted, because it is not possible to do so with the clutch in position.

2   In the case of the RM50, a separate kickstart driven gear engages with the clutch outer drum by way of dogs. The driven gear and plain bush should be fitted over the gearbox mainshaft end before the clutch outer drum is positioned. On RM60 and RM80 models, a plain bush supports the clutch, as on the RM50, but the driven gear is integral with the drum, as it is on the RM100, 125 and 250. The RM100, 125, 250 and 400 employ a needle roller bearing to support the clutch outer drum,

with a plain inner race in the case of the two larger machines.

3   Fit the driven gear, where appropriate, and then slide the clutch outer drum into position. On all models, fit the plain thrust washer which separates the clutch centre and drum, then fit the clutch centre. On the RM250 and RM400 models, fit the clutch pushrods through the centre of the gearbox mainshaft, ensuring that the rounded end of each pushrod faces outwards. On the RM400 model, a steel ball is fitted between the two pushrods.

4   Place the clutch plain and friction plates into position, starting with a friction plate, and then fitting plain and friction plates alternately. Place the clutch centre nut and tab washer on the end of the mainshaft, and tighten the clutch centre nut to the recommended torque setting. The clutch centre should be prevented from turning in a similar manner to that used during removal. Do not omit to secure the nut by bending up the locking tab.

5   Fit the headed pushrod (RM250 and 400 only) and place the clutch thrust bearing and plain thrustwasher in position. It is essential that the thrustwasher is placed between the bearing and the clutch cover to prevent undue wear. Place the clutch cover in position, then fit and tighten the springs and screws. The screws can be prevented from slackening by applying a small quantity of thread locking fluid to each before fitting.

6   The remaining models employ a headed 'pull-rod' or rack, which is fitted from the inner face of the clutch pressure plate. A thrust bearing is fitted between the pull-rod head and the pressure plate. On RM50, RM60 and RM80, conventional compression springs are employed, and are fitted in the same manner as those of the RM250 and 400.

7   RM100 and RM125 models employ extension springs to retain the pressure plate. Place the pressure plate in position, then engage the looped spring end with the wire hook arrangement used during dismantling. Pull the spring loop through the pressure plate, and slide the anchor pin into place. This operation should be repeated to secure the remaining springs.

8   Fit the small O-ring over the crankshaft end (RM100, 125, 250 and 400 models) and fit the crankshaft pinion spacer. Lubricate the oil seal lip with grease before the spacer is positioned. Fit the crankshaft pinion, locking washer and securing nut. With the crankshaft immobilised in the same way as was used during dismantling, tighten the securing nut to the appropriate torque setting. Bend up the tab washer to prevent the nut from slackening in use, where appropriate.

9   On all but the RM250 and 400 models, refit the right-hand outer casing using a new gasket. As the cover is fitted, the toothed section of the clutch 'pull-rod' should engage with the operating shaft in the cover. It may be necessary to reposition the operating arm if this is still in position. In the case of RM250 and RM400 machines, leave the cover off until the clutch has been adjusted.

29.2a Larger models use similar retainer plates (RM100)

29.2b Screws should be coated with locking fluid (RM100)

29.2c RM250, 400 arrangement is similar (RM400)

29.2d Do not omit gearbox bearing retainers (RM100)

29.3a Selector mechanism should align as shown (RM100)

29.3b Fit the combined neutral detent and drain plug (RM400)

29.4 Kickstart idler pinion is secured by a circlip (RM100)

30.2a Fit plain thrustwasher ... (RM100)

30.2b ... followed by clutch needle roller bearing (RM100)

30.2c RM250, 400 uses similar arrangement (RM400)

30.3a Fit clutch outer drum into position (RM80)

30.3b Fitting RM100 clutch outer drum (RM100)

30.3c Place thrustwasher over end of shaft (RM100)

30.3d RM250, 400 employ single washer (RM400)

30.3e Place clutch pushrod(s) into hollow shaft (RM400)

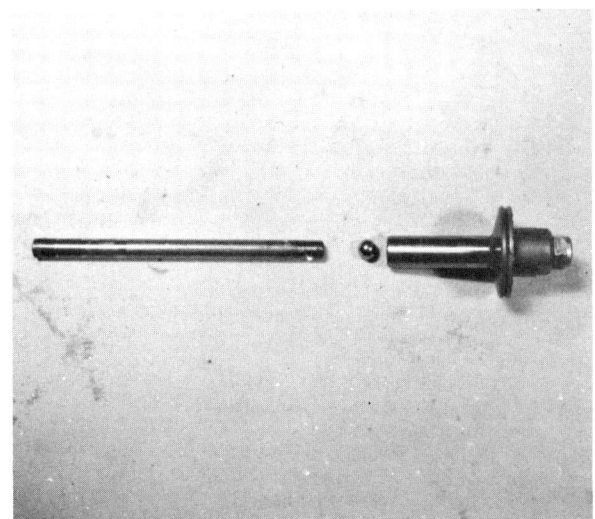

30.3f Note position of steel ball – RM400 only (RM400)

30.3g Place clutch centre into position (RM80)

30.4a Fit clutch plates in alternating sequence (RM400)

30.4b Fit and tighten securing nut

30.5a Note headed pushrod and bearing – RM250/400

30.5b Fit clutch cover, springs and securing screws (RM400)

30.6a Fit 'pull-rod' – all models except RM250/400 (RM100)

30.6b Place clutch cover in position (RM80)

30.8a Fit O-ring and spacer to crankshaft end (RM100)

30.8b Place crankshaft pinion over splines ... (RM100)

30.8c ... or Woodruff key, as appropriate (RM400)

30.8d Fit securing nut and tab washer (RM400)

30.8e RM80 crankshaft pinion ... (RM80)

30.8f ... and securing nut (RM80)

31 Engine reassembly: refitting the flywheel magneto – RM50 model

1   Place the stator assembly in position, and fit the three retaining screws. Do not tighten the screws fully at this stage. Place the rotor over the crankshaft end, having first fitted the Woodruff key which locates it.

2   Refering to Chapter 3 for details, check the contact breaker gap and ignition timing setting, then tighten the stator screws and secure the rotor to the crankshaft.

32 Engine reassembly: refitting the CDI stator and rotor – all models except RM50

1   Fit the Woodruff key to its slot in the crankshaft, and then place the rotor in position. Fit the plain and spring washers, then fit and tighten the securing nut. Place the stator assembly over the rotor, checking that it lines up correctly to allow the wiring to be routed properly. One of the elongated holes in the stator periphery will be seen to have an engraved line. This line should be arranged so that it is central to the securing screw. This will ensure that the system is timed correctly. Fit and tighten the stator securing screws.

32.1a Fit Woodruff key in crankshaft end ... (RM400)

32.1b ... then place rotor in position

32.1c Fit rotor with screw central in slotted holes (RM400)

33 Engine reassembly: refitting the gearbox sprocket

1   Fit the small O-ring over the end of the gearbox layshaft end, followed by the sprocket spacer, ensuring that the seal lip is greased first. Place the sprocket, splined washer and securing nut in position on the shaft. The nut should be fitted finger-tight at this stage, leaving final tightening until the engine has been installed in the frame. The sprocket can then be held by applying the rear brake whilst the nut is secured.

34 Engine reassembly: refitting the piston and rings

1   Position the engine to rest on the base of the crankcase. Pad the mouth of the crankcase with clean rag prior to fitting the piston and piston rings, so that any displaced parts will be prevented from falling in.
2   Replace the caged needle roller bearing in the small end, lubricate it thoroughly, then fit the piston and gudgeon pin,

checking to ensure that it is replaced securely. Note that the piston has an arrow stamped on the crown, which must face forwards.
3   If the gudgeon pin is a tight fit in the piston bosses, the piston can be warmed with warm water to effect the necessary temporary expansion. Oil the gudgeon pin and piston bosses before the gudgeon pin is inserted, then fit the circlips, making sure that they are engaged fully with their retaining grooves. A good fit is essential, since a displaced circlip will cause extensive engine damage. Always fit new circlips, NEVER re-use the old ones.
4   Check that the piston rings are fitted correctly, with their ends either side of the ring pegs. If this precaution is not observed, the rings will be broken during assembly.

33.1a Fit O-ring and sprocket spacer ... (RM400)

33.1b ... then place sprocket over splines (RM400)

33.1c Note recess in securing nut (RM100)

34.2a Fit and lubricate small end bearing ... (RM100)

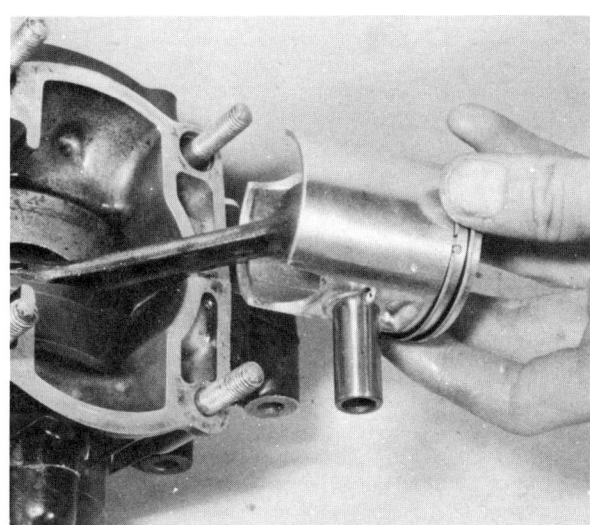

34.2b ... and assemble piston (RM100)

34.2c Arrow must face towards exhaust port (RM80)

34.4 Check that ring ends engage on pegs (RM100)

35 Engine reassembly: refitting the cylinder barrel

1   Place a new cylinder base gasket over the retaining studs and lubricate the cylinder bore with clean engine oil. Arrange the piston so that it is at top dead centre (TDC) and lower the cylinder down the retaining studs until contact is made with the piston. The rings can now be squeezed one at a time until the cylinder barrel will slide over them, checking to ensure that the ends are still each side of the ring peg. Great care is necessary during this operation, since the rings are brittle and very easily broken.

2   Although the cylinder barrel has a good lead-in, to facilitate entry of the piston rings, a piston ring clamp can be used as an alternative to the hand feed method. Here again, care must be taken to ensure that the rings are correctly positioned in relation to the piston ring pegs.

3   When the rings have engaged fully with the cylinder bore withdraw the rag packing from the crankcase mouth and slide the cylinder barrel down the retaining studs, so that it seats on the new base gasket (no gasket cement).

35.1a Feed piston into cylinder bore ... (RM80)

35.1b ... and lower barrel into position (RM400)

36 Engine reassembly: refitting the cylinder head

1   Place a new cylinder head gasket on the top of the cylinder barrel, using a smear of grease to retain it in position. Fit the cylinder head, taking care that the cylinder head gasket is not displaced or distorted during the initial tightening down.

2   The RM50, 60 and 80 models employ four holding studs which retain the cylinder barrel and head. There are two additional short studs at the rear of the cylinder barrel. On the larger models, six studs and nuts secure the cylinder base and six separate studs and nuts retain the cylinder head. In the case of the former models, gradually tighten all six nuts down evenly in a diagonal sequence to the specified value.

3   On the larger models, tighten the cylinder base nuts first, then tighten the cylinder head nuts in the sequence shown in the accompanying diagram, to the correct torque value. Replace the sparking plug in order to prevent any extraneous material from dropping into the engine whilst it is being refitted into the frame.

Cylinder head nut torque settings

RM50 and RM60	*13.0 – 16.0 lbf ft (180 – 220 kgf m)*
RM80, 100, 125, 250 and 400	*16.5 – 19.5 lbf ft (230 – 270 kgf m)*

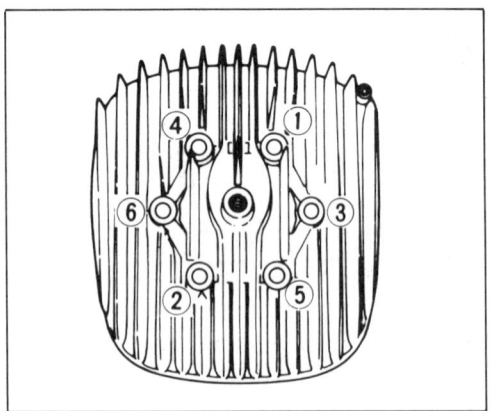

Fig. 1.28 Cylinder head nut tightening sequence

36.2a Cylinder head is retained by six studs ... (RM400)

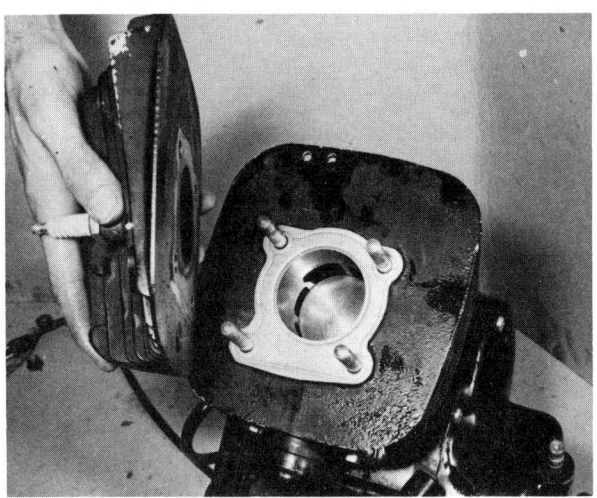
36.2b ... or four studs as shown (RM80)

36.3 Engine unit ready for installation (RM400)

37 Refitting the engine/gearbox unit into the frame

1   Check that the frame is supported securely and that nothing is in a position which would impede engine installation. It is advisable to obtain some assistance so that the machine can be steadied whilst the engine unit is lifted into the frame. The engine is not unduly heavy, and can be lifted into position by one person, leaving it resting on the frame cradle.

2   The engine mounting bolts can now be refitted. The RM50, 60 and 80 engine unit is secured by three bolts, whilst that of the RM100 and 125 is retained by engine plates at the front, these being secured by four bolts. The RM250 unit is retained by a total of six bolts, whilst the RM400 employs seven. Assemble the engine plates (where fitted) and the engine mounting bolts loosely. Once all bolts are in position, fit new self-locking nuts and tighten all bolts securely.

37.2a Footrest lever is secured by bolt – RM50, 60, 80 (RM80)

37.2b RM100 engine upper rear mounting bolt (RM100)

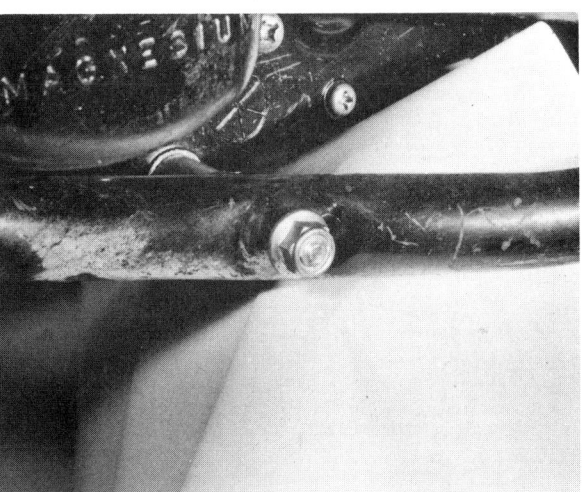
37.2c RM400 lower engine mounting bolt (RM400)

37.2d Do not omit lower rear mounting bolt (RM400)

38.3 Check timing, then fit outer casing (RM80)

38 Engine reassembly: refitting the drive chain and left-hand engine casing

1   Check that the O-ring, spacer and gearbox sprocket are in position on the gearbox layshaft end, and fit the tab washer and securing nut. Run the final drive chain around the gearbox sprocket, arranging the ends of the chain at the rear wheel sprocket so that they lie at adjacent teeth. Fit the joining link, side plate and retaining clip, ensuring that the closed end of the latter faces in the direction of chain travel.

2   With the chain installed, apply the rear brake to hold the gearbox sprocket then tighten the sprocket securing nut to 21.5 – 36.0 lbf ft (300 – 500 kgf m) on RM50, 60 and 80 models, or 29.0 – 43.0 lbf ft (400 – 600 kgf m) on all other models. Do not forget to secure the nut by bending up the locking tab.

3   On the smaller machines, the one-piece engine casing can be refitted, assuming that the ignition timing, if disturbed, has been re-set. On the larger machines, refit the slotted sprocket guard.

39.1a Spark arrester is retained by rubber-mounted bolt (RM100)

39 Engine reassembly: refitting the exhaust system and carburettor

1   The exhaust pipe and silencer assembly are a one-piece construction, and it will be necessary to manoeuvre it into position by threading it through the frame. Engage the silencer end in the spark arrester, and the exhaust pipe on its mounting stub on the cylinder barrel. The silencer is secured by a retaining bolt at its centre. The silencer is attached to the spark arrester by tension springs or a screw clamp arrangement, a similar spring arrangement being used to retain the exhaust pipe to the cylinder barrel. The retaining springs can be fitted using the wire hook device employed during dismantling.

2   The carburettor is refitted by reversing the removal sequence. It tends to be somewhat difficult to position, and a certain amount of patience and ingenuity will be called for. On the larger models, do not forget to swing the rear suspension oil reservoirs back into position after the carburettor has been refitted.

3   Place the throttle valve assembly into position, ensuring that the needle enters the needle jet and that the throttle valve guide pin locates correctly, then screw down the mixing chamber top. Check that the carburettor is vertical before the retaining clips are tightened.

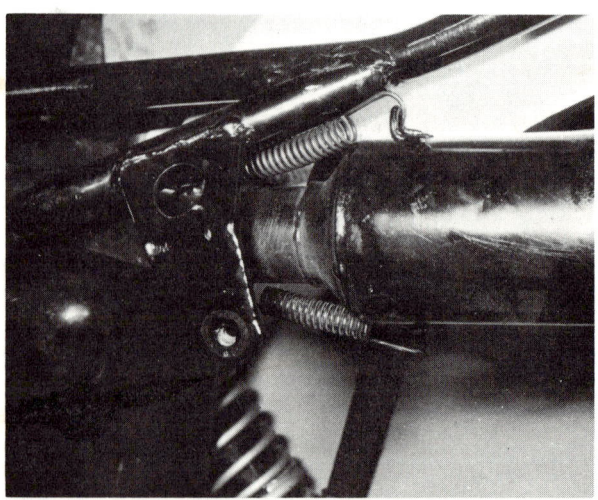

39.1b Springs secure spark arrester to silencer (RM400)

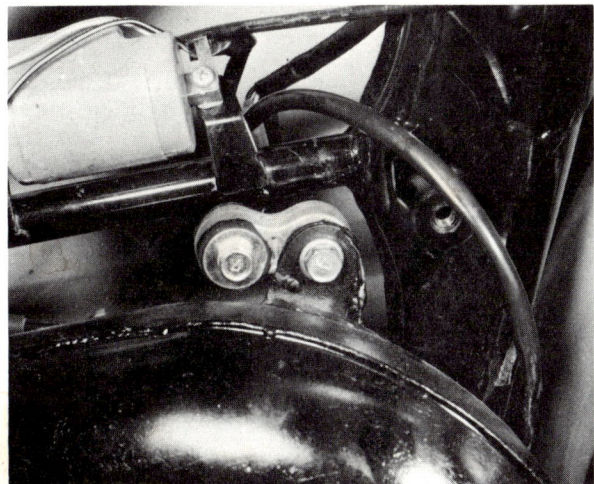

39.1c Silencer front mounting arrangement (RM400)

40 Engine reassembly: completion and final adjustments

1   Check that the air filter element is clean and in sound condi-tion, then replace it in the air cleaner case. Ensure that there are no air leaks between the filter and the carburettor, because any dust drawn into the engine will cause rapid wear.

2   Reconnect the clutch cable and arm, and adjust it to give about 4 mm free play in the cable. Coarse adjustment can be obtained by moving the operating arm on its splined shaft, fine adjustment being provided by the cable adjuster. Ensure that the clutch and throttle cables are routed correctly to give smooth operation. There should be no tight bends, and the cables should not hang in a position where they are likely to become snagged in use.

3   Trace the ignition leads from the engine, routing them through the front engine mounting, and reconnect them at the connectors beneath the top frame tube. The leads should be fixed to the frame with PVC tape or wiring clips. Refit the spark-ing plug lead.

4   Refit the gearchange pedal and kickstart lever, ensuring that they are positioned at the correct angle for easy operation. It is advisable to use a thread locking fluid on the pinch bolt threads to prevent them from loosening in use. Refit the fuel tank, ensuring that the rubber mounting rubbers are fitted correctly to prevent the tank from chafing on the frame tubes. Connect the fuel pipe between the fuel tap and the carburettor. Fit the seat and side covers.

5   Remove the gearbox filler plug, and add the recommended quantity of SAE20W/40 engine oil. The quantity of oil required varies according to the machine. See the accompanying table for details.

Gearbox oil capacities

Model	cc	Imp pint	US pint
RM50*	700	1.23	1.48
RM60*	700	1.23	1.48
RM80*	750	1.32	1.59
RM100	800	1.41	1.69
RM125	800	1.41	1.69
RM250	800	1.41	1.69
RM400	1000	1.76	2.11

*Recommended quantity in rebuilt (dry) engine. Use 50 cc (0.09 Imp pint (0.11 US pint) less oil at subsequent oil changes.

41 Starting and running the rebuilt engine

1   When the initial start-up is made, run the engine slowly for the first few minutes, especially if the engine has been rebored or a new crankshaft fitted. Check that all the controls function correctly and that there are no oil leaks before taking the machine out on test. The exhaust will emit a high proportion of white smoke initially during the first few miles, as the excess oil used whilst the engine was reassembled is burnt away. The volume of smoke should gradually diminish until only the customary light blue haze is observed during normal running. It is wise to carry a spare sparking plug during the first run since the existing plug may oil up due to the temporary excess oil.

2   Remember that a good seal between the piston and the cylinder barrel is essential for the correct functioning of the engine. A rebored two-stroke will require more careful running in, over a longer period, than its four-stroke counterpart. There is a far greater risk of engine seizure during the first one hundred miles if the engine is permitted to work hard.

3   Do not tamper with the exhaust system, or run the engine without the baffles fitted to the silencer. Unwarranted changes in the exhaust system will have a very marked effect on engine performance, invariably for the worse. The same advice applies to dispensing with the air cleaner or the air cleaner element.

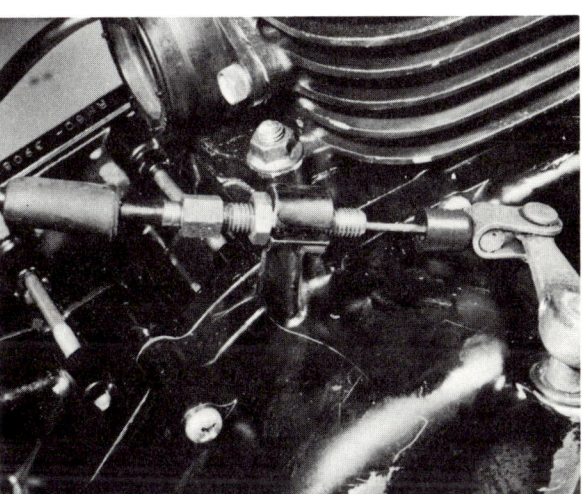

40.2 Connect and adjust clutch cable (RM80)

40.5 Do not omit to fit and tighten drain plug (RM80)

42 Fault diagnosis: engine

Symptom	Cause	Remedy
Engine will not start	Defective sparking plug	Remove plug and lay it on cylinder head. Check whether spark occurs when engine is kicked over.
	Dirty or closed contact breaker points (RM50)	Check condition of points and whether gap is correct.
	Air leaks at crankcase or worn crankshaft oil seals	Apply full choke and check whether petrol is reaching the plug.
	Lack of compression	Check for stuck piston ring, or worn ring, cylinder bore or piston.
Engine runs unevenly	Ignition and/or fuel system fault	Check as though engine will not start.
	Blowing cylinder head	Oil leak should provide evidence.
	Incorrect ignition timing	Check and if necessary adjust.
Lack of power	Incorrect ignition timing	See above.
	Fault in fuel system	Check system and vent in filler cap.
	Loss of compression	See above.
White smoke from exhaust	Too much oil	Correct fuel mixture.
	Drive side oil seal failed	Dismantle engine and fit new seal.
Engine overheats	Pre-ignition and/or weak mixture	Check carburettor settings, also grade of plug fitted. Check for air leaks at inlet manifold.
Engine runs on	Carburettor slide worn, air leak	Renew worn parts.

43 Fault diagnosis: clutch

Symptom	Cause	Remedy
Engine speed increases but machine does not respond	Clutch slip	Check whether clutch adjustment still has free play. Check thickness of linings and replace if near wear limit.
Difficulty in engaging gears, gear changes jerky and machine creeps forward, even when clutch is withdrawn fully	Clutch drag	Check clutch adjustment to eliminate excess play. Check whether clutch centre and outer drum have indented slots.
	Clutch assembly loose on mainshaft	Check tightness of retaining nut.
Operating action stiff	Bent pushrod	Replace.
	Dry pushrod	Lubricate.
	Damaged, trapped or frayed control cable	Check cable and replace if necessary. Make sure cable is lubricated and has no sharp bends.

44　Fault diagnosis: gearbox

Symptom	Cause	Remedy
Difficulty in engaging gears	Selector forks or rods bent, roller broken Broken springs in gear selector mechanism Clutch drag Cam barrel or pawl spring and plunger stuck	Replace. Check and replace. See next entry. See next entry.
Machine jumps out of gear	Worn dogs on ends of gear pinions Sticking camplate plunger. Broken selector fork rollers	Strip gearbox and replace worn parts. Remove plunger cap and free plunger assembly.
Kickstart does not return	Broken return spring	Remove left hand crankcase cover and replace spring. On RM400 models, the crankcases must be separated to effect repair.
Kickstart slips or jams	Worn ratchet assembly	Remove left hand crankcase cover, dismantle kickstart assembly and replace. On RM400 models the crankcases must be separated to effect repair.
Gearchange lever does not return to normal position	Broken return spring	Renew return spring after dismantling clutch to gain access.

Chapter 2 Fuel system and lubrication

Contents

Specifications

	RM50N,T	RM60N,T	RM80N,T	RM100N
Petrol tank				
Capacity	5.2 litres (1.1 Imp gall 1.4 US gall)	5.2 litres (1.1 Imp gall 1.4 US gall)	5.2 litres (1.1 Imp gall 1.4 US gall)	6.5 litres (1.4 Imp gall, 1.7 US gall)
Carburettor				
Make	Mikuni	Mikuni	Mikuni	Mikuni
Type	VM20SS	VM20SS	VM28SS	VM30SS
Main jet	105	115	160 (170)	190
Jet needle	4J29–4	4J29–3	5DP39–3	5DP11–2
Needle jet	0–8	P–0	P–6	R–4
Cut-away	2.0	1.5 (2.0)	2.5	2.5
Pilot jet	17.5	17.5	45 (50)	30
Mixture screw	2 turns out	2 turns out	$1\frac{1}{2}$ turns out	$1\frac{1}{2}$ turns out
Float level	20–22 mm	20–22 mm	25 ± 1 mm (23 ± 1 mm)	7.3–8.3 mm
Needle position	4th groove	3rd groove	3rd groove	2nd groove

	RM100T	RM125N,T	RM250N,T	RM400N,T
Petrol tank				
Capacity	6.5 litres (1.4 Imp gall, 1.7 US gall)	6.5 litres (1.4 Imp gall, 1.7 US gall)	8.5 litres (1.9 Imp gall, 2.2 US gall)	8.5 litres (1.9 Imp gall, 2.2 US gall)
Carburettor				
Make	Mikuni	Mikuni	Mikuni	Mikuni
Type	VM32SS	VM32SS	VM36SS	VM36SS
Main jet	250	250	290	270
Jet needle	5DP17–2	6DT5–2 (6DP17–2)	6FJ6–3	6FJ6–3
Needle jet	S–0	S–0	R–6	R–6
Cut-away	2.5	2.5	2.0	2.5
Pilot jet	30	25 (35)	60	50
Mixture screw	$1\frac{1}{2}$ turns out	$1\frac{1}{2}$ turns out	$1\frac{1}{2}$ turns out	$1\frac{1}{2}$ turns out
Float level	8.3–9.3 mm	8.8 mm	13.9 mm	13.9 mm
Needle position	2nd groove	2nd groove	3rd groove	3rd groove

Note figures in brackets are for T model

Petrol/oil mixing quantities

Petrol (Imp pint)	Oil (Imp pint)	Oil (Imp fl. oz.)	Oil (Imp cu in)	Oil (cc)
1	0.05	1	1.73	28.41
2	0.10	2	3.47	56.82
3	0.15	3	5.20	85.23
4	0.20	4	6.92	113.64
5	0.25	5	8.65	142.05
6	0.30	6	10.38	170.46
7	0.35	7	12.11	198.87
8	0.40	8	13.84	227.28

Gasoline (US pint)	Oil (US pint)	Oil (US fl. oz)	Oil (US cu in)	Oil (cc)
1	0.05	0.80	1.44	23.66
2	0.10	1.60	2.88	47.32
3	0.15	2.40	4.33	70.97
4	0.20	3.20	5.76	94.63
5	0.25	4.00	7.20	118.29
6	0.30	4.80	8.64	141.95
7	0.35	5.60	10.08	165.60
8	0.40	6.40	11.52	189.26

Engine lubrication

Type	Pre-mixed petrol and oil (petroil)
Mixing ratio	20:1 (5%)
Oil grades	Shell Super M
	Castrol R30
	Golden Spectro Synthetic Blend
	B.P. Racing
	Bel-Ray MC-1 Two-cycle racing lubricant

Note: When changing oil type drain and flush the entire fuel system. Mixing vegetable and mineral oils will cause the formation of sludge which can block the carburettor jets

1 General description

1   The fuel system comprises a steel or plastic petrol tank from which the fuel mixture is gravity-fed to the Mikuni carburettor via a simple on/off tap with an integral mesh filter.
2   All models are fitted with a Mikuni slide carburettor, the larger models making use of an independent float system, whilst the RM50, 60 and 80 employ a conventional paired-float arrangement. Air is drawn through a large capacity oiled foam filter element housed in a water resistant casing.
3   The engine is lubricated by oil pre-mixed with the petrol. The crankshaft main, big end and small end bearings are lubricated in this manner, as is the cylinder wall. Excess oil is ultimately burned and expelled with the exhaust gases.

2 Fuel tank: removal and replacement

1   It is often necessary to remove the fuel tank to gain access to the various engine and frame components which it normally masks. It is also useful to remove the tank if attention to the fuel tap is required, because this will obviate the need to drain off its contents. The method of removal is similar irrespective of whether the tank is of steel or plastic construction.
2   In the case of the RM50, 60 and 80, the rear of the tank is secured by a single retaining screw, the front of the tank being located by circular rubber blocks fitted on either side of the top frame tube. On the larger machines, a bracket is attached to each side of the front of the tank, and a retaining bolt is used to secure this to the frame via a rubber mounting washer. The rear of the tank is held by a rubber strap.
3   Before attempting to remove the tank, it will be necessary to release the seat by removing its retaining bolts. This will give access to the rear of the tank. Do not forget to turn the fuel tap off and remove the feed pipe before removing the tank.

3 Fuel tap: removal, dismantling and replacement

1   It is seldom necessary to remove the tap unless it has become clogged with debris or requires attention due to leakage. It should be noted that it will be necessary to remove the tank, positioning it so that the fuel level is below the tap if draining is to be avoided.
2   On RM50, 60 and 80 models, the tap is retained by a gland nut to the threaded stub on the underside of the tank. On larger machines, a flange fitting is used, two screws being employed to retain the tap to the tank. Leakages can occur around the tap lever, the gland nut on the smaller models, or around the fixing flange on larger models.
3   The tap lever is retained by two small screws and a retainer plate (RM50, 60 and 80) and by a single screw on the larger models. Leakage here is almost invariably caused by wear or damage to the seal. Leaks around the gland nut or flange fitting can be cured by careful use of a **fuel resistant** sealing compound. On no account use an RTV silicone sealant, because this is attacked by fuel and will only cause more problems.

4 Fuel pipe: examination

1   The single petrol feed pipe is made from thin-walled plastic, and is of the push-on type, retained by a wire clip. Renewal is seldom required unless the plastic becomes hard or splits. Always replace the pipe in the same position as when it was removed, as the plastic sometimes takes a permanent form of the fitting over which it is connected. It is unlikely that the wire retaining clips will need renewal due to fatigue as the main seal between the pipe and union is effected by an interference fit.
2   When renewing the feed pipe, always ensure that plastic or synthetic rubber tubing is obtained. Natural rubber is not fuel resistant, and will break up internally, blocking the carburettor jets.

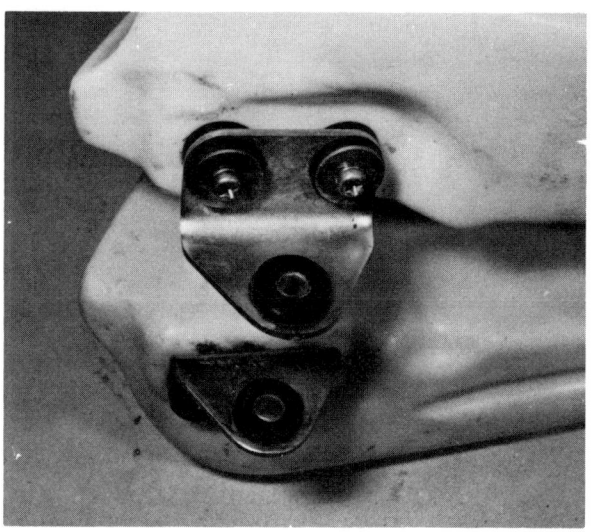

2.2 Fuel tank is secured by rubber-mounted brackets (RM400)

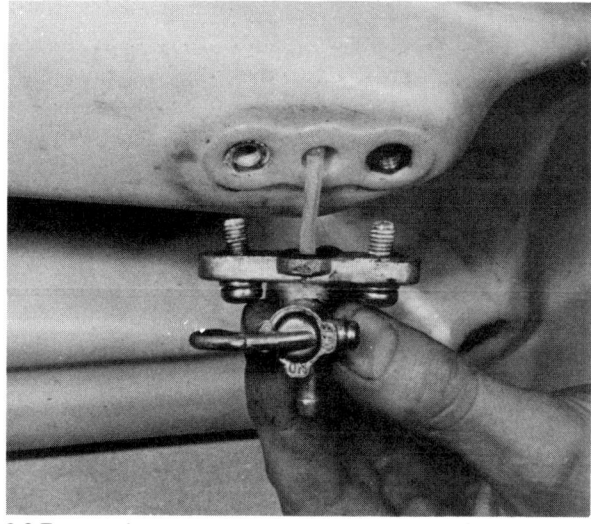

3.2 Tap may be removed for cleaning or overhaul (RM400)

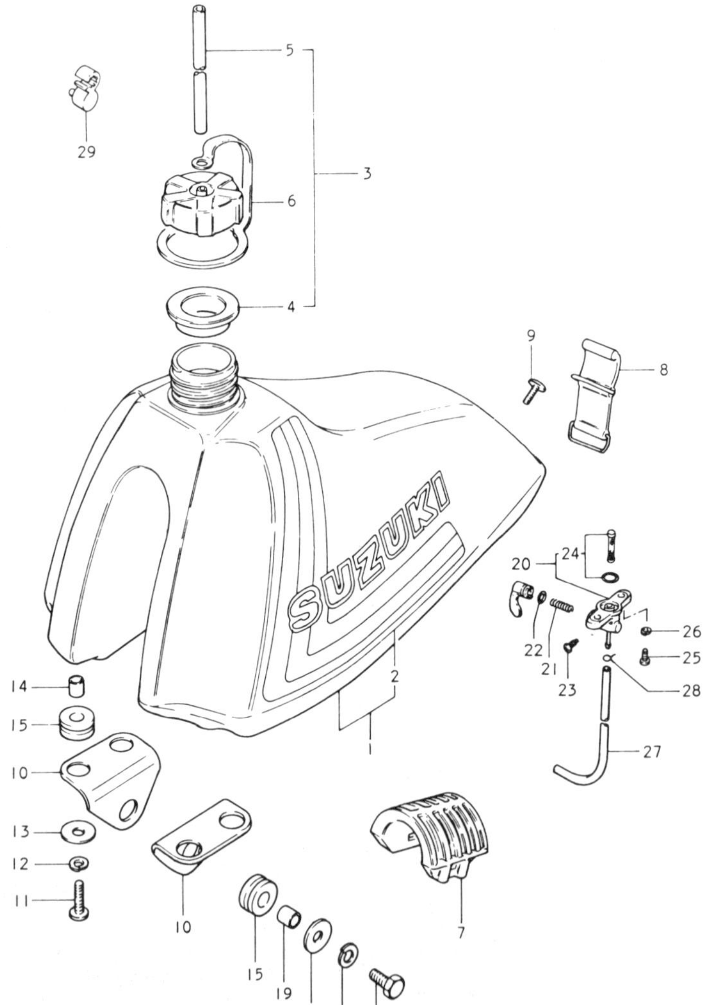

Fig. 2.1 Fuel tank

1 Fuel tank
2 Tank decal – 2 off
3 Filler cap assembly
4 Gasket
5 Breather pipe
6 Strap
7 Frame cushion – 2 off
8 Rear fixing band
9 Screws
10 Mounting bracket – 2 off
11 Screw – 4 off
12 Spring washer – 4 off
13 Washer – 4 off
14 Spacer – 4 off
15 Grommet – off
16 Bolt – 2 off
17 Spring washer – 2 off
18 Washer – 2 off
19 Spacer – 2 off
20 Fuel tap body
21 Spring
22 O-ring
23 Screw
24 Filter assembly
25 Screw – 2 off
26 Spring washer – 2 off
27 Fuel delivery pipe
28 Clip – 2 off
29 G-Clamp

5 Carburettor: removal and replacement

1   The carburettor is secured by the intake and air cleaner hoses, these being clamped at each end by screw clips. Before the carburettor is removed, turn the fuel tap off, and prise off the fuel pipe. Unscrew the carburettor top, and withdraw the throttle valve assembly. Unless this requires attention, it can be left undisturbed and lodged clear of the carburettor.

2   Slacken the retaining clips at each side of the carburettor. The carburettor can now be released by twisting it clear of the air cleaner and intake hoses. This is not particularly easy and will require a certain amount of manoeuvering. Reassembly is a straightforward reversal of the removal sequence.

5.1a Carburettor is retained by hose clips (RM100)

5.1b Throttle valve assembly can be left attached to cable (RM100)

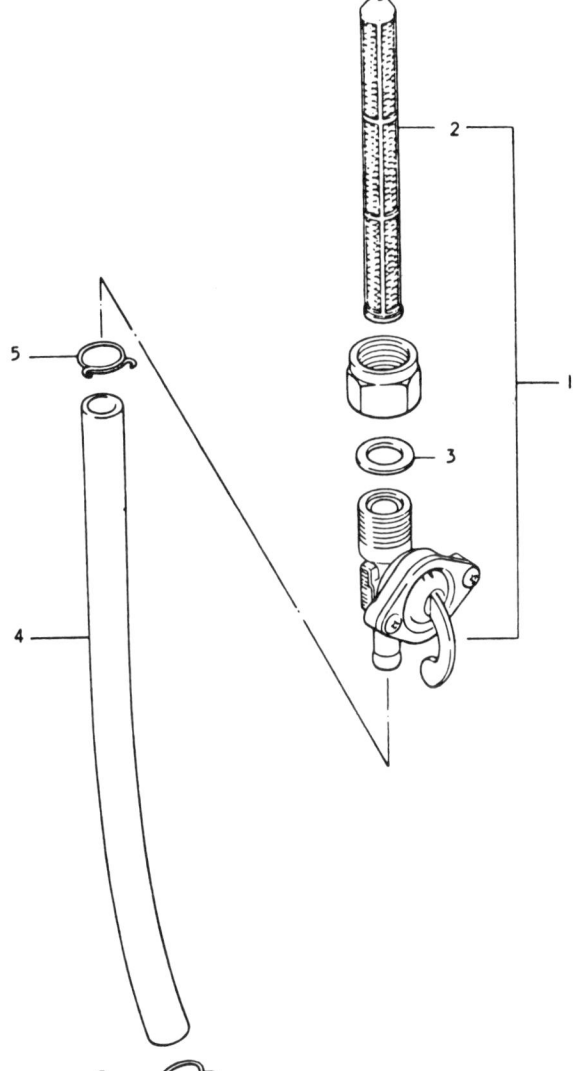

Fig. 2.2 Fuel tap

1   Fuel tap assembly
2   Fuel filter
3   Sealing washer
4   Delivery pipe
5   Clip – 2 off

5.2 It may be helpful to release filter hose (RM80)

6 Carburettor: dismantling and reassembly

1   Before the carburettor is dismantled, it should be scrupulously cleaned to prevent dirt from contaminating the various jets and small drillings. This is of particular importance in the case of motocross machines, where such contamination is likely.

2   Remove the four screws which retain the float bowl. Lift the float bowl away, noting that there will probably be some residual fuel left in it. It will be noted that the RM100, 125, 250 and 400 models have independent float systems. The floats are supported by metal rods projecting up from the bottom of the float bowl. The floats will drop out if the bowl is inverted and the plastic retaining caps removed. The floats act upon a pivoted metal arm which opens and closes the float valve assembly. This system means that either float can operate the valve independently of the other, and maintain a more constant fuel level in a larger carburettor than the conventional paired float arrangement.

3   On the RM50, 60 and 80 the problems of maintaining a constant fuel level are less pronounced due to the smaller float bowl capacity, and a conventional paired float arrangement is employed. To release the float assembly, or the operating arm in the case of the independent float models, displace the pivot pin using a piece of wire.

4   The float valve assembly on the independent float carburettors consists of a threaded valve body. This can be unscrewed from the carburettor body if it requires attention. The valve body also retains the baffle plate which is fitted to reduce fuel surge. A wire clip retains the valve needle in the centre of the body. The needle incorporates a spring-loaded pin which serves to damp out fluctuations in the height of the floats over rough terrain, thus reducing damage to the sealing faces which might otherwise occur.

5   On the smaller models, the valve needle will drop free as the float assembly is removed. The valve body is retained by a shaped retainer plate which is secured by a single cross-head screw. No baffle plate is fitted on the smaller models.

6   On all models, the main jet is screwed into the bottom of the needle jet, and in normal use projects into a small reservoir formed by the float bowl drain plug. A collar around the main jet effectively closes this reservoir, although it remains connected to the rest of the float bowl. This is to provide a small well of fuel which will be unaffected by the constant movement of the rest of the fuel in the float bowl. This prevents the fuel from frothing around the jet and ensures a limited supply to prevent stalling when the float bowl's contents is thrown away from the jets over very rough terrain. It will be noted that the main jet is easily accessible when the carburettor is installed on the machine, and thus can be changed or cleaned between races.

7   On all but RM50 and 60 models, remove the main jet, using a suitable socket or box spanner, and lift away the collar. The needle jet can now be displaced by pushing it up into the mixing chamber. On RM50 and 60 models the main jet screws into the needle jet which itself screws into the mixing chamber. The pilot jet is located in the adjacent projection of the carburettor body, and may be unscrewed for cleaning or examination.

8   The throttle valve and jet needle form an assembly, and will have been left attached to the throttle cable and carburettor top. To release the valve, the return spring should be compressed against the carburettor top and held there while the inner cable is disengaged from its locating slot in the valve. It may prove necessary to displace the needle assembly slightly to produce adequate clearance on the smaller models. A slightly different retention method is employed on the independent float types, and the accompanying line drawings should be consulted for further details.

9   The various components are refitted in the reverse order of that given for dismantling, using new O-rings and gaskets as required. It is important that all of the carburettor components are completely clean prior to reassembly, as any residual dirt will inevitably find its way into a jet or drilling, causing problems when the machine is run. Take care not to overtighten any jets or screws, because these and the carburettor body threads are easily damaged. The float height setting should be checked before the float bowl is refitted, as described in Section 8 of this Chapter.

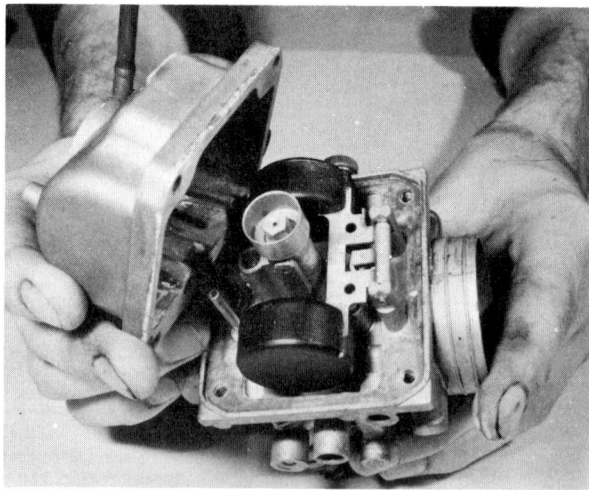

6.2a Float bowl removal (RM80)

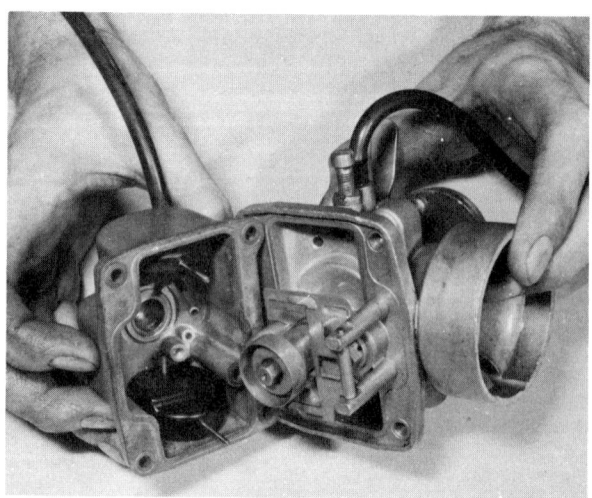

6.2b Float bowl removal (RM100)

6.2c Float bowl removal (RM400)

6.3a Displace pin to release float assembly ... (RM80)

6.3b ... or operating arm, as appropriate (RM100)

6.4a Clip secure valve needle – larger models (RM100)

6.4b Valve seat secures fuel baffle (RM100)

6.5 Valve seat and retainer plate – smaller models (RM80)

6.6a Main jet screws into carburettor body ... (RM100)

6.6b ... and holds anti-surge collar (RM80)

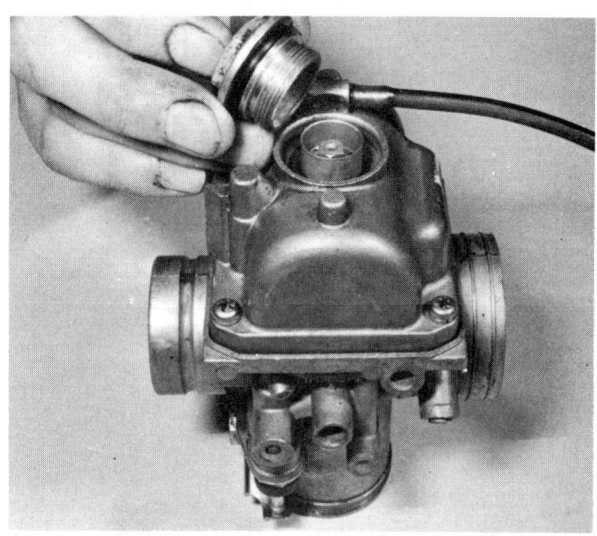

6.6c Cap in float bowl permits quick jet changes (RM80)

6.7a Needle jet is secured by main jet ... (RM400)

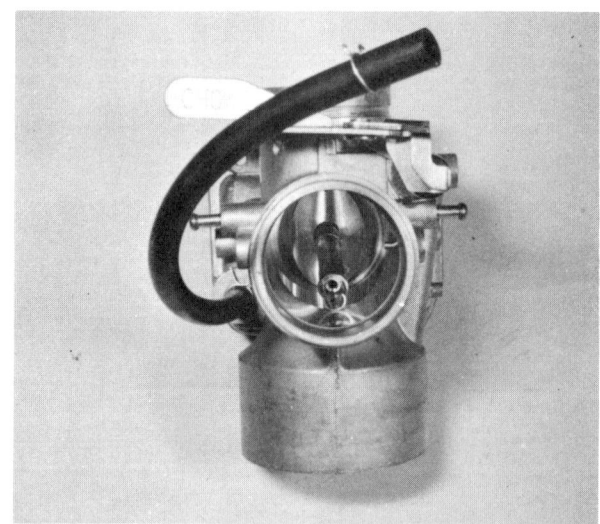

6.7b ... and can be removed upwards (RM400)

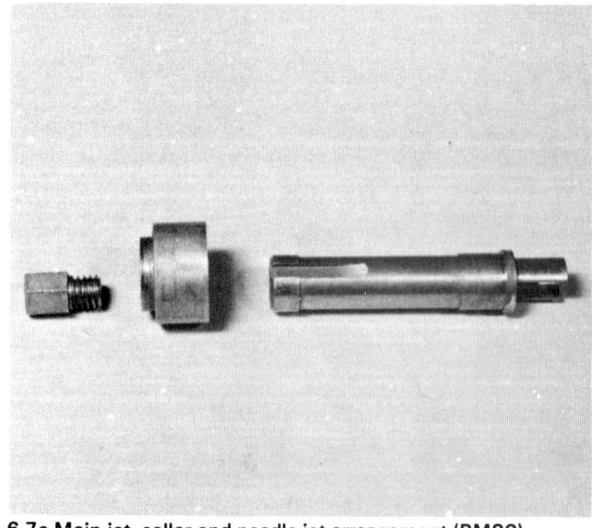

6.7c Main jet, collar and needle jet arrangement (RM80)

6.7d Pilot jet is located in drilling (arrowed) (RM400)

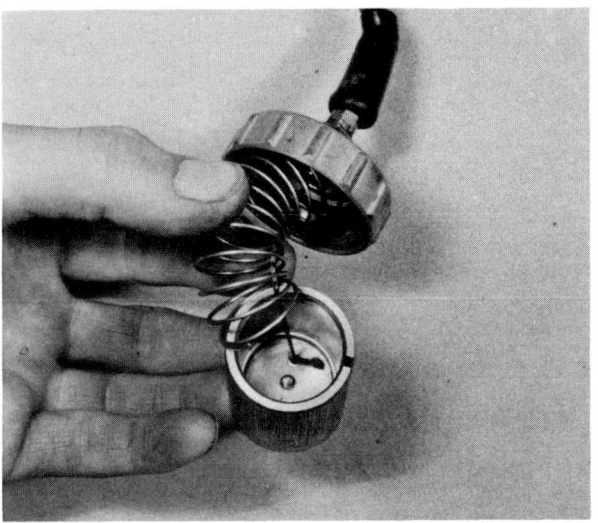

6.8a Displace return spring to free ... (RM80)

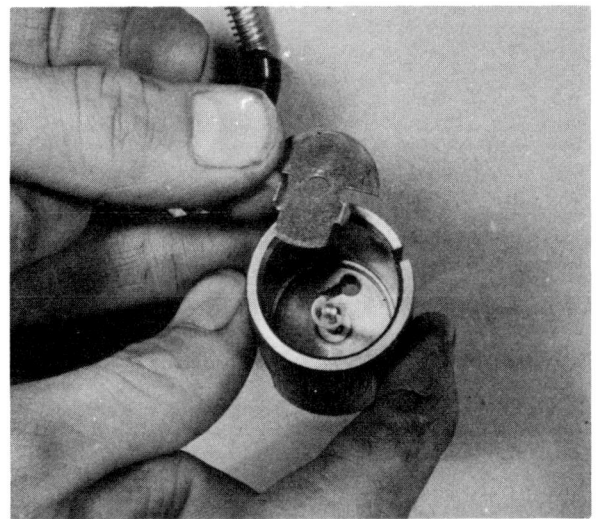

6.8b ... cable, plate and needle assembly (RM80)

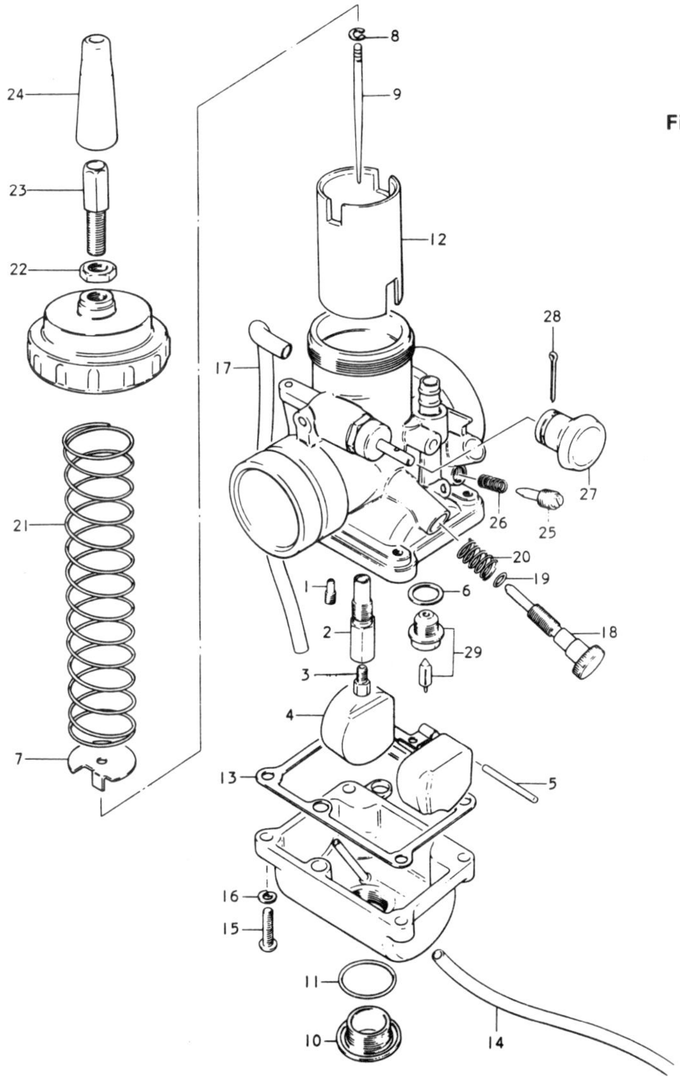

Fig. 2.3 Carburettor – RM 50 and 80 models

1 Pilot jet
2 Needle jet
3 Main jet
4 Float
5 Float pivot pin
6 Valve seat gasket
7 Spring seating
8 Needle clip
9 Jet needle
10 Drain plug
11 Drain plug gasket
12 Throttle valve
13 Float chamber gasket
14 Overflow pipe
15 Screw – 4 off
16 Spring washer – 4 off
17 Air vent pipe
18 Throttle stop screw
19 O-ring
20 Spring
21 Throttle valve return spring
22 Locknut
23 Cable adjuster
24 Dust cap
25 Pilot air screw
26 Spring
27 Knob
28 Split pin
29 Needle valve assembly

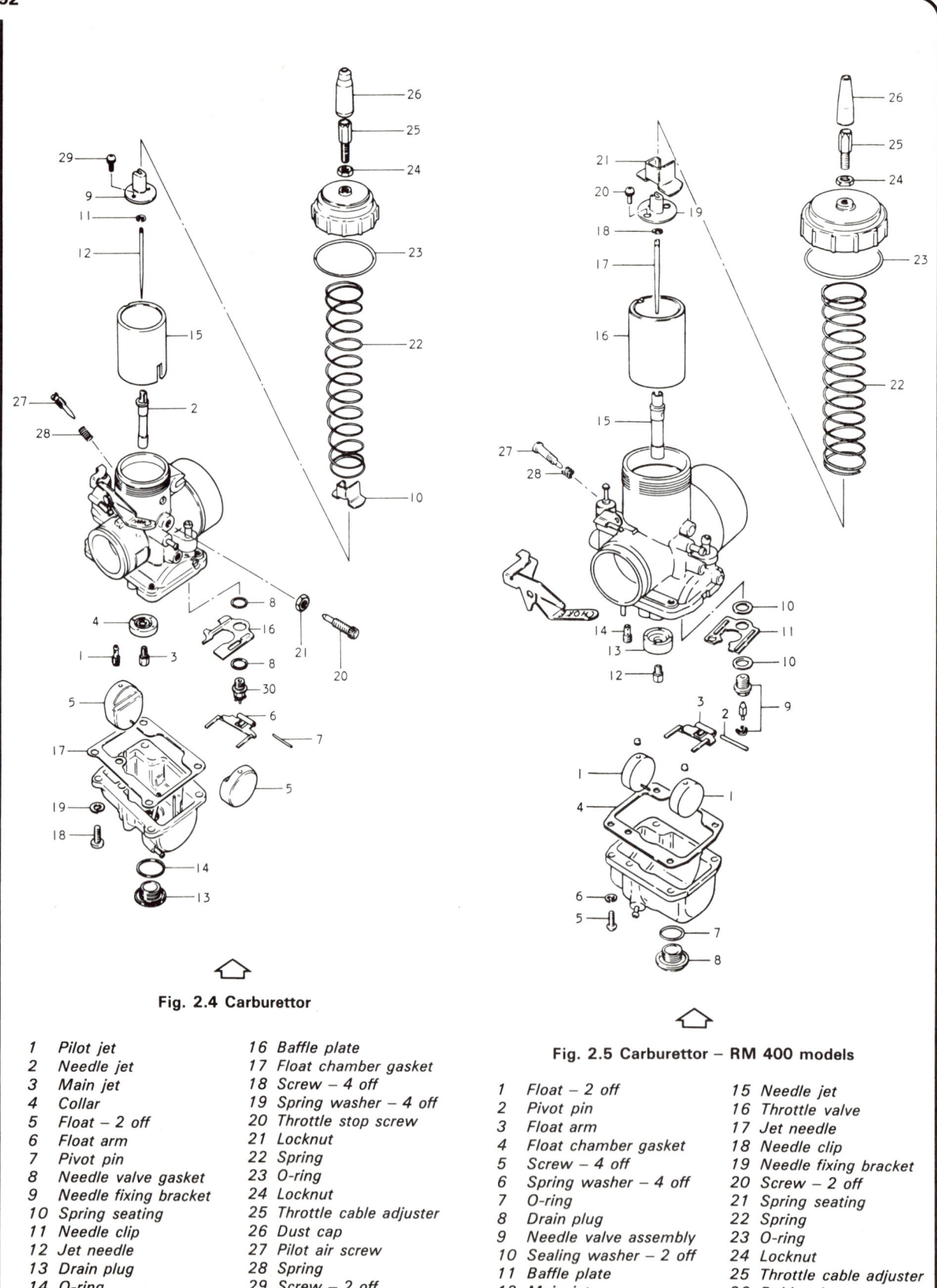

Fig. 2.4 Carburettor

1 Pilot jet
2 Needle jet
3 Main jet
4 Collar
5 Float – 2 off
6 Float arm
7 Pivot pin
8 Needle valve gasket
9 Needle fixing bracket
10 Spring seating
11 Needle clip
12 Jet needle
13 Drain plug
14 O-ring
15 Throttle valve

16 Baffle plate
17 Float chamber gasket
18 Screw – 4 off
19 Spring washer – 4 off
20 Throttle stop screw
21 Locknut
22 Spring
23 O-ring
24 Locknut
25 Throttle cable adjuster
26 Dust cap
27 Pilot air screw
28 Spring
29 Screw – 2 off
30 Needle valve assembly

Fig. 2.5 Carburettor – RM 400 models

1 Float – 2 off
2 Pivot pin
3 Float arm
4 Float chamber gasket
5 Screw – 4 off
6 Spring washer – 4 off
7 O-ring
8 Drain plug
9 Needle valve assembly
10 Sealing washer – 2 off
11 Baffle plate
12 Main jet
13 Collar
14 Pilot jet

15 Needle jet
16 Throttle valve
17 Jet needle
18 Needle clip
19 Needle fixing bracket
20 Screw – 2 off
21 Spring seating
22 Spring
23 O-ring
24 Locknut
25 Throttle cable adjuster
26 Rubber boot
27 Air adjusting screw
28 Spring

7 Carburettor: examination and renovation

1 Examine the throttle valve for signs of wear or scoring. This should not normally be a problem unless the machine has been used with an inefficient air cleaner system. Any dust drawn through the carburettor is highly abrasive, and apart from the risk of engine damage, rapid wear of the carburettor and throttle valve will take place. If signs of wear are noted, check for play between the valve and its bore in the carburettor. If a lot of play is found it will be necessary to renew the valve, and in extreme cases, the carburettor body. Air leaks around the valve will cause erratic running at low to intermediate throttle settings.

2 Check that the jet needle is straight and undamaged by rolling it on a dead flat surface such as a sheet of glass. Any score marks denote wear, and indicate the need for renewal along with the needle jet. The latter is prone to mechanical wear from the needle, and eventually erosion by the fuel drawn through it. As a general rule, the needle jet should be renewed whenever the needle is replaced, because the degree of wear in the jet orifice is difficult to assess visually or to measure.

3 The main and pilot jets are unlikely to suffer pronounced wear during their normal life, and should only require checking for obstructions. On no account try to clear a blocked jet orifice with wire, as this can easily score the drilling and alter the fuel flow characteristics. This can slow down the fuel delivery rate and thus upset the mixture, even if the size of the hole is not affected. A blast of compressed air is the best means of cleaning a jet, and a foot or hand pump will usually suffice. As a last resort, a fine nylon bristle may be used without fear of damaging the jet.

4 Check the float valve assembly for wear which will be apparent by a ridge being formed on the tapered face of the needle. It is advisable to renew both the needle and the valve body if wear is extensive. A leaking needle valve can cause flooding and is often the cause of problems with the engine 'gassing up' at low speeds. Make sure the seating faces are quite clean, because foreign matter will also cause persistent and annoying flooding problems.

5 The various drillings and passages in the carburettor body should be cleaned out with a blast of compressed air. Make sure that all of the carburettor components are absolutely clean before commencing reassembly, because any residual dirt will inevitably find its way to the jet orifices if it is not removed.

8 Carburettor: checking the float height

1 It is important that the fuel level in the float chamber is maintained at the correct setting, because any pronounced variation will affect the mixture strength throughout the operating range. There will be some change in the level during normal use, as wear takes place on the needle valve assembly and pivot, and it follows that the float level should be checked periodically as a precursor to carburettor adjustment.

2 In the case of the RM50, 60 and 80 models, the float height is measured between the gasket face of the carburettor body and the furthest edge of the float, as shown in the accompanying illustration (Fig. 2.6). The carburettor should be in the inverted position during this measurement check. Where necessary, adjustments can be made by bending the small metal tang which operates on the float needle. Make sure that the float assembly is kept level by checking the height against both floats.

3 In the case of the RM100, 125, 250 and 400, measure the distance between the operating arm ends and the underside of the main jet cup, again with the carburettor inverted. The prescribed heights are as follows.

RM50, 60N,T	20–22 mm (0.76–0.84 in)
RM80N	24–26 mm (0.94–1.02 in)
RM80T	22–24 mm (0.87–0.95 in)
RM100N	7.3–8.3 mm (0.29–0.33 in)
RM100T	8.3–9.3 mm (0.33–0.37 in)
RM125N,T	8.8 mm (0.35 in)
RM250, 400N,T	13.9 mm (0.55 in)

4 In all cases, the small amount of travel of the spring-loaded pin in the valve needle is ignored, so when taking the measurement, the float assembly or arm should be lifted, and then lowered gently until it **just** contacts the pin. Measurement should be made at this setting rather than with the weight of the arm or floats compressing the spring and pin.

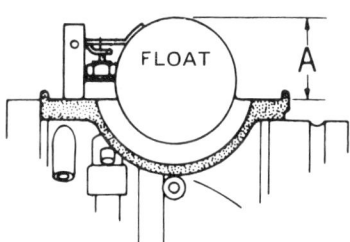

Fig. 2.6 Float height adjustment – conventional float type

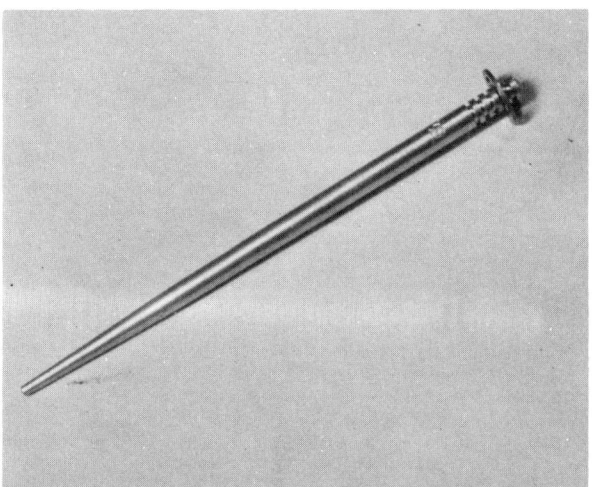

7.2a Check needle for wear and for straighteness (RM80)

7.2b Renew needle and needle jet as a pair (RM80)

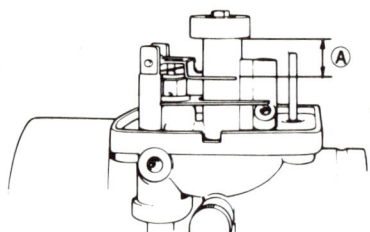

Fig. 2.7 Float height adjustment – independent float type

9 Carburettor: checking the settings

1   The various jet sizes, throttle valve cutaway and needle position are predetermined by the manufacturer and should not require modification. Check with the specifications list at the beginning of this Chapter if there is any doubt about the values fitted.

2   As a rough guide, up to $\frac{1}{8}$ throttle is controlled by the pilot jet, $\frac{1}{8}$ to $\frac{1}{4}$ by the throttle valve cutaway. $\frac{1}{4}$ to $\frac{3}{4}$ throttle by the needle position and from $\frac{3}{4}$ to full by the size of the main jet. These are only approximate divisions, which are by no means clear cut. There is a certain amount of overlap between the various stages.

3   Slow running is controlled by a combination of the throttle stop and pilot jet settings. Adjustment should be carried out as explained below. Remember that the characteristics of the two-stroke engine are such that it is extremely difficult to obtain a slow, reliable tick-over at low rpm particularly in the case of competition machines.

4   To set the idle speed mixture, the engine should be started and run until normal operating temperature is reached. Set the throttle stop screw to give the slowest possible idle speed. Turn the pilot mixture screw in by a fraction of a turn at a time, until the engine starts to falter. Now back the screw off progressively, noting the number of turns required to reach the point where the engine again starts to run erratically. The correct position for the pilot mixture screw is mid-way between these two extremes. This should be within about $\frac{1}{2}$ turn from the position recommended in the Specifications.

5   A range of optional main jet sizes is available, providing adjustment to each side of the standard setting. The main jet can be checked by riding the machine at high speed under normal racing conditions, then killing the engine quickly. The sparking plug should be removed, and its colour checked, comparing it with the sparking plug condition chart which will be found later in this manual. If the mixture is correct, the plug electrodes will be a brownish-grey or tan colour. Black, oily electrodes indicate an excessively rich mixture, whilst a blistered, white appearance indicate a weak (lean) mixture. If necessary, fit a new jet one size richer or weaker as required, and repeat the running test after cleaning the sparking plug. Main jets are available in the following optional sizes.

Optional main jet sizes

Model	Size
RM50:	100, 110, 115, 120 or 125
RM60:	110, 120, 125, 130 or 135
RM80:	145, 160, 170, 180 or 190
RM100:	170, 180, 190, 200 or 210
RM125:	230, 240, 260, 270 or 280
RM250:	270, 280, 300, 310 or 320
RM400	250, 260, 280, 290 or 300

6   The needle and needle jet control the mixture strength between $\frac{1}{4}$ and $\frac{3}{4}$ throttle settings, and thus will have a noticeable effect throughout most of the throttle range. If either or both components wear, the mixture will become progressively richer. Small amounts of wear can be compensated for by moving the needle down one or two notches. If wear is evident in the form of obvious scoring, or a flat on the side of the needle, the needle and needle jet should be renewed as a pair. Wear in the needle jet orifice is not readily apparent or easily measured. It is safe to assume that a worn needle will indicate a similarly worn needle jet.

7   Guard against the possibility of incorrect carburettor adjustments which will result in a weak mixture. Two-stroke engines are very susceptible to this type of fault, causing rapid overheating and often subsequent engine seizure. Changes in carburation leading to a weak mixture will occur if the air cleaner is removed or disconnected, or if the silencers are tampered with in any way. Above all, do not add extra oil to the petrol, in the mistaken belief that it will aid lubrication. The extra oil will only reduce the petrol content by the ratio of oil added, and therefore cause the engine to run with a permanently weakened mixture.

10 Reed valve assembly: general description

1   Like many modern two-stroke engines, the Suzuki RM models make use of a reed valve arrangement to control induction timing. On the RM models, the reed valve forms a supplementary induction route, allowing mild port timing to be used to enhance low and mid range power, whilst the reed valve allows the engine to 'breathe' freely at higher engine speeds. This arrangement permits a wider spread of power than would be available by piston porting alone.

2   To gain access to the reed valve assembly it will be necessary to remove the cylinder head and barrel as described in Chapter 1. The valve assembly is retained by screws to the underside of the cylinder barrel flange. The reed valve unit will require little attention during the life of the machine, but when the engine is dismantled for overhaul, the valve unit should be checked for obvious signs of damage, such as cracked reed petals. After extended periods of use, the valve may wear leaving a permanent gap between the valve petal and seat. If this exceeds 0.2 mm (0.008 in) the valve assembly must be renewed.

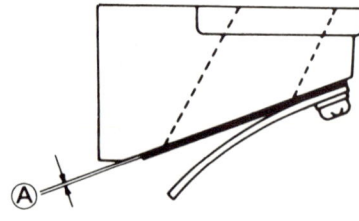

Fig. 2.8 Reed valve to case clearance

A: below 0.2 mm (0.008 in)

10.2a Two-petal reed valve assembly – smaller models (RM80)

10.2b ... or 3-petal unit – larger models (RM400)

10.2c Check for weak or damaged petals (RM80)

11 Air cleaner: removing and cleaning the element

1 The air cleaner assembly consists of a moulded plastic casing mounted below the seat and connected to the carburettor by a flexible hose. An oil-impregnated foam element is mounted inside the casing. The oil on the foam surface will trap dust particles which would otherwise be drawn into the engine. It will be appreciated that once the oil film has become clogged by accumulated dust, the effect of the filter will be impaired. If not cleaned regularly, it will restrict the air flow into the engine.

2 The filter arrangements used on the various models are similar in principle, but there are variations in construction. In the case of the RM50 and 60, access to the filter is gained after removing the left-hand side panel. The foam element consists of a flat circular sheet and is sandwiched between the air cleaner case and its cover. On all other models access to the filter is gained after removing the seat. The RM80N has a flat rectangular element, similar to that used on the smaller machines, whilst that of the RM80T is of the cylindrical type. The RM100, 125, 250 and 400 each have cylindrical elements supported by plastic frames.

3 The element should be removed from its supporting frame for cleaning. The manufacturers recommend a non-flammable cleaning solvent for this operation. Failing this, a strong detergent solution may be used as long as the element is dried carefully after rinsing out all traces of the detergent solution. When clean and dry, immerse the element in clean engine oil or, if preferred, air filter oil. Squeeze the element to remove excess oil, then refit it in the casing. It is important to ensure that the element seals effectively, and that air cannot find its way into the engine without first passing through the filter element.

4 Eventually, the foam will deteriorate and become less effective. If ageing or cracking become apparent, the element must be renewed immediately. It is useful to have one or more spare elements which can be kept clean and oiled ready for installation at the circuit.

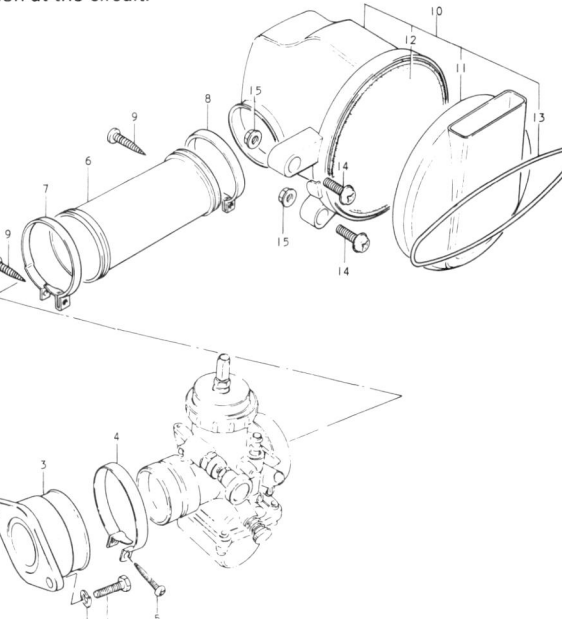

Fig. 2.9 Air cleaner assembly – RM 50 and 60 models

1	Bolt – 2 off	9 Screw – 2 off
2	Spring washer – 2 off	10 Air cleaner assembly
3	Inlet pipe	11 Air cleaner cap
4	Clamp	12 Element
5	Screw	13 O-ring
6	Air cleaner tube	14 Screw – 2 off
7	Clamp	15 Nut – 2 off
8	Clamp	

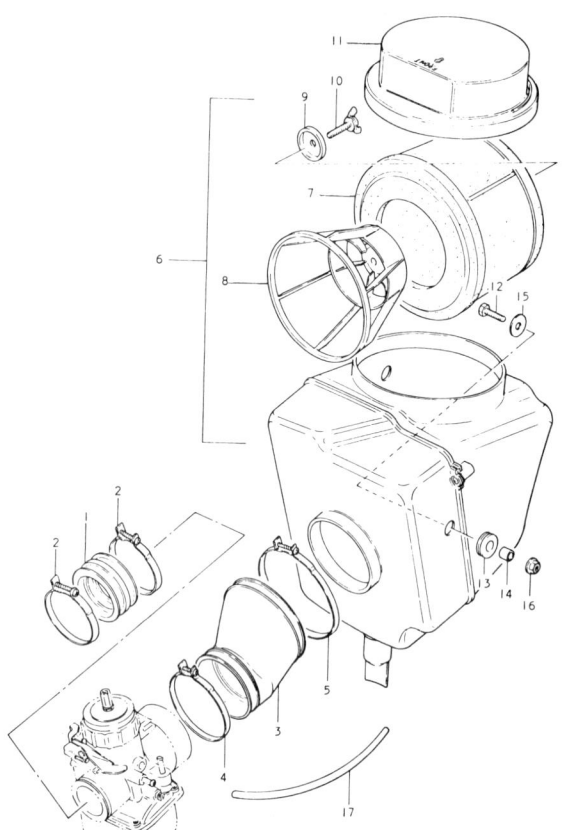

Fig. 2.10 Air cleaner assembly – RM 100 models

1	Inlet hose	10	Screw
2	Hose clamp	11	Casing top
3	Transfer hose	12	Bolt
4	Hose clamp	13	Grommet
5	Hose clamp	14	Spacer
6	Air cleaner assembly	15	Washer
7	Element	16	Nut
8	Element frame	17	Drainage pipe
9	Washer		

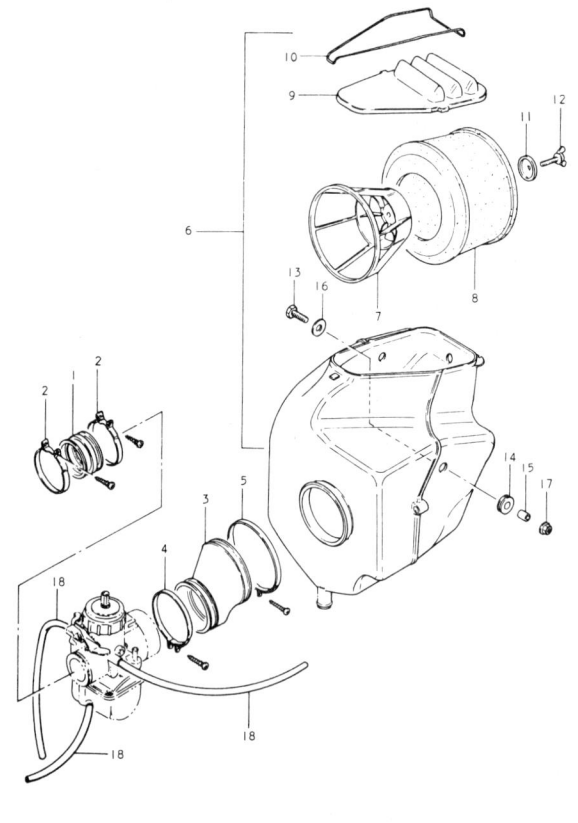

Fig. 2.11 Air cleaner – RM 250 and 400 models

1	Inlet hose	10	O-ring
2	Clamp – 2 off	11	Washer
3	Transfer hose	12	Screw
4	Hose clamp	13	Bolt – 3 off
5	Hose clamp	14	Grommet – 3 off
6	Air cleaner assembly	15	Spacer – 3 off
7	Element frame	16	Washer – 3 off
8	Element	17	Nut – 3 off
9	Casing cap	18	Breather pipe

12 Engine lubrication

1   The engine internals are lubricated by a proportion of oil which is pre-mixed with the petrol. It is important to ensure that the recommended mixture ratio of 20:1 (twenty parts of petrol to one part of oil) is adhered to. If less oil is used, the bearings and cylinder wall will be inadequately lubricated, and engine seizure is likely to result. Conversely, adding extra oil will result in the amount of petrol available for combustion being reduced, with the result that the mixture strength will become weak. This will cause the engine to run far too hot, and apart from the resulting poor performance, the piston may become holed.
2   A list of recommended lubricants will be found in the preliminary sections at the front of this manual. It should be stressed that vegetable and mineral based oil must never be allowed to become mixed, as the two can combine to form a rubbery sludge which is remarkably effective in blocking carburettor jets. To preclude this, remove the tank and flush with neat petrol before changing to a different type of oil.

13 Exhaust system: removal and maintenance

1   The exhaust system fitted to the Suzuki RM models is designed to suit the engine characteristics, and as with all two-stroke machines, plays an important part in extracting the best level of performance from the machine. Like all off-road machines, the system is fitted in such a way that it is kept clear of the underside of the frame, and is thus protected from damage.
2   Depending on the model, the one-piece system is secured by one or more frame mounting bolts, and by tension springs at the exhaust port. This enables the complete system to be detached quickly and easily for attention to the engine or to the exhaust system itself. The spark arrester should be released from the silencer tailpipe to allow the system to be disengaged from the machine.
3   The exhaust pipe and silencer are one unit and if a large amount of carbon has built up inside it is necessary to fill the silencer with a solution of caustic soda after blocking up one

end. If possible, leave the caustic soda solution within the silencer overnight, before draining off and washing out thoroughly with water.

4   Caustic soda is highly corrosive and every care should be taken when mixing and handling the solution. Keep the solution away from the skin and more particularly the eyes. The wearing of rubber gloves and goggles is advised whilst the solution is being mixed and used.

5   The solution is prepared by adding 3 lbs of caustic soda to 1 gallon of COLD water, whilst stirring. Add the caustic soda a little at a time and NEVER add the water to the chemical. The solution will become hot during the mixing process, which is why cold water must be used.

6   Make sure the used caustic soda solution is disposed of safely, preferably by diluting with a large amount of water. Do not allow the solution to come into contact with aluminium castings because it will react violently with this metal.

7   Slight damage, such as small cracks or rust holes, can be repaired by brazing a patch over the affected area. The system is finished with a matt black heat-dispersant finish which will flake off in use. This can be restored by wire-brushing and degreasing the system, and spraying it with a suitable aerosol paint finish. It follows that this should be of a type suitable for use on exhaust systems, such as Sperex VHT or similar.

8   After-market exhaust systems, where available, must be treated with a degree of caution. Although they can effect some improvement at particular engine speeds, there is inevitably a drop in performance elsewhere in the engine speed range. It is essential to ensure that the system is of well-known and reputable manufacture. It should be noted that some adjustment of the carburettor jetting will probably be required. This should be checked with the supplier when the system is purchased.

13.2a Exhaust system is secured by bolts ... (RM80)

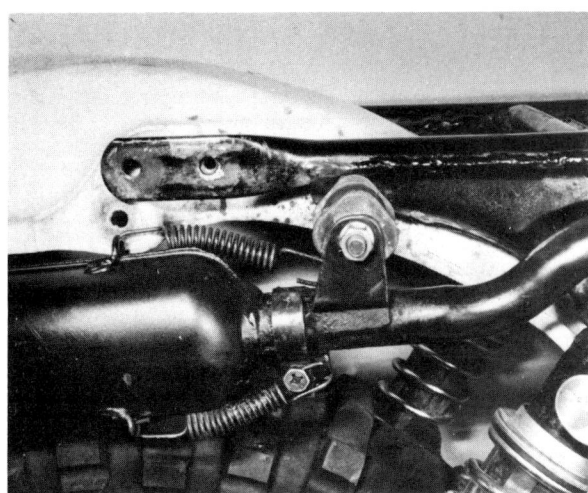

13.2b ... front and rear (RM80)

14 Fault diagnosis: fuel system

Symptom	Cause	Remedy
Excessive fuel consumption	Air cleaner choked or restricted	Clean or replace element.
	Fuel leaking from carburettor	Check all unions and gaskets.
	Badly worn or distorted carburettor	Replace.
	Carburettor settings incorrect	Re-adjust. Check settings with Specifications.
Idling speed too high	Throttle stop screw in too far	Adjust screw
	Carburettor top loose	Tighten.
	Air leaks in carburettor	Check and renew worn parts.
Engine sluggish. Does not respond to throttle	Throttle slide worn	Renew.
Engine dies after running for a short while	Blocked vent hole in filler cap	Clean.
	Dirt or water in carburettor	Remove and clean.
General lack of performance	Weak mixture, float needle sticking in seat	Remove float chamber and check needle seating.
	Air leak at carburettor or leaking crankcase seals	Check for air leaks or worn seals.
Excessive white smoke from exhaust	Too much oil in petrol or oil has separated	Mix in recommended ratio only. Shake mixture vigorously in can.
Engine 'four-strokes' – will not pull cleanly	Mixture excessively rich	Check and adjust.
Engine runs hot, spitting from exhaust	Mixture excessively weak	Check and adjust.

Chapter 3 Ignition system

Contents

Specifications

Ignition system
    Type ....

RM50N,T

Coil and contact breaker

Ignition coil
    Primary winding resistance ....
    Secondary winding resistance ....

0.75 Ohms approx
5.70 Ohms approx

Contact breaker
    Gap ....

0.3 – 0.4 mm (0.012 – 0.016 in)

Static timing
    Piston position BTDC ....

0.90 – 1.40 mm (0.035 – 0.055 in)

Timing advance
    Full advance ....

18° BTDC

Sparking plug
    Make ....
    Type ....
    Gap ....

NGK   Nippon Denso (ND)
B-7HS   W22FS
0.6 – 0.7 mm (0.024 – 0.028 in)

RM60N,T

Ignition system
    Make ....
    Type ....

Suzuki PEI (pointless electronic ignition)
CDI (capacitor discharge ignition)

Ignition coil
    Primary winding resistance ....
    Secondary winding resistance ....

0.75 Ohms approx
5.70 Ohms approx

CDI source coil
    Low speed windings ....
    High speed windings ....

370–450 Ohms
20 – 25 Ohms

Timing advance ....

18° BTDC at 10 000 rpm

Sparking plug

	NGK	Nippon Denso (ND)
Make	NGK	Nippon Denso (ND)
Standard type	B8HS	W24FS
Hot type	B7HS	W22FS
Cold type	B9HS	W27FS
Gap	0.6 – 0.7 mm (0.024 – 0.028 in)	

RM80N,T

Ignition system

Make	Suzuki PEI (pointless electronic ignition)
Type	CDI (capacitor discharge ignition)

Ignition coil

	N model	T model
Primary winding resistance	4 ohms approx	0-1 ohms approx
Secondary winding resistance	13 k ohms approx	10-11 k ohms approx

CDI coils

Exciter coil	80 ohms approx	70-80 ohms approx
Low speed coil	290 ohms approx	250-300 ohms approx
High speed coil	56 ohms approx	50-60 ohms approx

Timing advance . . . . 18.5° BTDC at 11000 rpm

Sparking plug

	NGK	Nippo Denso (ND)
Make	NGK	Nippo Denso (ND)
Standard type	B8ES	W24ES
Hot type	B7ES	W22ES
Cold type	B9ES	W27ES
Gap:		
N	0.6 – 0.7 mm (0.024 – 0.028 in)	
T	0.6 – 0.8 mm (0.024 – 0.031 in)	

RM100N,T

Ignition system

Make	Suzuki PEI (pointless electronic ignition)
Type	CDI (capacitor discharge unit)

Ignition coil

Primary winding resistance	0.7 Ohms approx.
Secondary winding resistance	13 k Ohms approx.

CDI Coils

Low speed coil	170 Ohms approx
High speed coil	290 Ohms approx
Timing advance:	
N model	10.5° BTDC @ 11000 rpm
T model	17.5° BTDC @ 10000 rpm

Sparking plug

	NGK	Nippon Denso (ND)
Make	NGK	Nippon Denso (ND)
Standard type	B9EV	W27ES-G
Hot type	B8EV	W24ES-G
Cold type	B10EV	W31ES-G
Gap	0.5 – 0.6 mm (0.020 – 0.024 in)	

RM125

Ignition system

Make	Suzuki PEI (pointless electronic ignition)
Type	CDI (capacitor discharge ignition)

Ignition coil

Primary winding resistance	1 Ohm approx.
Secondary winding resistance	13 K ohms approx.

CDI coils

	N models	T models
Exciter coil	120 ohms approx	65-85 ohms approx
Low speed coil	320 ohms approx	250-350 ohms approx
High speed coil	60 ohms approx	50-65 ohms approx

Timing advance . . . . 12° BTDC @ 10000 rpm | 16° BTDC @ 10000 rpm

Sparking plug

	NGK	Nippon Denso (ND)
Make	NGK	Nippon Denso (ND)
Standard type	B9EV (B9EGV – T models)	W27ES-G
Hot type	B8EV (B8EGV – T model)	W24ES-G
Cold type	B10EV (B10EGV – T model)	W31ES-G
Gap	0.5 – 0.6 mm (0.020 – 0.024 in)	

RM250

Ignition system

Make	Suzuki PEI (pointless electronic ignition)
Type	CDI (capacitor discharge ignition)

Ignition coil

Primary winding resistance	several ohms
Secondary winding resistance	over 10 K Ohms

CDI coils

Low speed coil	several hundred Ohms
High speed coil	10 – 30 Ohms approx
Timing advance:	
N model	6° BTDC @ 8000 rpm
T model	10.5° BTDC @ 8000 rpm

Sparking plug

	NGK	Champion
Make	NGK	Champion
Standard type	B9EGV	N-2G
Hot type	B8EGV	N-3G
Cold type	B10EGV	N-59G
Gap	0.5 – 0.6 mm (0.020 – 0.024 in)	

RM400

Ignition system

Make	Suzuki PEI (pointless electronic ignition)
Type	CDI (capacitor discharge ignition)

Ignition coil

	N model	T model
Primary winding resistance	0.7 ohms approx	0-1 ohms approx
Secondary winding resistance	13 K ohms approx	10-11 K ohms approx

CDI coils

Low speed coil	290 ohms approx	250-300 ohms approx
High speed coil	170 ohms approx	150-200 ohms approx

Timing advance

Timing advance	17.5° BTDC @ 6000 rpm	15° BTDC @ 6000 rpm

Sparking plug

	NGK	Nippon Denso (ND)
Make	NGK	Nippon Denso (ND)
Standard type	B8EV	W24ES-G
Hot type	B7EV	W22ES-G
Cold type	B9EV	W27ES-G
Gap	0.5 – 0.6 mm (0.020 – 0.024 in)	

1 General description

The ignition system fitted to all of the RM models except the RM50, is of the Suzuki PEI type. Coils in the generator assembly feed low tension current to the CDI unit, where it charges a capacitor. A small magnet in the rotor acts as an electronic triggering device, sending a small electrical pulse to a thyristor (or silicon-controlled rectifier) in the CDI unit, which in turn allows the capacitor to discharge through the ignition coil primary windings. This induces a high tension pulse in the secondary windings, and this is then fed to the sparking plug. A low-speed and high-speed pulser coil arrangement provides a progressive advance as the engine speed rises.

On the RM50, a contact breaker assembly is used to trigger the spark. The low tension currect is fed to the ignition coil primary windings. As the contact breaker points separate, the electromagnetic field in the ignition coil collapses, causing a high tension pulse in the secondary windings. The contact breaker assembly is operated by a cam arrangement attached to the generator rotor.

2 Contact breaker: examination and adjustment – RM50

1   Access to the contact breaker assembly can be gained by removing the left-hand outer cover which is retained by screws. This will reveal the flywheel rotor, which has two large elongated holes in its outer face to permit inspection and adjustment of the contact breaker assembly.
2   Using a small screwdriver, open the contact breaker assembly against its spring pressure, so that the condition of the contact faces may be checked. A piece of fine emery cloth backed by a thin piece of tin may be used to remove any light surface deposits, but if burnt or pitted, the assembly must be removed for further examination, and if necessary, renewal. Refer to Section 3 for further details.
3   Turn the engine over slowly until the contact breaker is at its fully open position, then measure the gap, using a feeler gauge. If correct, a 0.35 mm (0.014 in) feeler gauge will be a light sliding fit between the contact faces. If this is not the case, slacken the fixed contact securing screw just enough to allow the fixed contact to be moved by inserting a screwdriver

between the stops in the casing.

4   Move the fixed contact by the necessary amount to obtain the correct contact breaker gap. Tighten the retaining screw, then re-check the gap. It is important that the setting is accurate. Before refitting the cover, apply one or two drops of oil to the lubricating wick, taking care not to allow excess oil to foul the contact points.

3   Contact breaker assembly: removal, renovation and replacement – RM50

1   If the contact breaker points are found to be burned, pitted or badly worn, they should be removed for dressing. If, however, it is necessary to remove a substantial amount of material before the faces can be restored, new contacts should be fitted.
2   To gain access to the contact breaker assembly, it will be necessary to remove the left-hand outer casing and the flywheel rotor. Refer to Chapter 1, Section 6 for details. The contact breaker assembly is retained by a single screw to the stator plate. Before the assembly can be removed, it is first necessary to detach the coil and condenser lead from the spring blade of the moving point. They are retained by a nut, which should be replaced to avoid displacing or losing the two insulating washers, after the spring blade has been removed from the support post.
3   Using a small electrician's screwdriver, prise off the circlip which retains the moving contact assembly to its pivot pin. Remove the plain washer, followed by the moving contact complete with insulating washers. Make a note of the order in which components are removed, as they are easily assembled incorrectly.
4   The fixed contact is retained by a single screw located at the outer edge of the stator, or backplate. On no account should the three stator mounting screws be slackened, or the ignition timing will be lost.
5   The points surfaces may be dressed by rubbing them on an oilstone or fine emery paper, keeping the points square to the abrasive surface. If possible, finish off by using Crokus paper to give a polished surface, which is less prone to subsequent pitting. Make sure all traces of abrasive are removed before reassembly.
6   Reassemble the contact breaker assembly by reversing the dismantling sequence, taking care that the insulating washers are replaced correctly. If this precaution is not observed, it is easy to inadvertently earth the assembly rendering it inoperative. The pivot pin should be greased sparingly, and a few drops of oil applied to the cam lubricating wick.
7   If the contact breaker is being renewed due to excessive burning of the contacts, this is likely to have been caused by a faulty condenser. Refer to the next section if this is suspected.

4   Condenser: location, checking and renewal – RM50

1   A condenser is included in the contact breaker circuit to prevent arcing across the contact faces as they separate. It is connected in parallel with the contact set, and if the condenser fails in service, ignition problems will undoubtedly arise.
2   If the engine is difficult to start, or if misfiring occurs, it is possible that the condenser is at fault. To check whether the condenser has failed, observe the points whilst the engine is running, after removing the left-hand crankcase cover. If excessive sparking occurs across the contact points and they have a blackened or burnt appearance, it may be assumed the condenser is no longer serviceable.
3   The condenser is attached to the stator and is retained by a single screw through the strap soldered to the body of the condenser and by the lead wire attached to the screw and nut passing through the end of the moving contact return spring. Remove the screw and nut so that the terminal end is freed. Because it is impracticable to repair a defective condenser, a new one must be fitted.

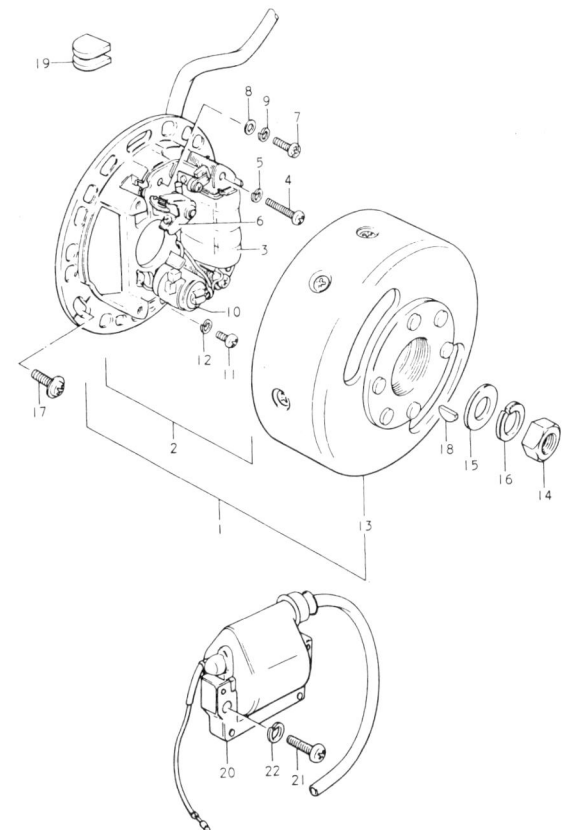

Fig. 3.1 Flywheel generator and ignition coil

1 Magneto assembly	*12 Spring washer – 2 off*
2 Stator assembly	*13 Flywheel rotor*
3 Primary coil	*14 Nut*
4 Screw – 2 off	*15 Washer*
5 Spring washer – 2 off	*16 Spring washer*
6 Contact breaker assembly	*17 Screw – 3 off*
7 Screw	*18 Woodruff key*
8 Washer	*19 Grommet*
9 Spring washer	*20 Ignition coil assembly*
10 Condenser	*21 Screw – 2 off*
11 Screw – 2 off	*22 Spring washer – 2 off*

5   Ignition coil: location and testing – RM50

1   Ignition coils normally have a long and trouble-free working life. If, however, a persistent ignition fault cannot be resolved after checking the contact breaker condition and setting, the condenser and the ignition timing, it is possible that the coil has broken down. In many cases, the coil will not fail completely, but will operate inconsistently.
2   The coil is mounted beneath the frame's top tube, and can be reached after the petrol tank has been removed. The coil is retained by bolts and may be removed after releasing the low tension lead and high tension (sparking plug) lead.
3   For those owners suitably equipped and experienced in vehicle electrical systems, the coils primary windings can be checked with a multimeter set on the resistance or Ohms scale. Connect one of the probe leads to the low tension lead terminal and the other to earth. The reading should be about 0.75 Ohms, although this is not crucial. If, however, an infinitely high or low reading is shown, it is likely that there is either a break or short circuit in the windings.

4   The secondary windings can be checked by measuring the resistance between the high tension lead and earth. A reading of approximately 5.7 Ohms should be given, though again this is not an exact figure. If the coil appears to have failed it should be checked by a Suzuki dealer or Auto-electrician before it is condemned.

5   A quick, if inaccurate, check is to remove the high tension lead and cap, and arrange the bowed end of the lead about 5mm from earth (a cylinder head fin or stud). Kick the engine over and watch the lead. If all is well, a fat bluish spark should be seen. If it appears thin and yellow, it is likely that the coil is defective, and further testing should be undertaken.

6   In the event of failure, it will be necessary to purchase and fit a new coil. It is a sealed unit, and it is not possible to dismantle or repair it.

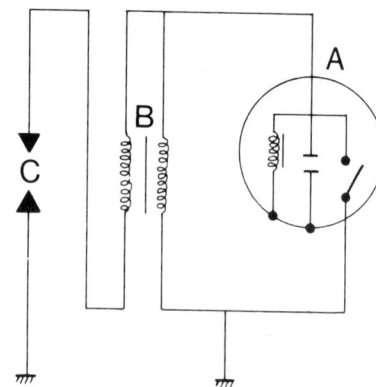

Fig. 3.2 Ignition circuit – RM 50 models

A   *Flywheel generator*
B   *Ignition coil*
C   *Sparking plug*

6   Ignition timing: checking and adjustment – RM50

1   Small high-performance two-stroke engines are extremely sensitive to ignition timing adjustment, and where coil and contact breaker ignition systems are used, regular checking and adjustment are necessary. If allowed to get badly out of adjustment, the engine will run very badly, and in extreme cases, engine damage will occur.

2   To carry out the timing check, it will be necessary to obtain a dial gauge or (DTI) and some means of establishing the exact position at which the contact breakers separate. The dial gauge can be purchased as a Suzuki tool, part No 09931-00112, or a similar device can be bought from most motorcycle shops. To find the contact opening position, a simple torch battery and bulb arrangement can be used, or a multimeter set on resistance. These are shown in the accompanying illustration.

3   Remove the sparking plug and fit the dial gauge and adaptor. Slowly turn the crankshaft whilst watching the dial gauge needle. As the piston approaches TDC, the gauge needle will begin to move. As TDC is reached, the gauge will stop momentarily, and then start to move the other way. There is a slight dead spot at TDC, and true TDC is at the centre of this. When TDC has been established, set the gauge scale at zero.

4   Set up the timing lamp or multimeter, connecting one lead to the contact breaker to coil connection and the other to earth (ground). Slowly rotate the flywheel rotor in a **clockwise** direction, so that all backlash in the engine components is taken up. As the piston nears TDC, the lamp or multimeter will indicate the exact point at which the contact breakers separate. If necessary, turn the rotor back and recheck this position carefully, ensuring that the rotor is moving clockwise when the check is made.

5   Note the reading of the dial gauge, which should show the piston to be 0.90 – 1.40 mm before the top dead centre (BTDC). If outside this range, it will be necessary to adjust the ignition timing setting accordingly. Fine adjustments can be made by varying the contact breaker gap between its permitted operating range of 0.3 – 0.4 mm (0.012 – 0.016 in). If this does not suffice, set the contact breaker gap at 0.35 mm (0.014 in), then remove the flywheel rotor as described in Chapter 1, Section 6.

6   Slacken the three screws which secure the stator to the crankcase. The stator can now be turned fractionally in either direction to advance or retard the ignition setting. Moving the stator clockwise will advance the ignition, whilst turning it in the oposite direction will retard the setting. Refit the rotor, but do not tighten the securing nut at this stage. Re-check the timing as described above, and repeat the adjustment sequence if necessary. When timed correctly, tighten the rotor securing nut to 300–400 kgf cm (13.0 – 16.0 lb f ft).

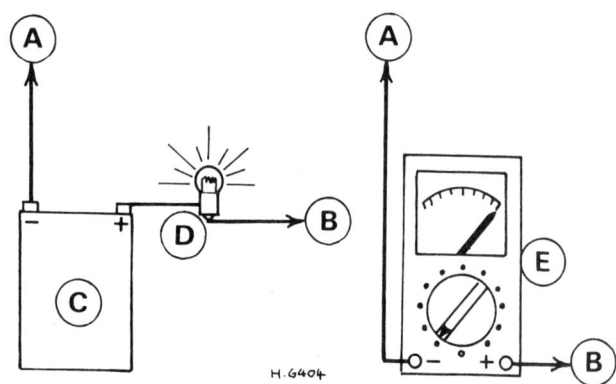

Fig. 3.3 Alternative methods of checking the ignition timing

A: *To contact breaker terminal*
B: *To earth*
C: *Battery*
D: *Bulb*
E: *Multimeter set on resistance*

7   Stroboscopic timing – RM50 model

1   The ignition timing can be checked quickly and with great accuracy using a stroboscopic timing lamp. This device produces a short pulse of light every time the sparking plug fires. When directed at the timing mark on the rotor periphery, the rapidly flashing light will appear to 'freeze' the line in one position. If the timing is correct, the line will match up with an index mark cast into the crankcase.

2   Before making the timing check, it is recommended that the timing and index marks are highlighted by applying some white paint. This will be of particular value if one of the cheaper low-intensity neon lamps is being used. Start the engine and allow it to run at idle speed, having first connected up the timing lamp as directed by the manufacturer.

3   The lamp should be directed at the index mark which is at the ten o'clock position when viewed from the left-hand side of the machine. If the timing mark does not align with the index mark, stop the engine and adjust the timing as described in the preceding section. After making the adjustment re-tighten the rotor centre nut and re-check the timing. If necessary repeat the adjustment procedure.

8 Ignition timing – all models except RM50

1 The CD1 ignition system used on all but the RM50 model requires no routine adjustment or testing. Once set correctly, the timing cannot alter unless the stator is disturbed. In this event, slacken the stator screws so that it can be moved. It will be noted that there is an engraved line close to one of the elongated fixing holes. The stator should be positioned so that the line corresponds with the centre of the screw hole, and the fixing screws secured to retain this setting.

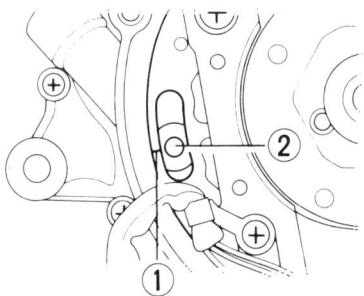

Fig. 3.4 Setting the ignition timing – RM 400 models

1: *Timing alignment mark*
2: *Centre of fixing hole*

8.1a Timing is correct when marks align as shown (RM400)

8.1b Marks may be found at bottom of stator (RM100)

9 Testing the CD1 system

1 The CD1 ignition system fitted to the RM models offers many advantages over the coil-and-contact breaker arrangement which it replaces. The absence of mechanical contact removes the necessity for routine servicing adjustment, and under normal circumstances the system should last indefinitely.

2 In the event of a fault developing in the system, it is possible to trace the defective component with the assistance of a suitable test meter. Ideally, the test meter should be capable of measuring Ohms, Kilo Ohms and Mega Ohms, for the complete test sequence to be carried out. Although not generally provided with a Mega Ohm range, for most practical purposes the inexpensive pocket multi-meter can be used for these tests. When measuring resistances expected to be in the Mega Ohm range use the meter in the Kilo Ohm range. A slight needle deflection heavily biased to no continuity should be expected. This, of course, is not accurate enough to provide conclusive test results but will indicate whether further testing may be required, using more accurate equipment.

3 Before testing commences it should be noted that the CD1 unit contains a capacitor which 'stores' the high tension current when the system is in operation. To avoid damage to the meter and possible shocks, the two terminals to be tested should first be shorted out with an insulated lead to discharge any residual charge.

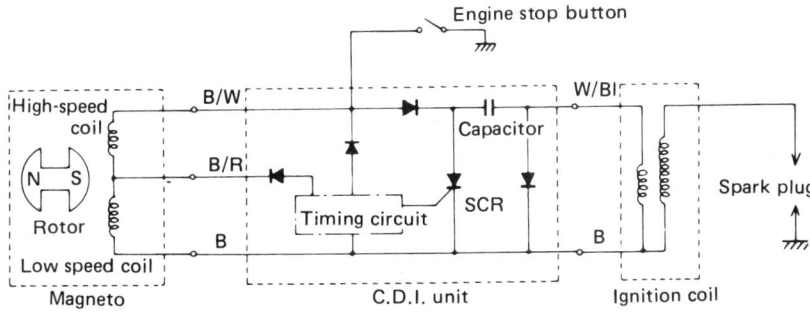

B	= Black	B/Y = Black with yellow tracer
B/W	= Black with white tracer	W/Bl = White with blue tracer
B/R	= Black with red tracer	

Fig. 3.5 CDI ignition circuit – RM 60 models

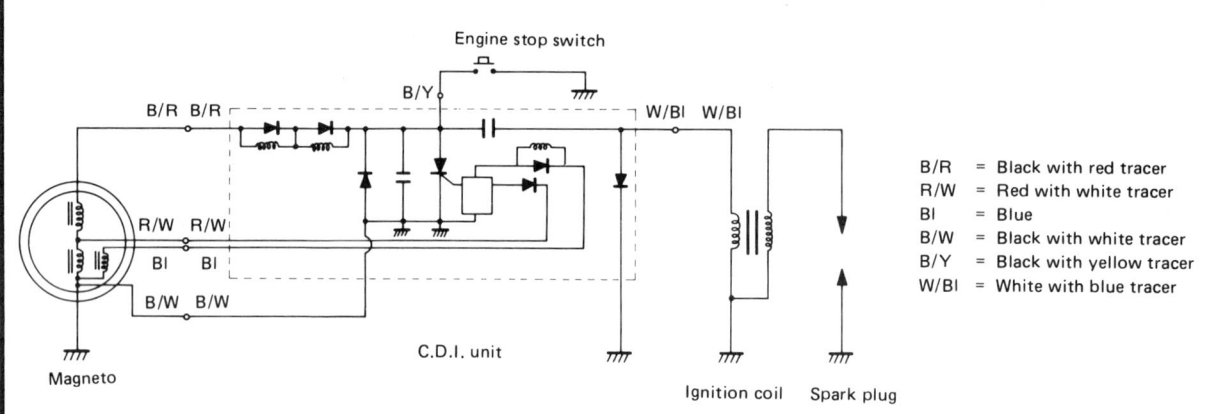

Fig. 3.6 CDI ignition circuit – RM 80 models

B/R = Black with red tracer
R/W = Red with white tracer
Bl = Blue
B/W = Black with white tracer
B/Y = Black with yellow tracer
W/Bl = White with blue tracer

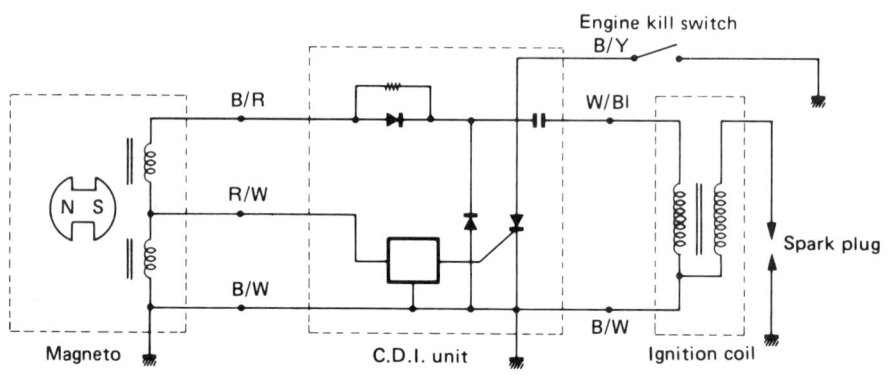

R/W = Red with white tracer
B/W = Black with white tracer
B/R = Black with red tracer

B/Y = Black with yellow tracer
W/Bl = White with blue tracer

Fig. 3.7 CDI ignition circuit – RM 100 models

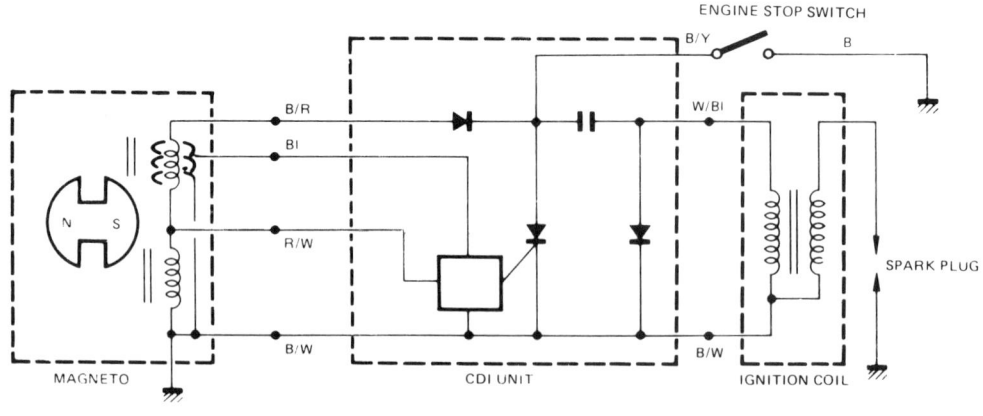

Bl = Blue
B/W = Black with white tracer
B/R = Black with red tracer

B/Y = Black with yellow tracer
W/Bl = White with blue tracer
R/W = Red with white tracer

Fig. 3.8 CDI ignition circuit – RM 125 models

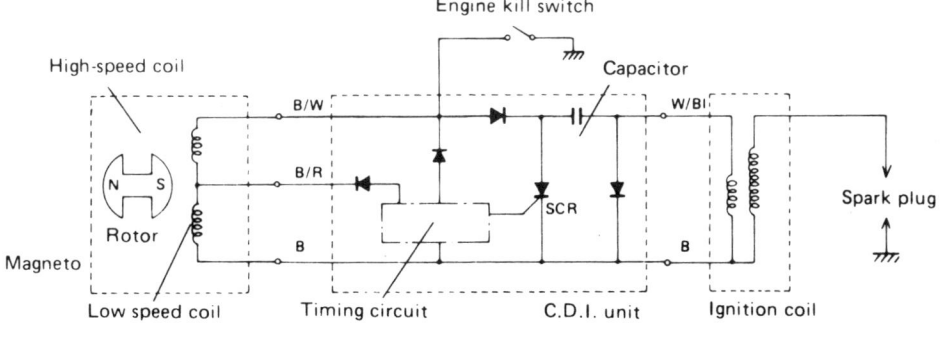

B   = Black
B/W = Black with white tracer
B/R = Black with red tracer
B/Y = Black with yellow tracer
W/Bl = White with blue tracer

Fig. 3.9 CDI ignition circuit – RM 250 models

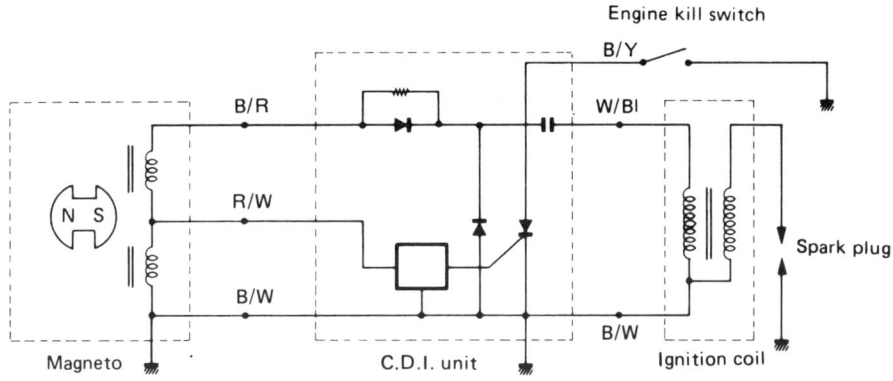

R/W = Red with white tracer
B/W = Black with white tracer
B/R = Black with red tracer
B/Y = Black with yellow tracer
W/Bl = White with blue tracer

Fig. 3.10 CDI ignition circuit – RM 400 models

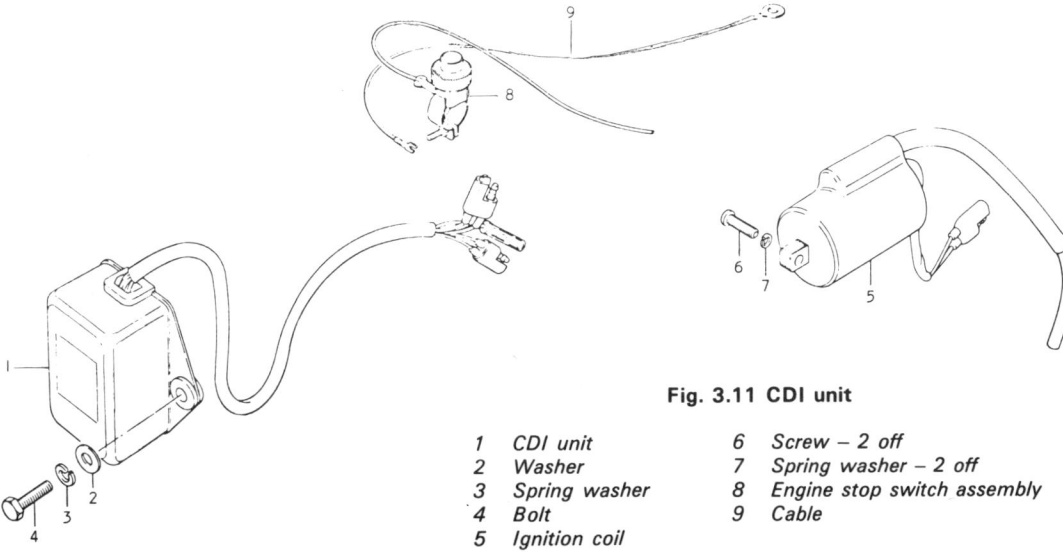

Fig. 3.11 CDI unit

1 CDI unit
2 Washer
3 Spring washer
4 Bolt
5 Ignition coil
6 Screw – 2 off
7 Spring washer – 2 off
8 Engine stop switch assembly
9 Cable

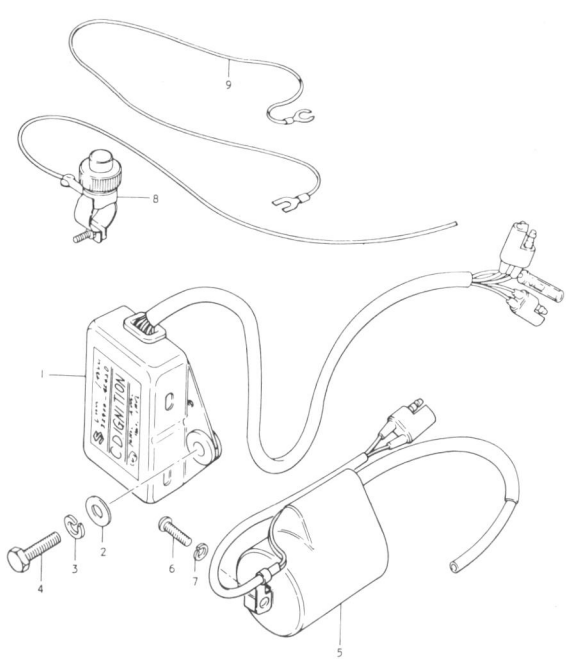

Fig. 3.12 CDI unit

1   CDI unit
2   Washer – 2 off
3   Spring washer – 2 off
4   Bolt – 2 off
5   Ignition coil assembly
6   Screw – 2 off
7   Spring washer – 2 off
8   Engine stop switch assembly
9   Cable

10 Testing the CDI unit

1   Trace and disconnect the leads from the frame-mounted CDI unit. Measure the resistance between the various terminal combinations shown in the appropriate table below. The abbreviated terms used in the table can be interpreted as follows:

ON: Indicates continuity
OFF: Indicates open circuit, or infinitely high resistance
CON: Needle should deflect momentarily, but settle back at the infinite end of the scale

The resistance values, where shown, are approximate, and only large discrepancies will indicate a fault in the unit. Do not omit to short the terminals to be tested before connecting the meter probe leads.

RM 60 and RM 250

Positive (+) probe connection

Negative (–) probe connection		B/W and B/Y	B/R	B (2 off)	W/BL
	B/W and B/y	–	OFF	OFF	CON
	B/R	OFF	–	OFF	About 5 M Ohms*
	B (2 off)	ON	ON	–	CON
	W/BL	ON	ON	ON	–

(*5M Ohms = 5 000 000 Ohms)

RM80

Positive (+) probe connection

Negative (– probe connection		B/Y	B/W	B/R	R/W	BL	W/BL
	B/Y	–	CON	ABOUT 2 M Ohms	CON	CON	CON
	B/W	ON	–	ABOUT 2 M Ohms	ON	ON	CON
	B/R	ON	CON	–	CON	CON	CON
	R/W	OFF	OFF	OFF	–	OFF	OFF
	BL	CON	CON	CON	CON	–	CON
	W/BL	ON	ON	About 2 M Ohms	ON	ON	–

RM100

Positive (+) probe connection

Negative (–) probe connection		B/W and B/Y	B/R	R/W	W/BL
	B/W and B/Y	–	About 2 M Ohms	ON	CON
	B/R	About 2 M Ohms	–	OFF	About 2 M Ohms
	R/W	OFF	OFF	–	OFF
	W/BL	About 2 M Ohms	About 2 M Ohms	About 2 M Ohms	–

RM 125

Positive (+) probe connection

Negative (–) probe connection		B/W	B/Y	B/R	R/W	W/BL	BL
	B/W	–	ON 3 K Ohm	About 2 M Ohms	ON 3 K Ohm	OFF	ON 20 K Ohm
	B/Y	CON	–	ON About 2 M Ohm	OFF	CON	OFF
	B/R	CON	9 K Ohm	–	CON	OFF	OFF
	R/W	OFF	OFF	ON About 2 M Ohm	–	OFF	OFF
	W/BL	ON 3 K Ohm	ON 9 K Ohm	ON About 2 M Ohm	ON 3 K Ohm	–	ON 50 K Ohm
	BL	ON 200 K Ohm	CON	ON 200 K Ohm	CON	ON 100 K Ohm	–

RM 400

Positive (+) probe connection

Negative (–) probe connection		B/W and B/Y	B/R	B (2 off)	W/BL
	B/W and B/Y	–	ON About 2 M Ohm	ON About 2 M Ohm	CON
	B/R	ON About 2 M Ohm	–	OFF	ON About 2 M Ohm
	B (2 off)	OFF	OFF	–	OFF
	W/BL	ON About 2 M Ohm	ON About 2 M Ohm	ON About 2 M Ohm	–

2   If the CDI unit appears to be defective it should be removed from the machine and taken to a Suzuki dealer for checking, and if necessary, renewal. It is a sealed unit, and cannot be dismantled or repaired if defective.

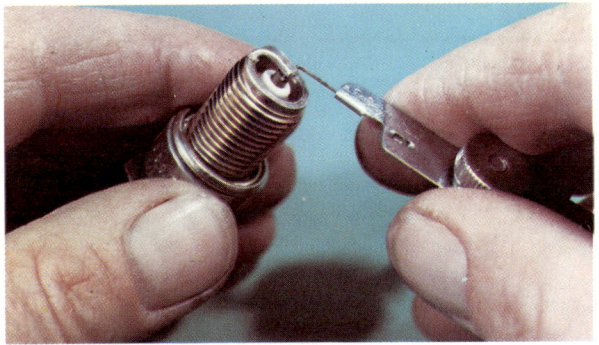

Spark plug maintenance: Checking plug gap with feeler gauges

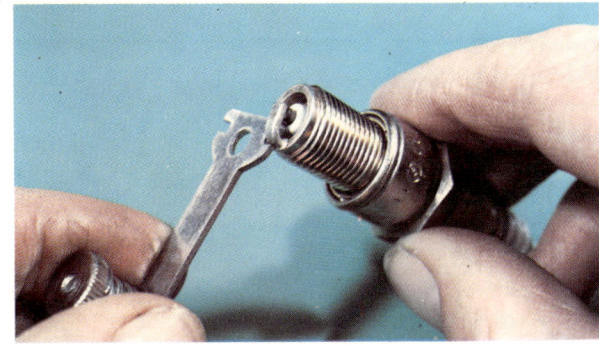

Altering the plug gap. Note use of correct tool

Spark plug conditions: A brown, tan or grey firing end is indicative of correct engine running conditions and the selection of the appropriate heat rating plug

White deposits have accumulated from excessive amounts of oil in the combustion chamber or through the use of low quality oil. Remove deposits or a hot spot may form

Black sooty deposits indicate an over-rich fuel/air mixture, or a malfunctioning ignition system. If no improvement is obtained, try one grade hotter plug

Wet, oily carbon deposits form an electrical leakage path along the insulator nose, resulting in a misfire. The cause may be a badly worn engine or a malfunctioning ignition system

A blistered white insulator or melted electrode indicates over-advanced ignition timing or a malfunctioning cooling system. If correction does not prove effective, try a colder grade plug

A worn spark plug not only wastes fuel but also overloads the whole ignition system because the increased gap requires higher voltage to initiate the spark. This condition can also affect air pollution

10.1a CDI unit may be mounted on headstock ... (RM100)

10.1b ... or behind side panel (RM80)

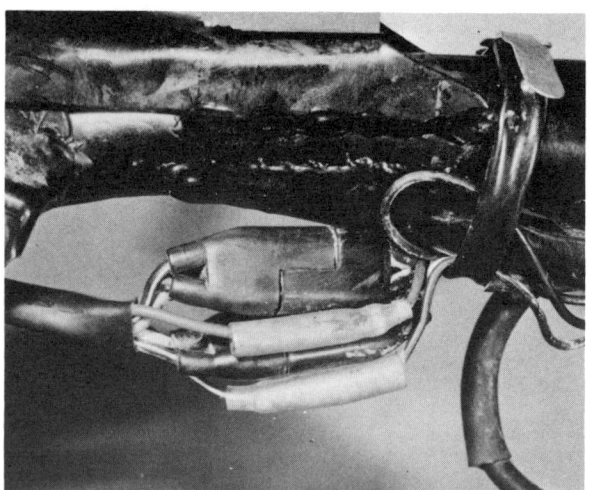

10.1c Connectors can be separated for testing (RM80)

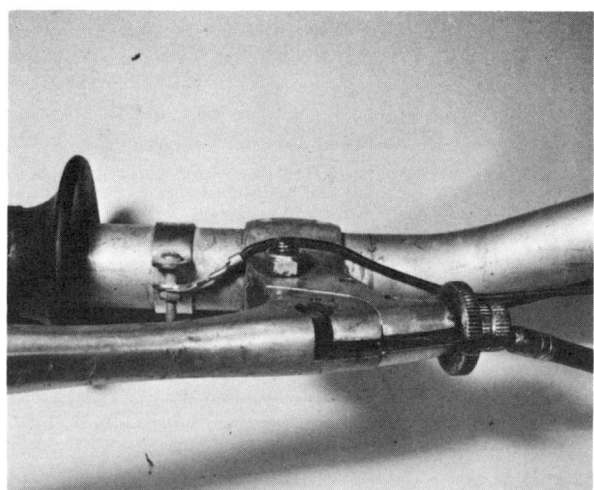

10.1d Check sound connection of earth lead (where fitted) (RM80)

11 Checking the ignition coil

1 The ignition coil can be checked by measuring the resistance of the primary and secondary windings, using a suitable multimeter. The primary windings are measured between the two low tension coil leads, whilst the secondary winding resistance is measured between one of the low tension leads and the high tension sparking plug lead. The resistance values shown are approximate, but if the readings indicate shorted or open circuits, the coil can be assumed to be defective.

RM 60

Primary windings (Black to White/blue)	0.75 Ohms
Secondary windings (HT to Black)	5.70 Ohms

RM 80

Primary windings (White/blue to Black/white)	0.40 Ohms
Secondary windings (HT to Black/white)	13 K Ohms

RM100

Primary windings (White/blue to Black/white)	0.7 Ohms
Secondary windings (HT to Black/white)	13 K Ohms

RM 125

Primary windings (White/blue to Black/white)	1.0 Ohm
Secondary windings (HT to Black/white)	13 K Ohms

RM 250

Primary windings (Black to White/blue)	Several Ohms
Secondary windings (HT to Black)	Over 10 K Ohms

RM 400

Primary windings (Black to White/blue)	0.7 Ohms
Secondary windings (HT to Black/white)	13 K Ohms

2 If the resistance readings vary drastically from the values given above, it is likely that the ignition coil is defective. The coil is a sealed unit, and in the event of failure will have to be renewed as repair is not practicable.

11.1 Ignition coil is mounted beneath fuel tank (RM400)

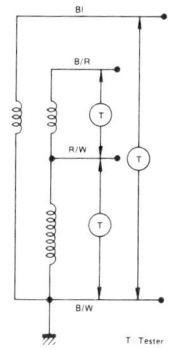

B/R : Black/red
R/W : Red/white
B/W : Black/white
Bl : Blue

Fig. 3.13 Typical flywheel generator test connections — RM 125 shown

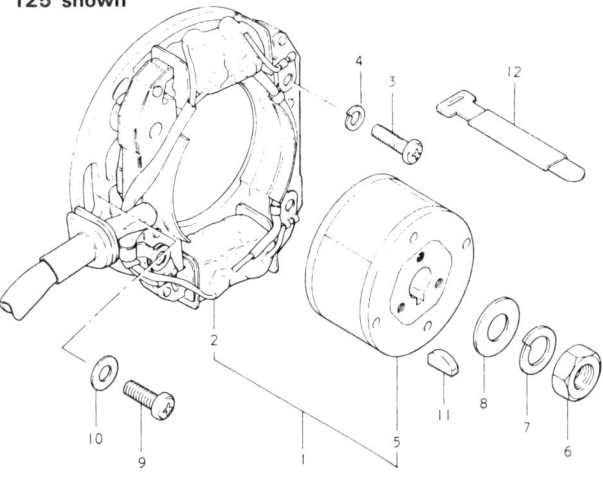

12 Checking the CDI source coils

1   The CDI ignition system is fed by two source coils mounted on the generator stator. A high-speed and low-speed coil are employed to give the correct timing settings at various engine speeds. The coil resistances can be measured at the output lead connector block, and compared with the figures given below. Whilst some variance is permissible, a completely open circuit or a short circuit will indicate the need for renewal. All values are approximate.

RM 60
Low-speed coil (Black to Black/red)	370-450 Ohms
High-speed coil (Black/red to Black/white)	20-25 Ohms

RM 80
Exciter coil (Black/red to Red/white)	80 Ohms
Low-speed coil (Black/white to Red/white)	290 Ohms
High-speed coil (Black/white to Blue)	56 Ohms

RM 100
Low-speed coil (Black/red to Red/white)	170 Ohms
High-speed coil (Red/white to Black/white)	290 Ohms

RM 125
Exciter coil (Black/red to Red/white)	120 Ohms
Low-speed coil (Red/white to Black/white)	320 Ohms
High-speed coil (Blue to Black/white)	60 Ohms

RM 250
Low-speed coil (Black to Black/red)	Several hundred Ohms
High-speed coil (Black/red to Black/white)	10-30 Ohms approx

RM 400
Low-speed coil (Black/white to Red/white)	290 Ohms
High-speed coil (Red/white to Black/red)	170 Ohms

Fig. 3.14 Flywheel generator — RM 100

1	Magneto assembly	7	Spring washer
2	Stator assembly	8	Washer
3	Screw – 4 off	9	Screw – 2 off
4	Spring washer – 4 off	10	Washer – 2 off
5	Flywheel	11	Woodruff key
6	Nut	12	Lead clip

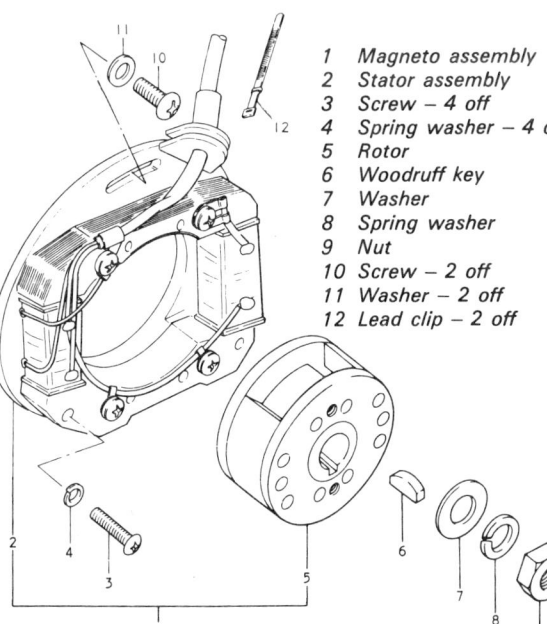

1   Magneto assembly
2   Stator assembly
3   Screw – 4 off
4   Spring washer – 4 off
5   Rotor
6   Woodruff key
7   Washer
8   Spring washer
9   Nut
10 Screw – 2 off
11 Washer – 2 off
12 Lead clip – 2 off

Fig. 3.15 Flywheel generator — RM 80 models

13 Sparking plug: checking and maintenance

1   A selection of sparking plug makes and grades is given in the specifications at the beginning of this Chapter. If the normal grade of plug proves too soft in use, characterised by erosion and burning of the plug electrodes, a harder or colder grade should be fitted. Conversely, if electrode fouling becomes a problem, a softer grade (hotter) plug will be required.

2   The electrode gap should be kept clean and set at the recommended clearance. The gap can be reset by carefully bending the outer, earth, electrode to obtain the required setting. The clearance is correct when the appropriate feeler gauge is a light sliding fit between the electrodes. Never bend the central electrode, otherwise the insulator will crack, causing engine damage if the broken particles fall in whilst the engine is running.

3   After some experience the sparking plug electrodes can be used as a reliable guide to engine operating conditions. See colour photographs.

4   Always carry a spare sparking plug of the correct type. The plug in a two-stroke engine lead a particularly hard life and are liable to fail more readily than when fitted to a four-stroke.

5   Never overtighten a sparking plug, otherwise there is risk of stripping the threads from the cylinder head, especially as it is cast in light alloy. A stripped thread can be repaired without having to scrap the cylinder head by using a 'Helicoil' thread insert. This is a low-cost service, operated by a number of dealers.

6   Before replacing a sparking plug into the cylinder head, coat the threads sparingly with a graphited grease to aid future removal. Use the correct sized spanner when tightening a plug, otherwise the spanner may slip and damage the ceramic insulator. The plug should be tightened sufficiently to seat firmly on its sealing washer, and no more.

7   Make sure that the plug insulating cap is a good fit and free from cracks. Apart from acting as an insulator from water and dirt it contains the suppressor for eliminating radio and TV interference.

14 Fault diagnosis: ignition system

Symptom	Cause	Remedy
Engine will not start	No spark at plug	Check sparking plug and coil connections. Check engine kill switch (where fitted). Check contact breaker points (RM50) or CDI system (other models).
	Weak spark at plug	RM50: check CB points and condenser. Check CDI system (where fitted). Try new plug.
	Engine flooded	Remove, dry and clean plug. Turn off fuel tap and spin engine to clear excess fuel. Refit plug and re-start.
Engine starts, but runs erratically	Intermittent or weak spark	Renew sparking plug. Check contact breaker points (RM50). Check ignition system connections.
	Ignition timing incorrect	Check and reset.
	Broken or damaged ignition leads Faulty kill switch	Check and renew. Clean or renew.
Engine difficult to start and runs sluggishly. Tends to overheat	Ignition timing incorrect	Check and adjust.
	Carburation fault	Check settings. Clean carburettor.

Chapter 4 Frame and forks

Contents

Specifications

Front forks

Type	Oil damped telescopic Air-assisted on RM125, 250 and 400

Oil capacity (per leg):

Conventional fork	
RM50N,T	65 cc (2.20/2.29 US/Imp fl oz)
RM60N,T	72 cc (2.43/2.53 US/Imp fl oz)
RM80N	150 cc (5.07/5.28 US/Imp fl oz)
RM80T	166 cc (5.61/5.84 US/Imp fl oz)
RM100N,T	270 cc (9.13/9.51 US/Imp fl oz)
Air assisted fork*	
RM125N (UK, US)	412 cc (13.92/14.50 US/Imp fl oz)
RM125N (Canada)	392 cc (14.24/13.80 US/Imp fl oz)
RM125T	404 cc (13.66/14.22 US/Imp fl oz)
RM250N	416 cc (14.05/14.65 US/Imp fl oz)
RM250T	400 cc (13.52/14.08 US/Imp fl oz)
RM400N	404 cc (13.66/14.22 US/Imp fl oz)
RM400T	400 cc (13.52/14.08 US/Imp fl oz)

*Nominal capacities only on these models. See level and pressure ranges below

Oil level range	
RM125	145 – 205 mm (5.71 – 8.07 in)
RM250	135 – 205 mm (5.31 – 8.07 in)
RM400	145 – 205 mm (5.71 – 8.07 in)
Air pressure range (RM125, 250 and 400 only)	
RM125	0 – 2.0 kg cm^2 (0 – 28 psi)
RM250	0 – 2.5 kg cm^2 (0 – 35 psi)
RM400	0 – 2.0 kg cm^2 (0 – 28 psi)

Rear suspension

Type	Swinging arm

Suspension units

RM50N,T .... Oil-damped coil spring
RM60N,T .... 5-way adjustable coil spring. Oil-damped
RM80N .... Gas/oil damped, coil spring
RM80T .... Gas/oil damped. 5-way adjustable coil spring
RM100N,T .... Gas/oil damped. 3-way adjustable coil spring
RM125N .... Gas/oil damped. 2-way adjustable damping. 3-way adjustable spring. Sealed dampers
RM250N .... Gas/oil damped. 2-way adjustable damping. 3-way adjustable spring. Sealed dampers
RM400N .... Gas/oil damped. 2-way adjustable damping. 3-way adjustable spring. Sealed dampers
RM125T .... Gas/oil damped. 4-way adjustable damping. 3-way adjustable spring. Gas/oil can be changed
RM250T .... Gas/oil damped. 4-way adjustable damping. 3-way adjustable spring. Gas/oil can be changed.
RM400T .... Gas/oil damped. 4-way adjustable damping. 3-way adjustable spring. Gas/oil can be changed.

1 General description

All RM models employ a welded tubular steel frame of conventional motocross design. The frames of each model are similar, though not generally identical, there being detail changes to accommodate the various engine and suspension arrangements.

The front forks are of the telescopic type on all models. In every case, oil damping is used, with air assistance in the case of the RM 125, 250 and 400 models, allowing a wide range of spring and damping adjustment.

Rear suspension is of conventional pivoted fork (or swinging arm) design. A wide range of rear suspension units is used. Those of the RM 50 are simple non-adjustable coil spring units with oil damping, whereas greater flexibility is found on the larger models, which have gas/oil units with adjustments for spring preload and damping.

2 Suspension adjustment

1 With the exception of the RM50 model, the RM series features a varying degree of adjustment of the suspension components, allowing the machine to be set up to comply with the requirements of the rider and circuit. Not surprisingly, the most sophisticated systems are to be found on the larger models, because the higher power and weight of these machines demand a wider range of settings than the smaller machines.

RM50
2 The front suspension is not normally adjustable on these models, but some modification of the forks' characteristics can be made as follows. If the fork springs prove inadequate, indicated by a constant tendency for the forks to 'bottom', the spring preload can be increased by fitting small spacers above the fork spring ends. This will help prevent bottoming, but will also make the suspension firmer and less compliant. Some experimentation will be necessary to find the correct thickness of the spacers required. The damping action of the front forks can be varied by trying fork oils of different grades. The standard recommendation is 65 cc of SAE 5W/20 or automatic transmission fluid (ATF) per leg. Many riders may choose to use one of the specially formulated fork oils such as that produced by Bel-Ray.
3 The rear suspension units of the RM50 are simple oil-damped coil spring units similar to those employed on small capacity road machines. Progressive-rate springs are fitted to provide an increasingly firm ride as the units are compressed. These units are non-adjustable sealed components, and cannot be set to give different spring or damper rates. In the event of the units wearing out in use, it may be worth considering the fitting of an adjustable replacement pair to afford greater versatility in the future.

RM60
4 The front forks of this model are similar to those fitted to the RM50, but of slightly heavier construction. Minor modifications can be made to vary the damping and springing characteristics as described in paragraph 2 of this section. The normal damping oil recommendation is 72 cc of SAE 5W/20 or ATF per leg.
5 The RM60's rear suspension units differ from those fitted to the RM50 in that they feature a 5-way adjustable spring preload setting. This is normally set at the centre position, but may be varied to suit rider weight or different terrain. The units can be re-set by turning the sleeve cam on the underside of the spring, using the C-spanner provided in the toolkit. Always ensure that the two units are set equally.

RM 80
6 The front forks are again of conventional oil-damped telescopic design, being similar to, but heavier than those of the two smaller models. Modifications described in paragraph 2 can be applied. The nominal damping oil quantity and grade is 150 cc of SAE 5W-20 or ATF per leg.
7 The rear suspension units are non-adjustable, but have the added refinement of being gas-pressurised. This pressure supplements the main springs to give a smoother and more progressive action over a wide range of loadings.

RM 100
8 This model uses yet another version of the conventional oil-damped telescopic front fork. For details of possible modifications refer to paragraph 2. The normal recommended quantity and grade of damping oil is 270 cc of SAE 5W/20 engine oil per leg.
9 The rear suspension units are gas-pressurised oil-damped components, similar to those fitted to the RM80. There is provision for spring preload adjustment at three different settings. To adjust the preload setting it will be necessary to remove the unit from the frame. Invert the unit on the workbench, and wedge a metal rod, such as a screwdriver shaft, between two spring coils on opposite sides of the spring. Grasp the ends of both rods, and simultaneously squeeze them together whilst pressing down to tension the spring. This will allow the lower spring seat to be removed (by an assistant, unless you happen to have three hands). The spring and upper spring seat can then be slid off to expose the spring clip fitted to the upper end of the damper body. The clip can be re-positioned as required, and the unit re-assembled in the reverse order of dismantling. Do not omit to set the remaining unit at the same position.

RM 125
10 The forks used on the RM125 are of oil-damped telescopic construction, and use air-assisted coil springs as the suspension medium. By altering the quantity of damping oil and the air pressure in each fork leg, an almost unlimited range of spring

and damping combinations is possible. It is important, however, to keep within the limitations prescribed by the manufacturers.

11 To set the damping oil to the required level, the machine should be supported by blocks or a suitable crate so that the front wheel is clear of the ground. Remove the dust caps from the top of each fork leg, and release all air pressure from the fork. Remove the fork cap bolt, spacer, spring seat and fork spring, noting that the bolt will be under some degree of spring pressure as it comes free.

12 It will now be necessary to fit the special oil level gauge, Suzuki part number 09943 – 74110, as the oil measurement is made with the fork fully compressed so that the oil is forced up into a specially graduated cylinder. Push the lower leg fully upwards and note the reading on the gauge. The level can be varied between 145 mm and 205 mm by adding or removing oil as required. The oil level in one leg must be kept within 5 mm of the other.

13 Once the best oil level has been established, it is advisable to drain and measure the quantity used. This will make subsequent oil changes much less complicated, and will obviously save time if the oil requires changing between races. Taken a stage further, the various oil levels can be equated to capacities for future reference, and this may enable the owner to borrow or hire a gauge for the initial level measurements, which can then be converted to capacities.

14 The forks are fitted with Schraeder valve inserts, similar to those used in tyre valves. Using a suitable pump, the air pressure in the fork legs can be raised to assist the normal coil springs. The action of air of a spring medium is more progressive than that of a coil spring, the two combining to give a form of suspension capable of responding to wider ranges of loadings than a normal coil spring fork.

15 The operational pressure range is 0 – 28 psi (0 – 2.0 kg cm^2), and this upper limit should not be exceeded in use. This caution should also be applied to the maximum oil level, as an excess of oil and/or air can cause seal failure, or in extreme cases, fork damage.

16 When applying pressure to the forks, it must be remembered that the pressure will rise quickly due to the small air space available. For this reason it is inadvisable to use an airline for this purpose, as compressed air is difficult to control, and may well destroy the fork seals. A safer method is to use a hand or foot pump. Small adjustments can be made by using one of the small syringe-type fork pumps available from most motorcycle shops.

17 When checking the air pressure, it should be noted that a small amount of air will be lost each time that the gauge is used. Care should be taken to avoid this as much as possible by removing the gauge quickly. It should be possible to measure the pressure loss and to take this into account. The pressure in each fork leg should be closely matched to that of the remaining leg. The maximum pressure differential is 1.4 psi (0.1 kg cm^2). As any weight on the front wheel will affect the pressure reading, the wheel should be raised clear of the ground first.

18 The rear suspension units are of the oil-damped coil spring variety, having a remotely-mounted gas reservoir which is clipped to the frame and connected to the appropriate suspension unit by way of a pressure hose. The reservoir consists of a steel cylinder containing pressurised nitrogen in its upper half. The lower part of the cylinder contains oil, separated from the nitrogen by a floating piston. It will be seen that gas pressure acts upon the piston and is then transmitted hydraulically to the inside of the suspension unit via the oil in the lower part of the reservoir and connecting hose. The reservoir is mounted remotely to minimise the tendency for heat to build up in use and thus degrade the operation of the units.

19 No gas pressure adjustment is possible in the case of the units fitted to the 'N' models, but spring preload can be altered by moving the circlip which locates the upper end of the spring. This can be tackled in a similar manner to that described for the RM 100 in paragraph 9 of this Section.

20 The damping effect can be set in two positions (N models) or four positions (T models) after the spring has been released

from the unit. This is accomplished by turning the damper rod. The three positions are indicated by a detent arrangement which will give a positive click as it engages. The positions are identified as follows for the N models. Positions A or B are the hardest damping settings, and the units are set at one of the positions during manufacture. The A and B settings are spaced about 45° apart and are indicated by click stops. Further movement, by about 120° will find C, the softest of the settings. Note that both units should be set up to give the same damping characteristics. Before the spring is refitted, push the damper rod inwards and twist it gently round so that the two mounting eyes align correctly.

21 The RM 125T model employs rear suspension units with four damping positions. These are spaced an equal distance apart, with a larger gap between 5 and 1. Positions 5 and 1 give the same damping characteristic. When selecting a new damping position, the damper rod must be turned clockwise, **never anti-clockwise**. See Fig. 4.2 for details of damping setting positions.

RM 250 and 400

22 The two larger models have similar suspension arrangements to that described for the RM 125 in paragraphs 10 - 20. The various adjustment sequences can be approached in the same way as described in the foregoing, noting the following operational limits.

	RM 250	*RM 400*
Front fork oil level range	135–205 mm	145–205 mm
Front fork air pressure range	0–25 kg cm^2 (0–35 psi)	0–2.0 kg cm^2 (0–28 psi)

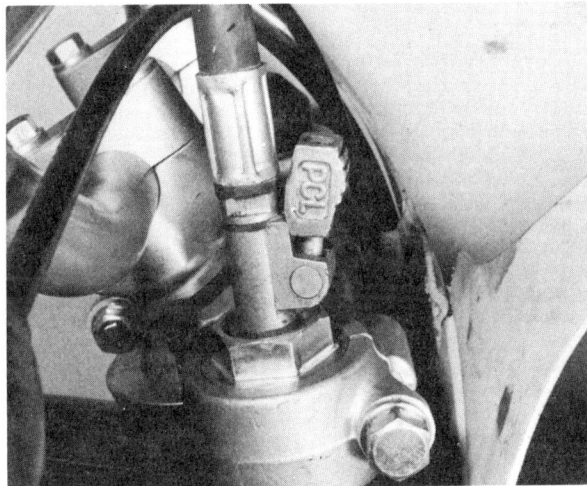

2.16 Air pressure can be adjusted on forks of larger models (RM400)

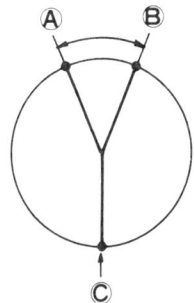

Fig. 4.1 Damper settings – RM 125, 250 and 400 N models

A and B: Hard damping setting
C: Soft damping setting

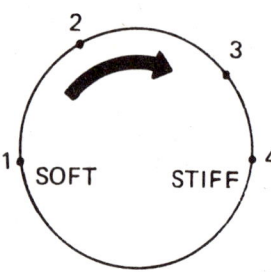

Fig. 4.2 Damper settings – RM 125, 250 and 400 T models

3.3 Disconnect brake and remove front wheel (RM100)

3 Front forks: removal and replacement

1   It is unlikely that it will be necessary to remove both fork legs whilst still attached to the lower yoke, unless accident damage makes this approach unavoidable. It is normally far easier to release each fork leg in turn after slackening the fork yoke clamp bolts, but if the stanchions have been badly bent, they can be left attached to the lower yoke and the assembly removed by dismantling the steering head. (See Section 6 for details).

2   Before the fork legs can be withdrawn, the machine must be supported in a stable position with the front wheel well clear of the ground. This can be accomplished with the aid of a stout wooden crate or blocks arranged beneath the crankcase. Make sure that there is no danger of the machine toppling whilst it is being worked on.

3   Detach the front brake operating cable at the brake plate end, having slackened off the cable adjuster to give adequate free play. Remove the wheel spindle split pin to allow the securing nut to be removed. Withdraw the wheel spindle and lower the wheel clear of the forks.

4   The fork legs can now be removed from the forks, leaving the handlebar assembly and mudguard in position. To gain better access, it may prove helpful to release the plastic number plate from the vicinity of the fork yokes. On RM 50 models, the stanchions are secured to the top yoke by the fork top bolts, and these must therefore be removed before the fork legs can be withdrawn. On all remaining models, a clamp arrangement is used on each yoke. In the case of the RM 125, 250 and 400 models, a double clamp bolt arrangement is used on the lower yoke.

5   If the forks are to be removed as a precursor to further dismantling, it is advisable to slacken the top bolts before the lower yoke clamp bolts are released. On the larger capacity machines, release the fork air pressure first. Slacken the remaining clamp bolts to release their grip on the stanchion, then remove each fork leg in turn by pulling it downward whilst twisting to help free it from the yokes.

6   The forks are refitted in the reverse order of that given above. With the exception of the RM50, ensure that the tops of the stanchions are positioned so that they are just flush with the top of the upper yoke. Before tightening the various bolts fully, allow the front wheel to take the weight of the machine and bounce the machine up and down a few times to ensure that everything assumes its natural position. The wheel spindle should be tightened fully, followed by the bottom yoke clamp bolts, and finally the upper yoke clamp bolts, or in the case of the RM50, the fork top bolts. Refer to the beginning of this Manual for the appropriate torque settings.

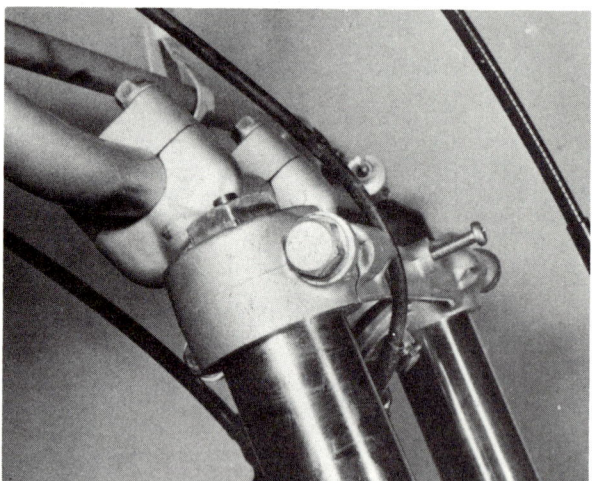

3.4a Stanchions are secured by clamp bolts (RM400)

3.4b Larger machines have double clamp on lower yoke (RM400)

4 Front forks: dismantling

1 It is recommended that each fork leg is dealt with independently of the other to remove the risk of parts becoming interchanged between the two assemblies. Before work starts, carefully clean each leg to make sure all accumulations of mud are removed. The fork top bolt should have been slackened off prior to the removal of the fork leg(s) from the yokes.

2 The accompanying line drawings will show that the forks on each model have subtle detail differences from the rest of the range. These do not materially affect the dismantling sequence described below. Start by draining off the damping oil. This is best done by removing the top bolt and spring, and pumping the inverted fork leg over a suitable drain tray.

3 As with most current types of telescopic fork, some difficulty may be experienced when attempting to remove the Allen bolt which secures the damper rod assembly, and consequently the stanchion, to the lower leg. The bolt passes up through the base of the lower leg, through an aluminium support piece (except RM50) and into the damper rod. As the latter is free to revolve, the bolt often resists any attempt to loosen it, the damper assembly turning inside the stanchion instead.

4 If this proves to be the case, it will be necessary to contrive some means of gripping the head of the damper rod so that the bolt can be unscrewed. A possible method is to refit the spring and top bolt to exert pressure on the damper. This will often prove sufficient, unless an excessive amount of locking fluid has been used on the bolt threads during assembly.

5 If this approach fails, carefully clamp the lower leg in a vice, taking care not to crush the soft alloy casting. Obtain a length of hardwood dowel just small enough to fit inside the fork stanchion. A coarse taper should be ground on one end. Slide the dowel into the stanchion until it bears against the damper rod. Pull the stanchion to its fully extended position, then mark the wood so that it can be sawn off to a length that will allow the top bolt to be used to apply pressure to the end of the dowel. After cutting the dowel to length, fit it inside the stanchion and apply pressure by tightening the top bolt. The Allen bolt should now prove quite easy to remove.

6 With the damper securing bolt removed, the stanchion and damper assembly can be withdrawn from the lower leg, having first removed the dust seal or gaiter. Invert the stanchion to displace the damper assembly, noting the disposition of the rebound spring and any spacers, where appropriate. Clean the various components carefully, then lay them out in order on a clean surface ready for examination.

4.1 Depress valve to release air pressure (where necessary) (RM400)

4.2a Remove fork top bolt, spring seat and spring (RM100)

4.2b Note spacer on RM400 forks (RM400)

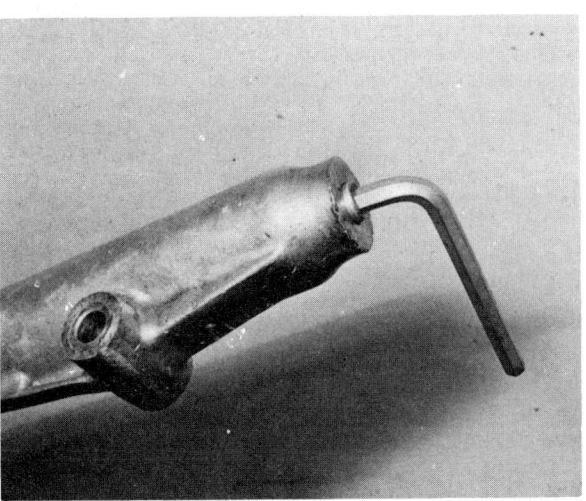

4.4 Slacken and remove damper holding bolt ... (RM100)

4.6a ... and withdraw stanchion from lower leg (RM400)

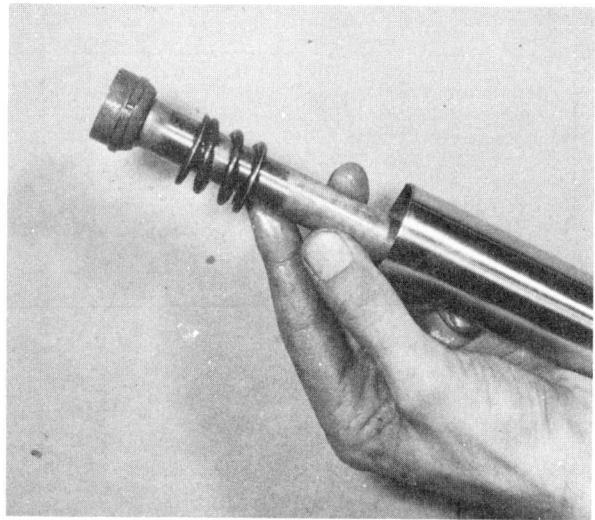

4.6b Damper assembly can be tipped out of stanchion (RM100)

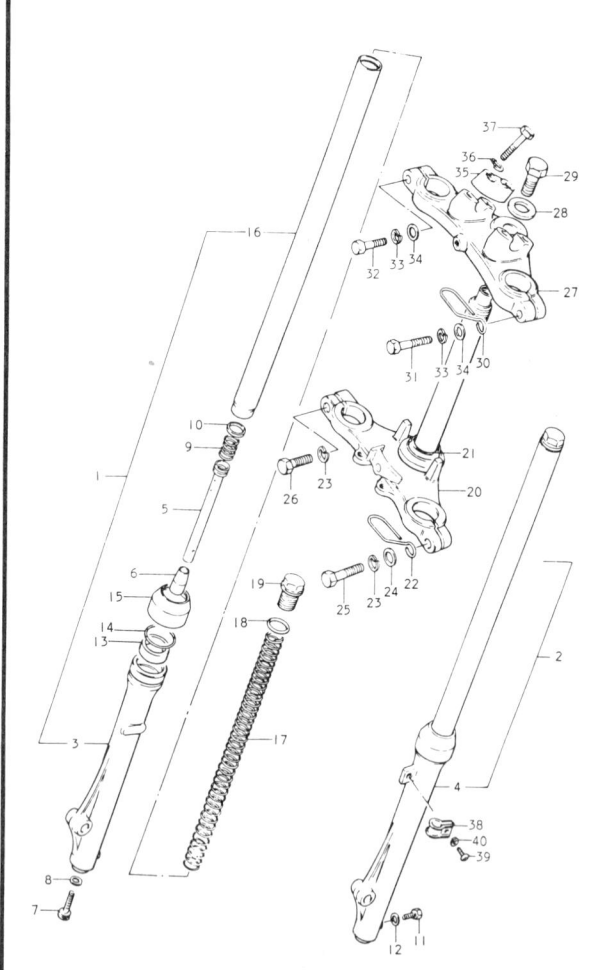

Fig. 4.3 Front fork assembly – RM 80, (RM 50 and 60 similar)

1   Right-hand fork assembly
2   Left-hand fork assembly
3   Right-hand lower leg
4   Left-hand lower leg
5   Damper rod – 2 off
6   Damper rod seat – 2 off
7   Bolt – 2 off
8   Sealing washer – 2 off
9   Rebound spring – 2 off
10   Piston ring – 2 off
11   Screw – 2 off
12   Sealing washer – 2 off
13   Oil seal – 2 off
14   Oil seal retaining ring – 2 off
15   Dust seal – 2 off
16   Stanchion – 2 off
17   Spring – 2 off
18   O-ring – 2 off
19   Top bolt – 2 off
20   Lower fork yoke
21   Steering head bearing lower cup
22   Cable clip
23   Spring washer – 2 off
24   Washer
25   Lower left-hand pinch bolt
26   Lower right-hand pinch bolt
27   Upper fork yoke
28   Washer
29   Crown bolt
30   Cable clip
31   Upper left-hand pinch bolt
32   Upper right-hand pinch bolt
33   Spring washer – 2 off
34   Washer – 2 off
35   Handlebar clamp – 2 off
36   Spring washer – 4 off
37   Bolt – 4 off
38   Cable clip
39   Screw
40   Spring washer

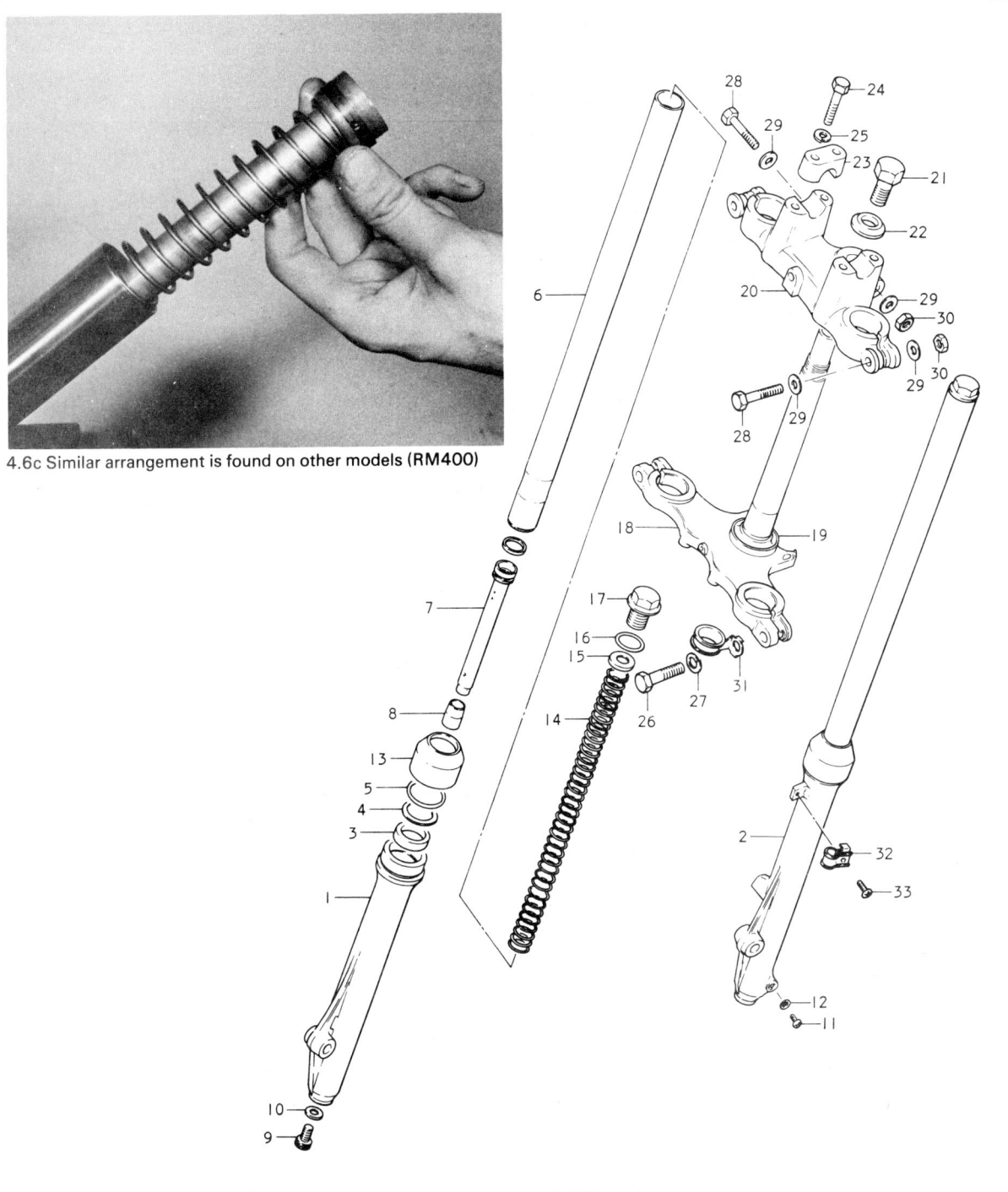

4.6c Similar arrangement is found on other models (RM400)

Fig. 4.4 Front forks – RM 100 models

1	Right-hand lower leg	12	Sealing washer – 2 off	23	Handlebar clamp – 2 off
2	Left-hand lower leg	13	Dust seal – 2 off	24	Bolt – 4 off
3	Oil seal – 2 off	14	Spring – 2 off	25	Spring washer – 4 off
4	Washer – 2 off	15	Spring seat – 2 off	26	Lower pinch bolt – 2 off
5	Circlip – 2 off	16	O-ring – 2 off	27	Spring washer – 2 off
6	Stanchion – 2 off	17	Top bolt – 2 off	28	Upper pinch bolt – 3 off
7	Damper rod – 2 off	18	Lower fork yoke	29	Washer – 6 off
8	Damper rod seat – 2 off	19	Bearing lower cup	30	Nut – 3 off
9	Bolt – 2 off	20	Upper fork yoke	31	Cable clamp
10	Sealing washer – 2 off	21	Crown bolt	32	Cable clamp
11	Drain screw – 2 off	22	Washer	33	Screw

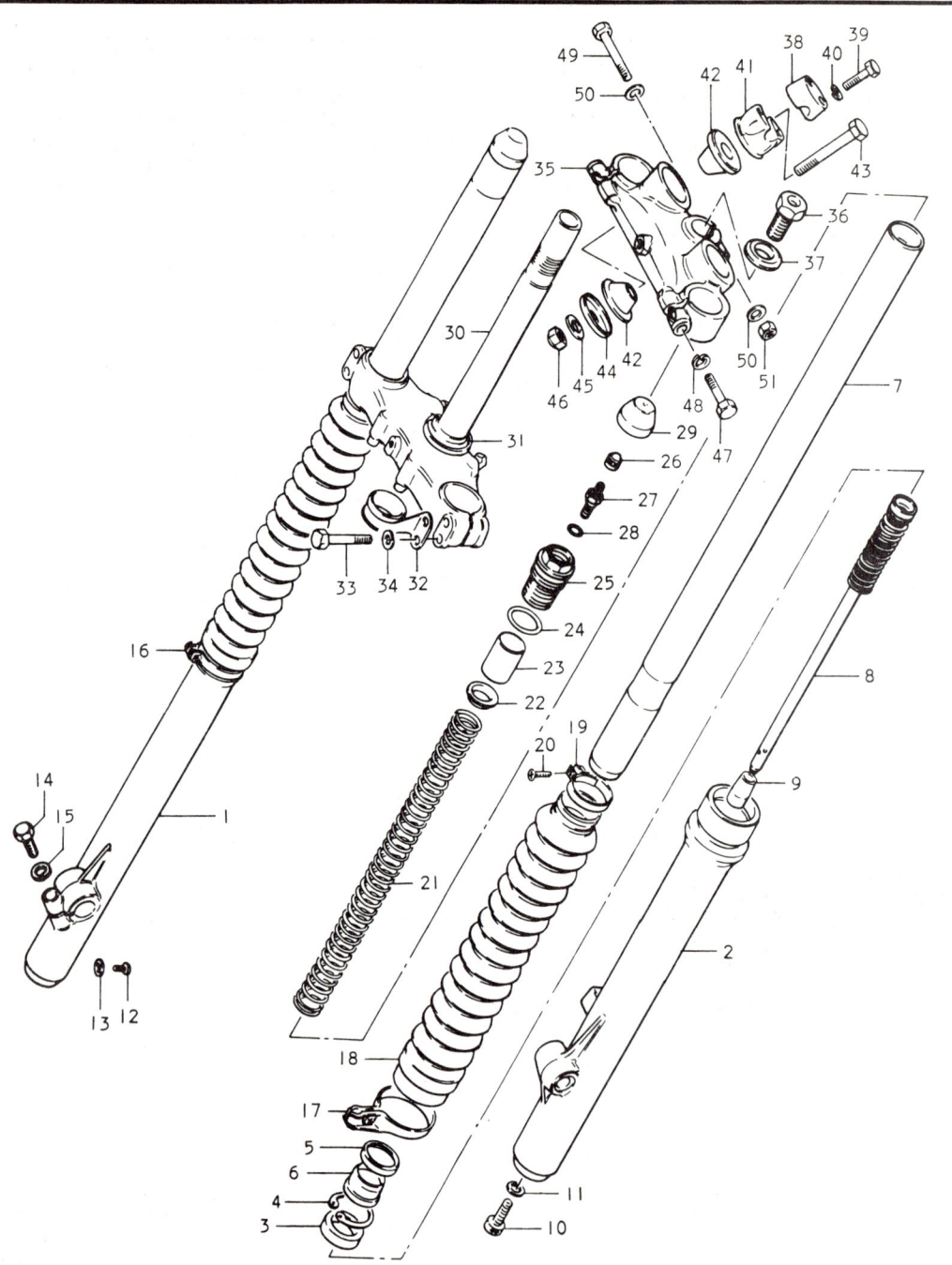

Fig. 4.5 Front forks – RM 400 (RM 125 and 250 similar)

1	Right-hand lower leg	18	Fork gaiter – 2 off	35	Upper fork yoke
2	Left-hand lower leg	19	Upper gaiter clamp – 2 off	36	Crown bolt
3	Oil seal – 2 off	20	Screw – 2 off	37	Washer
4	Circlip – 2 off	21	Fork spring – 2 off	38	Upper handle bar clamp – 2 off
5	Dust seal holder – 2 off	22	Spring seating – 2 off	39	Bolt – 4 off
6	Dust seal – 2 off	23	Spacer – off	40	Spring washer – 4 off
7	Stanchion – 2 off	24	O-ring – 2 off	41	Lower handlebar clamp – 2 off
8	Damper rod – 2 off	25	Top bolt – 2 off	42	Damping rubber – 4 off
9	Damper rod seat – 2 off	26	Dust cap – 2 off	43	Bolt – 2 off
10	Bolt – 2 off	27	Air valve – 2 off	44	Dust seal – 2 off
11	Sealing washer – 2 off	28	O-ring – 2 off	45	Washer – 2 off
12	Screw – 2 off	29	Top cap – 2 off	46	Nut – 2 off
13	Sealing washer – 2 off	30	Lower fork yoke	47	Upper pinch bolt – 2 off
14	Pinch bolt	31	Lower bearing cup	48	Spring washer – 2 off
15	Spring washer	32	Cable clip	49	Pinch bolt
16	Right-hand gaiter lower clamp	33	Lower pinch bolt – 4 off	50	Washer – 2 off
17	Left-hand gaiter lower clamp	34	Spring washer – 4 off	51	Nut

5   Front forks: examination and renovation

1   The parts most liable to wear over an extended period of service are the fork stanchions, lower legs and the oil seals, especially where gaiters are not fitted. Wear is normally accompanied by a tendency for the forks to judder when the front brake is applied and it should be possible to detect the increased amount of play by pulling and pushing on the handlebars when the front brake is applied fully. This type of wear should not be confused with slack steering head bearings, which can give rise to similar symptoms.

2   Renewal of the worn parts is quite straightforward. Particular care is necessary when renewing the oil seals. Both the seal and the fork tube should be greased, to lessen the risk of damage.

3   After an extended period of service the fork springs may take a permanent set. If the overall length has decreased it is wise to fit new components. Always fit new springs as a matched pair, never separately.

4   Check the outer surface of the fork stanchions for scratches or roughness. It is only too easy to damage the oil seals during reassembly, if these high spots are not eased down. The fork stanchions are unlikely to bend unless the machine is damaged in an accident. Any significant bend will be detected by eye, but if there is any doubt about straightness, roll the stanchions on a flat surface. If the stanchions are bent, they must be renewed. Unless specialised repair equipment is available, it is rarely practicable to straighten them to the necessary standard.

5   The dust seals must be in good order if they are to fulfil their proper function. Replace any that are split or damaged. Motocross machines are particularly vulnerable to stanchion damage. On the smaller machines where short dust seals are fitted, there is a tendency for abrasive mud to get trapped by the seal, leading to scored stanchions. More significant is the risk of damage by flying stones. One of the machines dismantled for photographic purposes in this Manual had severely damaged stanchions, and in consequence the seals had been ruined. The only remedy in these cases is to purchase and fit new stanchions.

6   The above problems can be avoided by fitting gaiters which will protect the stanchion from dirt and flying stones. Gaiters are inexpensive and can be obtained from most motorcycle dealers specialising in off-road machines.

7   It should be noted that the stanchions and oil seals of RM125, 250 and 400 machines must be in particularly good condition if air pressure is to be maintained. In the case of these models, new seals should be fitted as a precautionary measure.

5.1a Damper piston ring is located by small pin (RM400)

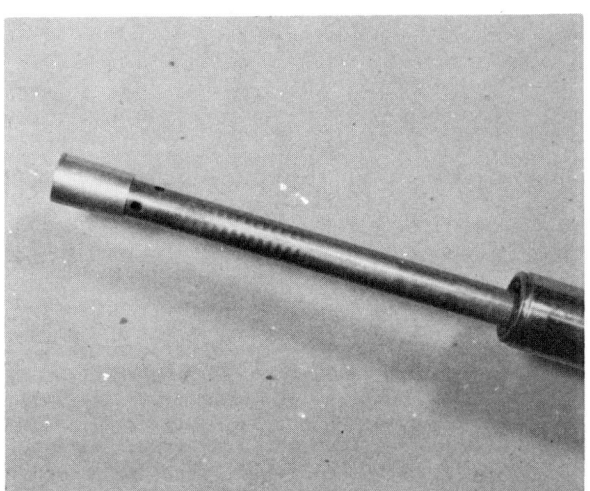

5.1b Check damper rod for straightness or scoring (RM100)

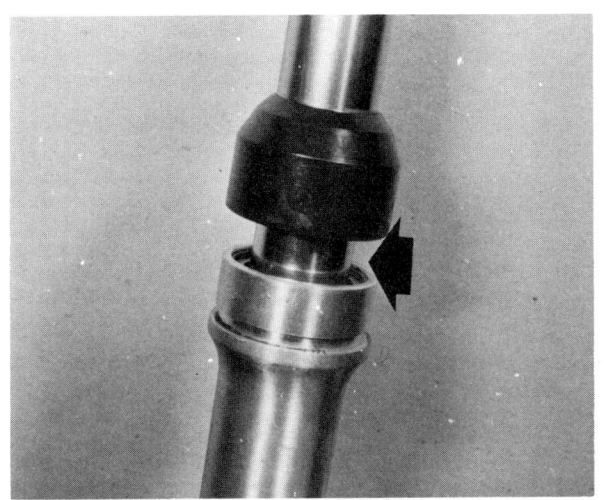

5.5 Dirt and water may build up here on ungaitered forks (RM100)

5.7a Fork seal fits as shown ... (RM100)

5.7b ... and is held by washer and circlip (RM100)

5.7c Elaborate seal is found on air fork models (RM400)

6 Steering head assembly: dismantling, renovation and reassembly

1   The steering head assembly comprises a top fork yoke, and a bottom yoke with an integral steering stem. The assembly pivots about the frame headstock supported by upper and lower cup and cone ball races. These components rarely require attention, other than occasional inspection and greasing of the bearings, unless accident damage has occurred. If strictly necessary, the fork legs can be left attached to the bottom yokes and removed with it, but it is far more convenient to remove the front fork legs first. See Section 3 for full details.

2   Slacken the four handlebar clamp bolts, then remove the clamp halves and lift the handlebar assembly clear of the top yoke. It is not necessary to detach the control cables, because these and the handlebar assembly can be lodged clear of the steering head. On machines so equipped, release the plastic front number plate.

3   Remove the bolts, spacers and spring washers which secure the front mudguard to the underside of the bottom yoke. The mudguard can then be placed to one side. Trace the routing of the leads from the CDI unit where this is mounted between the front yokes. Care must be taken not to damage the wiring or the unit during dismantling.

4   Slacken the upper yoke pinch bolts to free the fork stanchions, noting that this stage need only apply where the forks are still in position. On RM50 machines, remove the fork top bolts. On all models, remove the steering head top bolt. In the case of RM100, 125, 250 and 400 machines, this is secured by a clamp bolt which must be released before the top bolt is released.

5   The top yoke can now be freed by pulling it upwards. If it proves stubborn, a hide mallet can be used to jar it off the steering stem. Before the lower yoke is released, it should be noted that the lower bearing balls will drop free as the steering stem is unscrewed. Unless some provision is made to catch them, they will invariably bounce into the most inaccessible corners of the workshop when they hit the floor. As a safeguard against this, spread some rag on the floor immediately below the steering head, and be ready to catch the balls as they emerge.

6   Slacken the steering stem nut, whilst supporting the yoke until such time as a container can be held beneath it to catch the balls. Lower the yoke carefully. The upper race balls should

remain in position in the top of the headstock. These should be removed carefully and placed in **separate** containers.

7   Remove all traces of grease from the bearing cups in the headstock, and inspect their surfaces for wear or damage. The tracks where the balls have been running should be perfectly smooth and highly polished. If visibly damaged, it will be necessary to renew them. The cups can be driven out by passing a drift through the opposite side of the headstock and tapping around the underside of the cup. The new components are an interference fit in the headstock, and are quite simple to fit if care is taken to ensure that they enter the bore squarely. The lower cone will probably remain firmly attached to the steering stem, but can normally be dislodged by tapping with a suitable wedge, such as an old screwdriver, between it and the yoke. The cones should be checked in the same way as that described for the cups.

8   Keeping the upper and lower balls separate, wash each set in a cleaning solvent and check for pitting or any other marks. If any blemish is found, it is advisable to renew the entire set. If new cups and cones are fitted, the bearings should be renewed as a matter of course.

9   The steering head assembly is reassembled in the reverse order of that given for dismantling. When fitting the steel balls, they can be held in place with grease during assembly. Note that the small gap which will be found when all of the balls are fitted is intentional, and is to prevent the balls skidding against one another and thus wearing quickly. Before adjusting the bearings for free play, temporarily refit the fork legs to ensure that the yokes are correctly aligned.

10   Check the adjustment of the steering head bearings before the machine is used and again shortly afterwards, when they settle down. If the bearings are too slack, fork judder will occur. There should be no play at the headraces when the handlebars are pulled and pushed hard, with the front brake applied hard.

11   Overtight headraces are equally undesirable. It is possible to place a pressure of several tons on the head bearings by overtightening, even though the handlebars may seem to turn quite freely. Overtight bearings will cause the machine to roll at low speeds and give imprecise steering. Adjustment is correct if there is no play in the bearings and the handlebars swing to full lock either side when the machine is supported with the front wheel clear of the ground. Only a light tap on each end should cause the handlebars to swing.

6.2a Release handlebar assembly from top yoke ... (RM100)

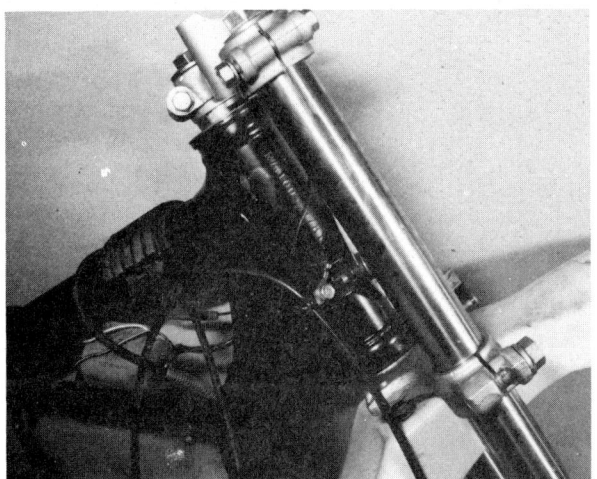

6.2b ... and position clear of steering head (RM100)

6.4 A: Steering stem bolt   B:Clamp bolt   C:Adjuster nut
(RM400)

7   Frame: examination and renovation

1   The frame is unlikely to require attention unless it is damaged as the result of an accident. In many cases, replacement of the frame is the only satisfactory course of action, if it is badly out of alignment. Comparatively few frame repair specialists have the necessary mandrels and jigs essential for the accurate re-setting of the frame a d, even then there is no means of assessing to what extent the frame may have been overstressed such that a later fatigue failure may occur.
2   The condition of the frame should be checked periodically, especially when damage is thought likely to have occurred. The various welded joints should be examined for signs of cracking, after the machine has been cleaned. It is worthwhile repainting any areas where paint has been removed. This will prevent rusting and can extend the life of the frame if dealt with promptly.
3   Minor frame repairs can be effected by welding or brazing, depending upon the area of the frame requiring attention. This operation is best left to an experienced welder who will know the best way to approach any particular breakage.

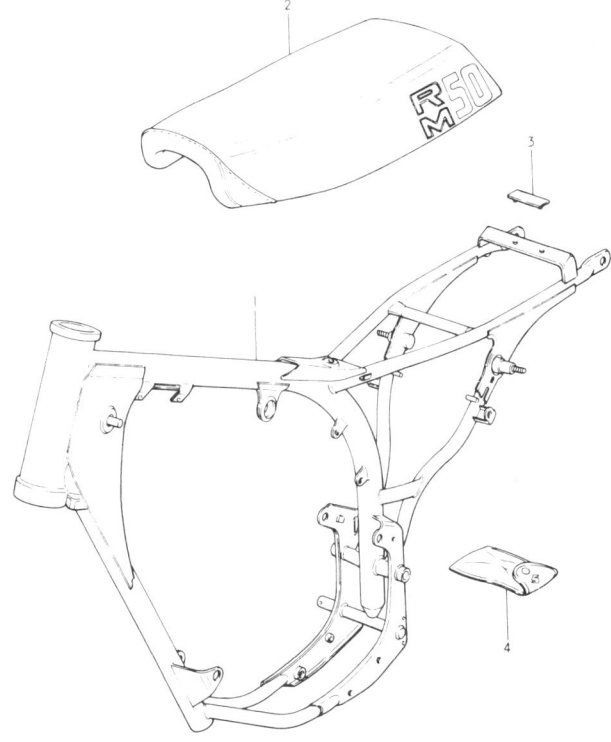

Fig. 4.6 Frame – RM 50 (RM 60 and 80 similar)

1   Frame
2   Seat
3   Rubber cushion
4   Tool roll

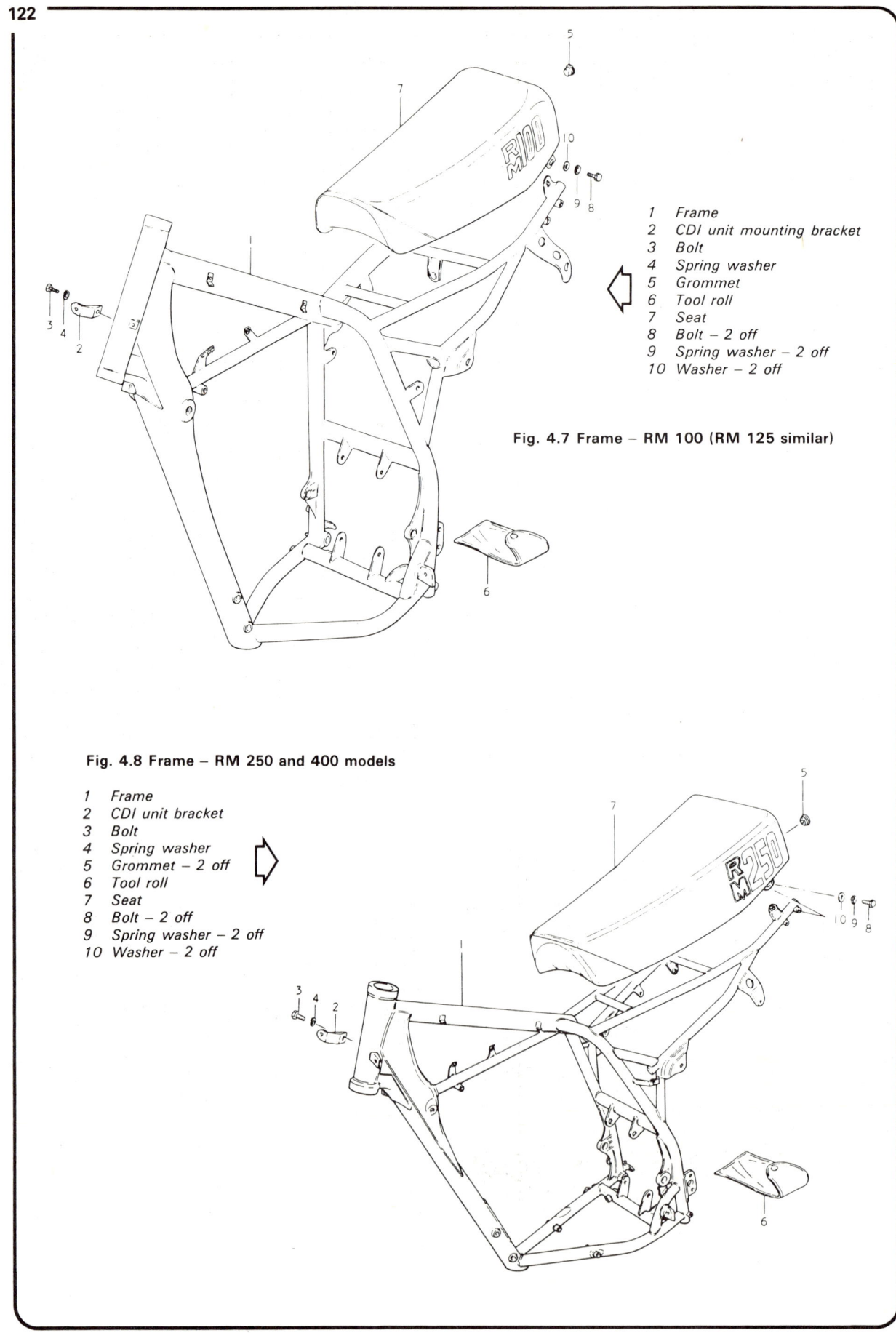

1 Frame
2 CDI unit mounting bracket
3 Bolt
4 Spring washer
5 Grommet
6 Tool roll
7 Seat
8 Bolt – 2 off
9 Spring washer – 2 off
10 Washer – 2 off

Fig. 4.7 Frame – RM 100 (RM 125 similar)

Fig. 4.8 Frame – RM 250 and 400 models

1 Frame
2 CDI unit bracket
3 Bolt
4 Spring washer
5 Grommet – 2 off
6 Tool roll
7 Seat
8 Bolt – 2 off
9 Spring washer – 2 off
10 Washer – 2 off

8 Swinging arm rear fork: removal, examination and renovation

1   Two types of swinging arm fork are used on the various RM models. The RM 50, 60 and 80 are equipped with a welded tubular steel fork, whilst that of the remaining models is fabricated from aluminium alloy or steel sections. Irrespective of the type used, it is attached to the frame by a pivot shaft mounted immediately behind the engine/gearbox unit.

2   All motocross machines are prone to suffer accelerated wear at the pivot bearings when compared to road going machines. Despite attempts to seal out water and dirt, this will inevitably work its way into the pivots. The rate of wear can be reduced by dismantling and cleaning the bearings on a regular basis. The frequency of this operation must depend on the type of terrain and amount of riding done, and is best left to the discretion of the rider. The procedure given below covers complete dismantling for full overhaul. Some riders may find it sufficient to leave the rear wheel and drive chain in place. The pivot shaft can then be withdrawn, and the bearings given some attention, but access will be rather limited.

3   To remove the fork for full overhaul, it is first necessary to place the machine on a suitable crate or stand so that the rear wheel is raised clear of the ground. Release the brake operating rod by unscrewing the adjuster nut and disengaging the rod from the trunnion in the brake arm. Refit the trunnion and nut to avoid their subsequent loss. Release the brake torque arm from the brake plate by releasing its retaining nut and bolt. It is helpful, though not essential, to remove the torque arm completely.

4   Turn the rear wheel until the drive chain joining link is located. Using pointed-nose pliers, displace the spring clip to allow the joining link to be separated. Reassemble the joining link on one end of the chain for safe keeping. The chain can now be run off the sprockets, and the opportunity should be taken to clean and relubricate it if time permits.

5   Remove the split pin from the end of the rear wheel spindle, then withdraw the spindle to allow the wheel to be disengaged from the swinging arm fork. Release the lower suspension unit mountings, leaving the swinging arm forks attached by the pivot

shaft alone. Slacken and remove the pivot shaft securing nut. The shaft can now be withdrawn to release the swinging arm assembly. If the shaft proves stubborn, it can be removed by driving it through with a suitable bar or long bolt. Care should be taken, however, to avoid damage to the threads.

6   On RM50 models, bonded rubber bushes are used, the assembly pivoting around the shaft. If left unlubricated for long periods, the inner steel bush may rust onto the pivot pin, and this tendency must be minimised by removing and greasing the pivot shaft at regular intervals. If the inner bush is worn or damaged, or if the rubber is cracked or damaged, the bonded bushes should be driven out of the fork eyes, and new components fitted. Regular preventative maintenance is essential with this arrangement.

7   The RM 80 uses plain inner and outer bearings, the former being pressed into the fork eye, whilst the latter fit around the pivot shaft. Once again, corrosion is a significant problem, and this situation is not improved if abrasive dust and water find their way in. If corrosion or scoring is evident it will be necessary to renew the inner and outer bushes, whose ground surfaces provide the bearing area for the swinging arm fork.

8   The inner bearings should push out of position unless badly corroded, in which case a certain amount of force may be required. The outer bushes are a press fit in the fork eyes and can be removed with a press or by using a suitable drift. It will be obvious that the dust seals, which provide some degree of protection, must be in good condition. Ideally, try to force as much grease as possible around the bearings to help exclude water.

9   The RM100 and all larger models are equipped with needle roller swinging arm pivot bearings. These vary in detail between the various models, as the accompanying line drawings show, but are basically the same in design. A caged needle roller race is fitted to either end of the fork brace tube. Plain tubular steel inner races are fitted inside the needle roller bearings, the pivot shaft running through the centres.

10   In the case of one of the machines dismantled for the photographic sequences, severe corrosion had completely ruined the bearings and inner races, necessitating renewal. The accompanying photograph indicates the severity of corrosion which will occur if the bearings are not greased regularly.

8.3 Remove rear wheel from frame – all models (RM400)

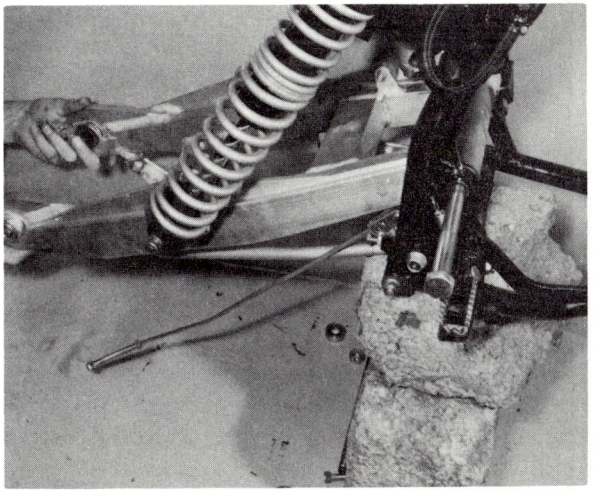

8.5a Withdraw pivot shaft to release swinging arm (RM400)

8.5b Similar arrangement found on other models (RM100)

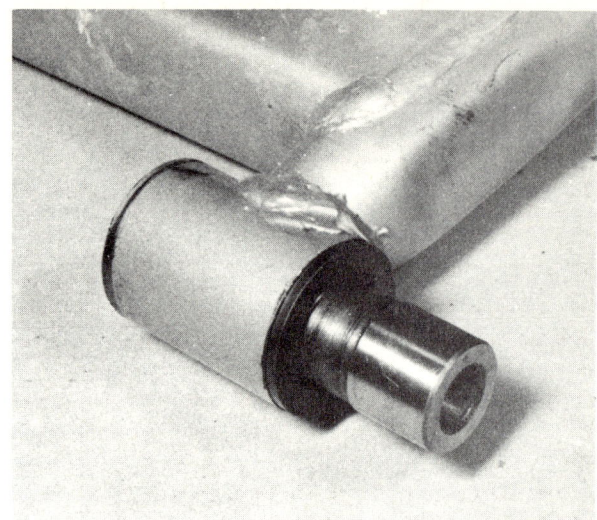

8.8a RM80 uses plain inner and outer bearings ... (RM80)

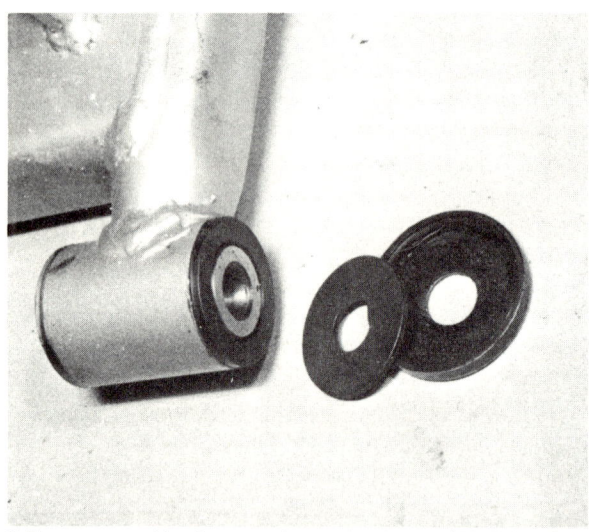

8.8b ... covered by thrustwasher and end cover (RM80)

8.9a Fit needle roller bearings in fork tube (RM100)

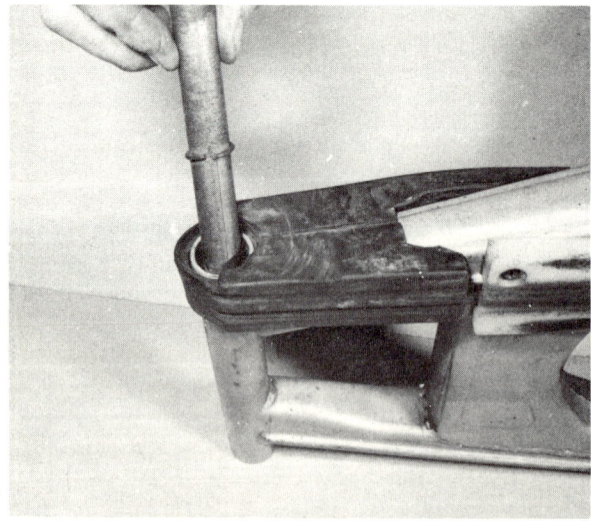

8.9b ... noting distance tube fitted between (RM100)

8.9c Plain inner bearings fit as shown ... (RM100)

8.9d ... followed by headed spacers (RM100)

8.9e Do not omit washer and end cap ... (RM100)

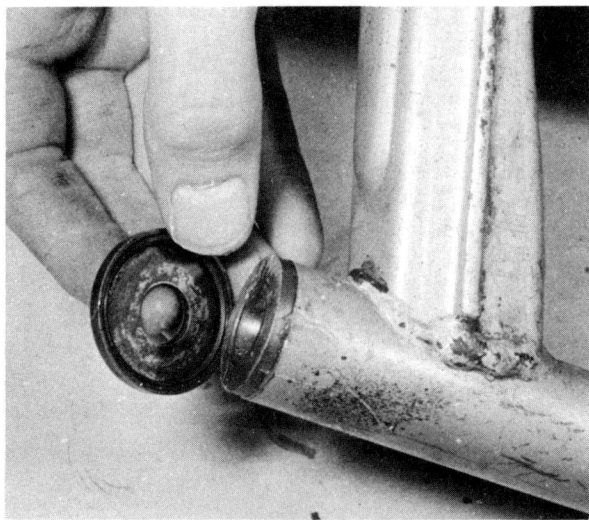

8.9f ... which seal bearings as shown (RM100)

8.10a The effect of water on bearing components (RM100)

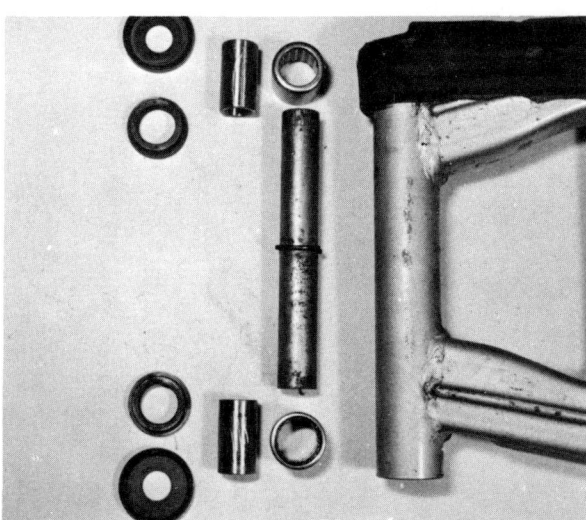

8.10b New components greased ready for installation (RM100)

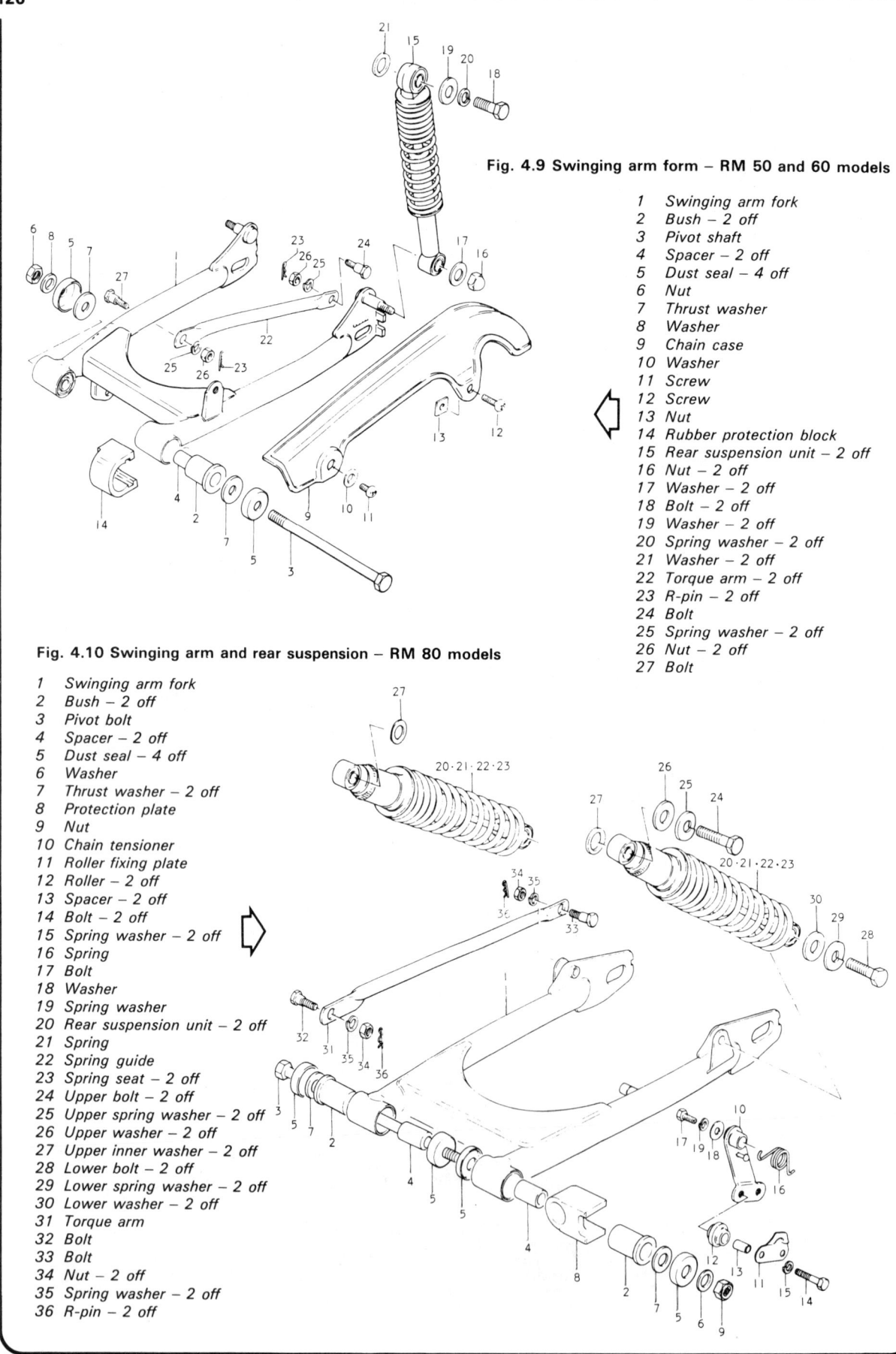

Fig. 4.9 Swinging arm form – RM 50 and 60 models

1   Swinging arm fork
2   Bush – 2 off
3   Pivot shaft
4   Spacer – 2 off
5   Dust seal – 4 off
6   Nut
7   Thrust washer
8   Washer
9   Chain case
10 Washer
11 Screw
12 Screw
13 Nut
14 Rubber protection block
15 Rear suspension unit – 2 off
16 Nut – 2 off
17 Washer – 2 off
18 Bolt – 2 off
19 Washer – 2 off
20 Spring washer – 2 off
21 Washer – 2 off
22 Torque arm – 2 off
23 R-pin – 2 off
24 Bolt
25 Spring washer – 2 off
26 Nut – 2 off
27 Bolt

Fig. 4.10 Swinging arm and rear suspension – RM 80 models

1   Swinging arm fork
2   Bush – 2 off
3   Pivot bolt
4   Spacer – 2 off
5   Dust seal – 4 off
6   Washer
7   Thrust washer – 2 off
8   Protection plate
9   Nut
10 Chain tensioner
11 Roller fixing plate
12 Roller – 2 off
13 Spacer – 2 off
14 Bolt – 2 off
15 Spring washer – 2 off
16 Spring
17 Bolt
18 Washer
19 Spring washer
20 Rear suspension unit – 2 off
21 Spring
22 Spring guide
23 Spring seat – 2 off
24 Upper bolt – 2 off
25 Upper spring washer – 2 off
26 Upper washer – 2 off
27 Upper inner washer – 2 off
28 Lower bolt – 2 off
29 Lower spring washer – 2 off
30 Lower washer – 2 off
31 Torque arm
32 Bolt
33 Bolt
34 Nut – 2 off
35 Spring washer – 2 off
36 R-pin – 2 off

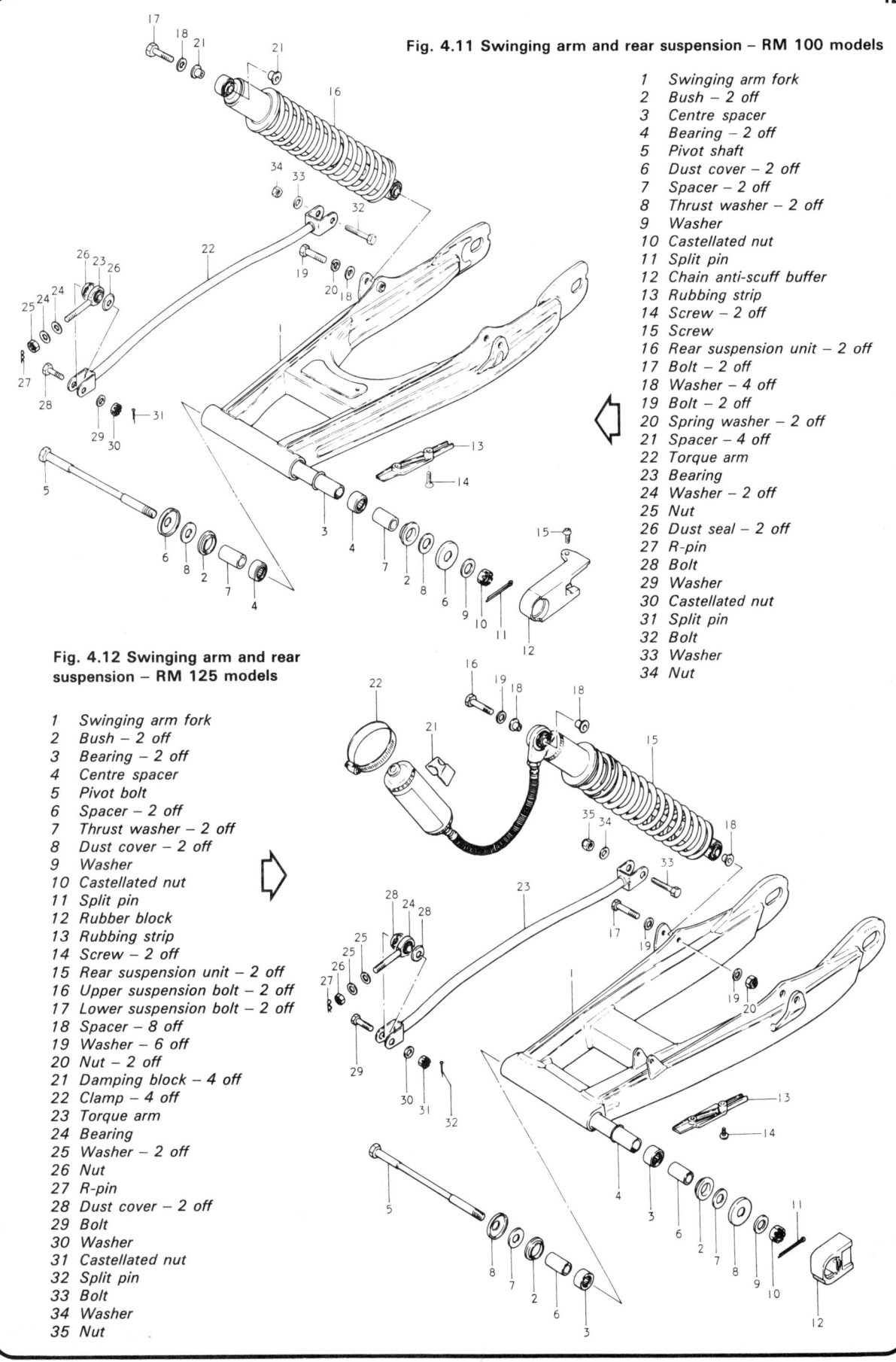

Fig. 4.11 Swinging arm and rear suspension – RM 100 models

1 Swinging arm fork
2 Bush – 2 off
3 Centre spacer
4 Bearing – 2 off
5 Pivot shaft
6 Dust cover – 2 off
7 Spacer – 2 off
8 Thrust washer – 2 off
9 Washer
10 Castellated nut
11 Split pin
12 Chain anti-scuff buffer
13 Rubbing strip
14 Screw – 2 off
15 Screw
16 Rear suspension unit – 2 off
17 Bolt – 2 off
18 Washer – 4 off
19 Bolt – 2 off
20 Spring washer – 2 off
21 Spacer – 4 off
22 Torque arm
23 Bearing
24 Washer – 2 off
25 Nut
26 Dust seal – 2 off
27 R-pin
28 Bolt
29 Washer
30 Castellated nut
31 Split pin
32 Bolt
33 Washer
34 Nut

Fig. 4.12 Swinging arm and rear suspension – RM 125 models

1 Swinging arm fork
2 Bush – 2 off
3 Bearing – 2 off
4 Centre spacer
5 Pivot bolt
6 Spacer – 2 off
7 Thrust washer – 2 off
8 Dust cover – 2 off
9 Washer
10 Castellated nut
11 Split pin
12 Rubber block
13 Rubbing strip
14 Screw – 2 off
15 Rear suspension unit – 2 off
16 Upper suspension bolt – 2 off
17 Lower suspension bolt – 2 off
18 Spacer – 8 off
19 Washer – 6 off
20 Nut – 2 off
21 Damping block – 4 off
22 Clamp – 4 off
23 Torque arm
24 Bearing
25 Washer – 2 off
26 Nut
27 R-pin
28 Dust cover – 2 off
29 Bolt
30 Washer
31 Castellated nut
32 Split pin
33 Bolt
34 Washer
35 Nut

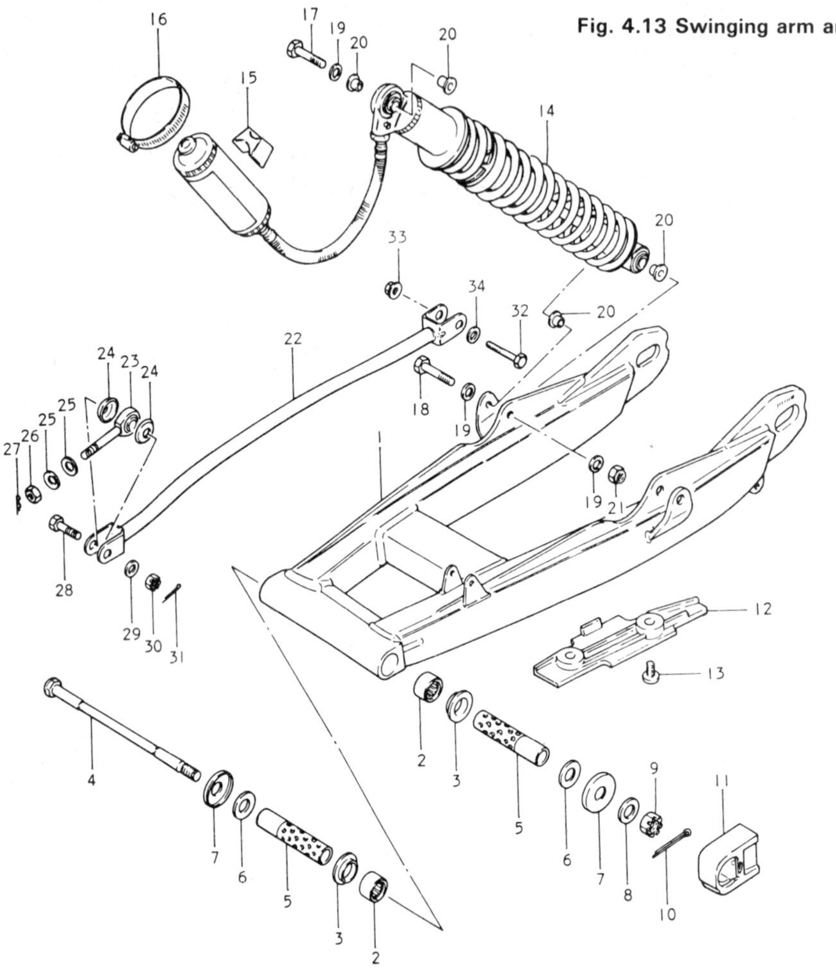

Fig. 4.13 Swinging arm and rear suspension – RM 250 and 400

1   Swinging arm fork
2   Bearing – 2 off
3   Shouldered bush – 2 off
4   Pivot bolt
5   Spacer
6   Thrust washer – 2 off
7   Dust cover – 2 off
8   Washer
9   Castellated nut
10 Split pin
11 Rubber block
12 Protection plate
13 Screw
14 Rear suspension unit – 2 off
15 Damping rubber – 4 off
16 Clamp – 4 off
17 Upper suspension unit bolt – 2 off
18 Lower suspension unit bolt – 2 off
19 Washer – 6 off
20 Spacer – 8 off
21 Nut – 2 off
22 Torque arm
23 Bearing
24 Dust seal – 2 off
25 Washer – 2 off
26 Nut
27 R-pin
28 Bolt
29 Washer – 2 off
30 Castellated nut
31 Split pin
32 Bolt
33 Nut

9   Rear suspension units: removal and renewal

1   The various models employ various types of rear suspension unit, ranging from the non-adjustable oil-damped coil
spring units of the RM50, to the remote-reservoir gas/oil types
fitted to the larger models. The range and methods of adjustment are covered in detail in Section 2 of this Chapter.

2   Apart from the RM 125, 250 and 400T models, the damper
units are of sealed construction. This applies to the N model
remote reservoir types, and no attempt should be made to
unscrew the hose connections between the damper and the
reservoir. In the event that this type of unit becomes ineffective,
the reservoir must be de-pressurised prior to its disposal. This is
accomplished by taping a plastic bag around the reservoir for
protection, and then drilling a small hole through the side wall,
about 10-20 mm from the top edge. This will allow the pressure
to be relieved harmlessly, the plastic bag catching any swarf or
oil forced out by the escaping gas.

3   The rear suspension units on all models are secured at the
upper and lower ends by a nut and bolt or stud arrangement.
Where remote reservoirs are used, these are held by plastic
cable clips to the frame tubes, immediately in front of the
suspension units. In the event of failure, the suspension units
should always be renewed as a pair, never singly.

4   The RM125, 250 and 400T employ modified rear suspension units which are designed to permit oil changes. These are
dealt with in detail in Section 10 of this Chapter.

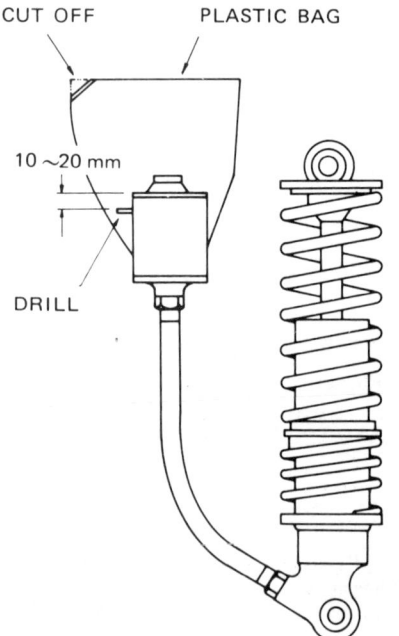

Fig. 4.14 De-pressurising sealed reservoir units prior to disposal

9.1 Larger models use nitrogen pressurised units (RM400)

9.3 Lower mounting has removable inner bush (RM400)

10 Rear suspension units: RM 125, 250 and 400T

1   The remote reservoir rear suspension units fitted to the 1980 (T) range have been redesigned to permit a wider range of damping settings. These modified units have also been adapted to allow the damping oil to be changed, whereas on the earlier models exhausted damping oil meant renewal of the complete unit. **Note:** Before attempting to change the damping oil, it must be understood that a cylinder of nitrogen gas will be required to re-pressurise the unit(s). This section is intended for owners who have access to this facility, or who can arrange for a Suzuki Agent to re-pressurise the units after the oil has been changed. It is assumed that the owner will have experience in handling compressed gases, or that this operation will be left to an expert.

2   Before the old damping oil can be removed, it is necessary to release the nitrogen pressure by depressing the pressure valve in the reservoir. Place some clean rag around the valve to catch any expelled oil. Carefully clamp the reservoir in a vice, taking great care to hold the unit near the hose end to avoid any risk of distorting the reservoir cylinder. The damper unit should be supported to avoid placing undue strain on the connecting hose.

3   Slowly unscrew the flexible connecting hose from the end of the reservoir, having first placed a suitable drain bowl or tray beneath the reservoir. As the union is slackened, any residual pressure will be released, together with some of the damping oil. As this may be expelled with some force, drape some rag around the union as it is slackened.

4   Hold the damper body and hose over the drain tray with the outlet and hose at the lowest point, then slowly pump the damper rod to expel the old damping oil. If time permits, the damper can be left completely overnight to drain. The damper should then be flushed out twice with new shock absorber oil to remove the remaining old oil and to clean the internal surfaces. On no account should any form of solvent be used during the flushing operation, as it may cause damage to the seals, leading to their subsequent failure.

5   Empty the oil from the reservoir and remove the pressure valve from its base. The reservoir should be flushed out with new damping oil in the same way as described above for the damper. Before proceeding further, check the condition of the O-rings which seal the pressure valve and hose union. If in good condition, these may be reused, but if marked in any way they should be renewed. The connecting hose is unlikely to be badly worn unless it has been chafing on the frame. If signs of damage are evident it should be renewed.

6   The floating piston which separates the damping oil from

the nitrogen under pressure must now be positioned exactly 44.0 $\pm$ 2.0 mm (1.73 $\pm$ 0.08 in) from the hose connection face of the reservoir. This is best accomplished by setting a vernier caliper to the required distance and using the projecting end to push the piston down into position. Do not use excessive force during this operation, but press gently and evenly on the piston. If the piston is found to be too far down, temporarily refit the pressure valve and use an air line or foot pump to force the piston upwards, then position as described above.

7   When the piston is in the correct position, refit the pressure valve, tightening it to 7.0 - 9.5 lbf ft (1.0 - 1.3 kgf m). Fill the reservoir completely with new damping oil, shaking it to remove any air bubbles, then place it to one side for the time being.

8   Using a length of plastic tubing, connect a funnel to the shock absorber hose. The funnel can be held by clamping it lightly in the vice. In the absence of a suitable length of tubing or a funnel, a cut down plastic squeeze pack of the type used for fork and gear oils will make a usable substitute. Holding the shock absorber with the outlet uppermost, fill the funnel with about 200 cc of oil, and then pump the damper rod to draw oil into the unit and to expel air. The pumping operation should be repeated for a few minutes to ensure the expulsion of all residual air.

9   When clear of air, extend the damper rod fully and release the hose from the funnel pipe. Taking care not to admit any air into the system, connect the hose to the primed reservoir as quickly as possible. Tighten the hose union to 11.0 - 14.5 lbf ft (1.5 - 2.0 kgf m).

10   The unit can now be re-pressurised using nitrogen. Do not use flammable gases or oxygen for this application. The manufacturer recommends nitrogen only, because compressed air may cause rusting inside the unit, whereas nitrogen is inert and will not permit any oxydisation to take place. Set the nitrogen bottle regulator to 228 psi (16 kg cm^2) and connect the adaptor to the pressure valve. Once the required pressure is reached, cover the adaptor to catch any oil spray, then release it from the reservoir. If in any doubt, leave the re-pressurisation to a qualified Suzuki Agent.

11   The following limits must be observed when dealing with refillable gas/oil shock absorbers. If insufficient or excessive pressure is used, damage may result.

Shock absorber oil grade   *Bel-Ray LT100 or equivalent*
Shock absorber oil quantity 192 cc (6.49/6.76 US/Imp fl oz)
                                                        (approximate value)

Absolute maximum nitrogen
pressure   *20 kg/cm^2 (2.0 MPa, 284 psi)*
Absolute minimum nitrogen
pressure   *10 kg/cm^2 (1.0 MPa, 142 psi)*
Standard nitrogen pressure   16 kg/cm^2 (1.6 MPa, 228 psi)

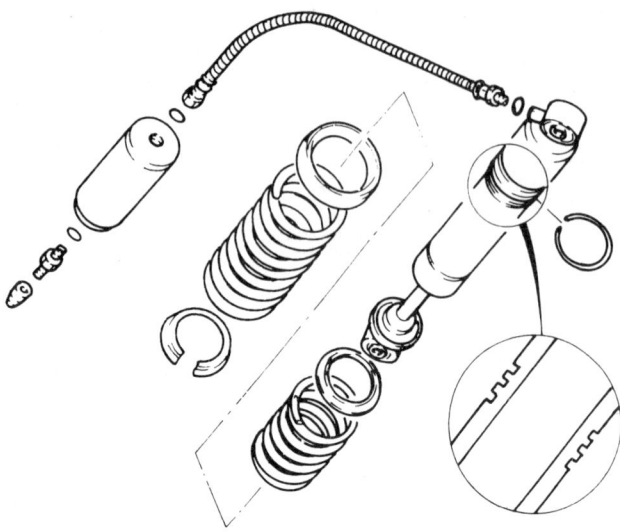

Fig. 4.15 Rear suspension unit – RM 125, 250 and 400 T models

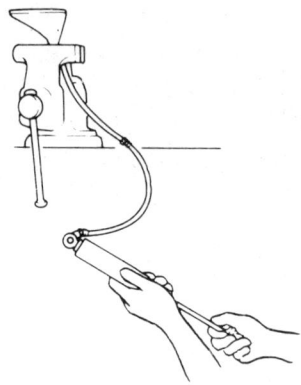

Fig. 4.18 Using funnel and tubing to fill rear shock absorber RM 125, 250 and 400 T models

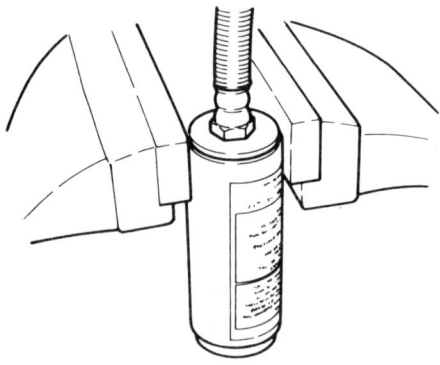

Fig. 4.16 Hold reservoir as shown when releasing hose – RM 125, 250 and 400 T models

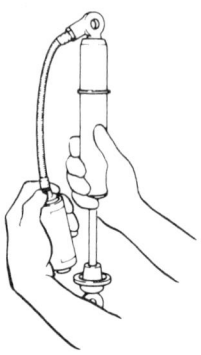

Fig. 4.19 Reservoir should be positioned below shock absorber when connecting hose – RM 125, 250 and 400 T models

11 Footrests: examination

1   The footrests are of the spring-loaded cleated steel variety, being designed to fold up if the machine is dropped. This serves to minimise the risk of damage. The footrests pivot on clevis pins which are retained by split pins to a support bar on the smaller machines or to small brackets on the larger models.
2   The footrests on motocross machines are subject to a fair amount of abuse, and it is important that they are checked regularly for wear or damage. It is advisable to ensure that the small return spring is renewed if it becomes broken or weak, as this will ensure that the footrest reverts to its normal position if displaced.

12 Rear brake pedal: examination and repair

1   The rear brake pedal is of welded steel construction and is secured to a pivot on the right-hand side of the machine. If it sustains damage when the machine is dropped, it is usually possible to straighten it if the damage is not too severe.
2   The affected area should be heated in a fire or with a blowlamp until it reached a dull cherry red colour. At this temperature the steel will be quite malleable, and the bend can be bent or hammered flat. Take care to avoid burns during this operation, and after straightening, paint the pedal to offset corrosion. Avoid trying to bend the pedal whilst it is cold, as this will strain the metal still further, and can result in breakage at a later date.

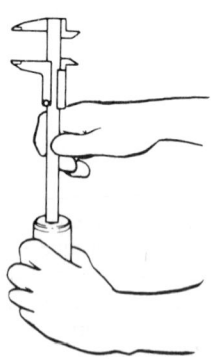

Fig. 4.17 Use vernier to set reservoir piston position – RM 125, 250 and 400 T models

11.1 Footrests are robust and spring-loaded (RM80)

13 Prop stand: examination

1   A prop stand (or side stand) is provided to support the machine when not in use. It is mounted on the left-hand side of the machine, pivoting on a lug attached to the footrest bar on the smaller machines, or to a bracket on the larger models.

2   It is vitally important that the pivot bolt is kept tight and in good condition at all times, as its failure during a race could have catastrophic consequences. This applies equally to the return spring, which should be renewed if it becomes stretched or broken.

3   If the stand becomes bent, it can be straightened in a similar manner to that described in Section 11, provided that care is taken to heat the area thoroughly first.

14 Kickstart lever: examination and renovation

1   The kickstart lever is splined and is secured to its shaft by means of a pinch bolt. The kickstart crank swivels so that it can be tucked out of the way when the engine is started. It is held in position on the swivel by a washer and circlip. A spring-loaded ball bearing locates the kickstart arm in either the operating or folded position; if the action becomes sloppy it is probable that the spring behind the ball bearing needs renewing. It is advisable to remove the circlip and washer occasionally, so that the kickstart crank can be detached and the swivel greased.

2   It is unlikely that the kickstart crank will bend in an accident unless the machine is ridden with the kickstart in the operating and not folded position. It should be removed and straightened, using the same technique as that recommended for the prop stand and brake lever.

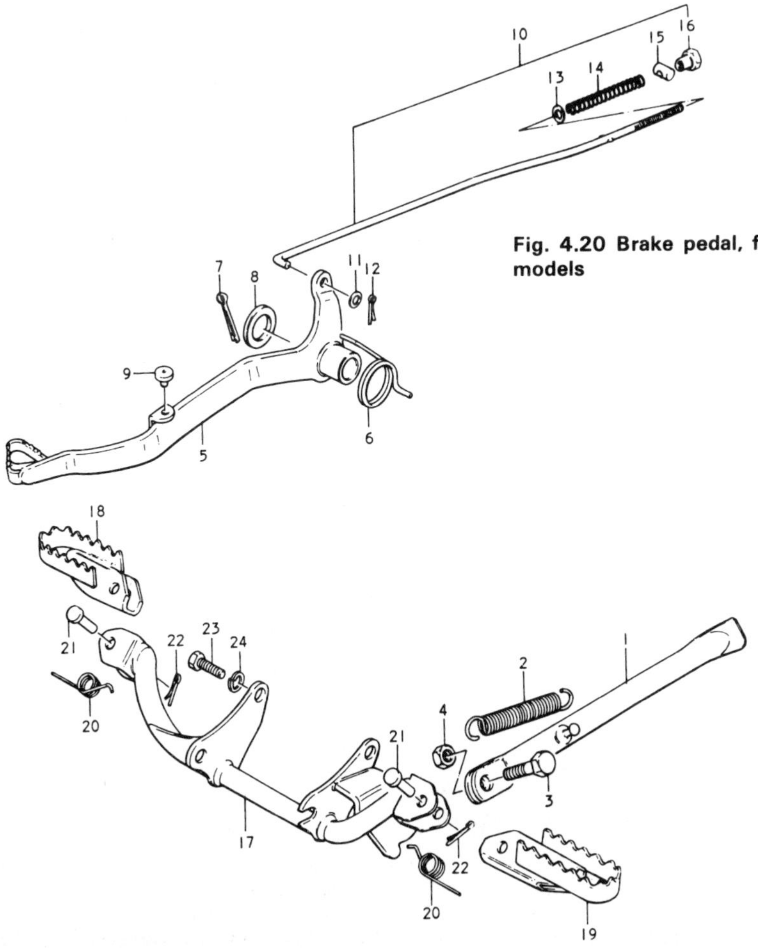

Fig. 4.20 Brake pedal, footrests and prop stand – RM 80 models

1   Prop stand
2   Prop stand return spring
3   Bolt
4   Nut
5   Rear brake pedal
6   Return spring
7   Split pin
8   Washer
9   Brake pedal stop
10 Brake operating rod assembly
11 Washer
12 Cotter pin
13 Split pin
14 Washer
15 Spring
16 Trunnion
17 Adjusting nut
18 Footrest bar
19 Right-hand footrest
20 Left-hand footrest
21 Footrest return spring – 2 off
22 Cotter pin – 2 off
23 Split pin – 2 off
24 Bolt – 2 off
25 Spring washer – 2 off

Fig. 4.21 Footrests, brake pedal and prop stand – RM 400 models

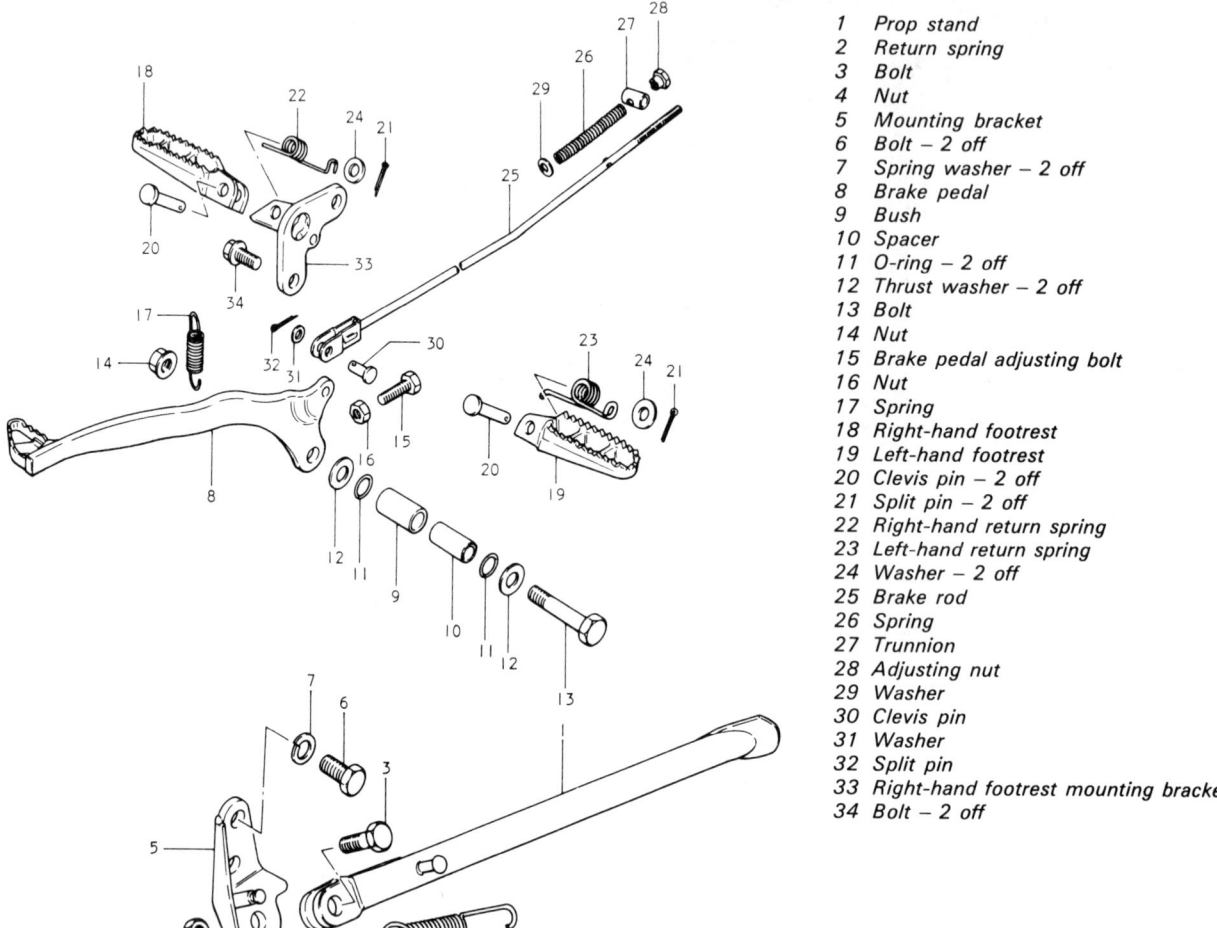

1   Prop stand
2   Return spring
3   Bolt
4   Nut
5   Mounting bracket
6   Bolt – 2 off
7   Spring washer – 2 off
8   Brake pedal
9   Bush
10 Spacer
11 O-ring – 2 off
12 Thrust washer – 2 off
13 Bolt
14 Nut
15 Brake pedal adjusting bolt
16 Nut
17 Spring
18 Right-hand footrest
19 Left-hand footrest
20 Clevis pin – 2 off
21 Split pin – 2 off
22 Right-hand return spring
23 Left-hand return spring
24 Washer – 2 off
25 Brake rod
26 Spring
27 Trunnion
28 Adjusting nut
29 Washer
30 Clevis pin
31 Washer
32 Split pin
33 Right-hand footrest mounting bracket
34 Bolt – 2 off

15 Fault diagnosis: frame and forks

Symptom	Cause	Remedy
Machine veers either to the left or the right with hands off handlebars	Bent frame Twisted forks Wheels out of alignment	Check, and renew. Check, and renew. Check, and re-align.
Machine rolls at low speed	Overtight steering head bearings	Slacken until adjustment is correct.
Machine judders when front brake is applied	Slack steering head bearings	Tighten, until adjustment is correct.
Machine pitches on uneven surfaces	Ineffective fork dampers Ineffective rear suspension units Incorrect suspension settings	Check oil content of front forks. Check whether units still have damping action. Check and adjust.
Fork action stiff	Fork legs out of alignment (twisted in yokes)	Slacken lower yoke clamps, and fork top bolts. Pump fork several times then retighten from bottom upwards.
Machine wanders. Steering imprecise Rear wheel tends to hop	Worn swinging arm pivot	Dismantle and renew bushes and pivot shaft

Chapter 5 Wheels, brakes and tyres

Contents

Specifications

Tyre size

	Front	Rear
RM50N,T	2.50–14–4PR	3.00–12–4PR
RM60N,T	2.50–14–4PR	3.00–14–4PR
RM80N (UK,US)	2.75–17–4PR	3.60–14–4PR
RM80N (Canada)	2.75–16–4PR	3.60–14–4PR
RM80T	2.75–17–4PR	4.10–14–4PR
RM100N,T	2.75–21–4PR	4.10–18–4PR
RM125N,T	3.00–21–4PR	4.10–18–4PR
RM250N,T	3.00–21–4PR	5.10–18–4PR
RM400N,T	3.00–21–4PR	5.10–18–4PR

Tyre pressures

RM50N,T	11–16 psi (0.8–1.1 kg cm^2/80–100 kPa)
RM60N,T	11–16 psi (0.8–1–1 kg cm^2/80–100 kPa)
RM80N,T	10–14 psi (0.7–1.0 kg cm^2/70–100 kPa)
RM125N, ...	10–14 psi (0.7–1.0 kg cm^2/70–100 kPa)
RM250N,T	10–14 psi (0.7–1.0 kg cm^2/70–100 kPa)
RM400T	10–14 psi (0.7–1.0 kg cm^2/70–100 kPa)
RM100N,T	10 psi (0.7 kg cm^2/70 kPa)
RM125T	10 psi (0.7 kg cm^2/70 kPa)
RM400N	10 psi (0.7 kg cm^2/70 kPa)

Note: The tyre pressures listed above are intended as a guide to the rider. Pressures can be varied to suit individual preference or particular track conditions. All pressures are measured with the tyre cold.

Brakes .... Single leading shoe (SLS) drum brake, front and rear

1 General description

The wheels fitted to the Suzuki RM range are of conventional wire spoked construction, using chromium plated steel or aluminium alloy rims. The diameter and section of the rims vary according to the models. Tyres are of the heavily blocked motocross pattern and are designed to give maximum traction without becoming clogged with mud. Simple single leading shoe (sls) drum brakes are fitted front and rear.

2 Wheels: examination and renovation

1 Place the machine firmly on blocks so that the wheel is raised clear of the ground. Spin the wheel and by using a pointer, such as a screwdriver, check the wheel rim alignment.

Small irregularities can be corrected by tightening the spokes in the affected area, although a certain amount of experience is advisable to prevent over-correction. Any flats in the wheel rim should be evident at the same time. These are more difficult to remove and in most cases it will be necessary to have the wheel rebuilt on a new rim. Apart from the effect on stability a flat will expose the tyre bead and walls to greater risk or damage if the machine is run with a deformed wheel.

2　Check for loose and broken spokes. Tapping the spokes is a good guide to tension. A loose spoke will produce a quite different sound and should be tightened by turning the nipple in an anticlockwise direction. Always recheck for run-out by spinning the wheel again. If the spokes have to be tightened an excessive amount, it is advisable to remove both tyre and tube by following the procedure in Section 10 of this Chapter. This is so that the protruding ends of the spokes can be ground off, to prevent them chafing the inner tube and causing punctures.

3　It should be noted that the wheels on motocross machines tend to suffer from the inevitable punishment of fast off-road riding. Once a spoke has become slightly loose, it will start to wear both the nipple and the rim hole, and will eventually break, placing an excessive load on the remaining spokes. For this reason, spoke tension should be checked after each event.

3　Front wheel: removal and replacement

1　Place the machine on blocks or a crate so that the front wheel is raised clear of the ground. Slacken off the front brake cable adjuster, and release the cable end from the brake lever at the front wheel.

2　Remove the split pin from the wheel spindle nut, then remove the castellated nut from the spindle end. Using a suitable tommy bar or a screwdriver blade, withdraw the wheel spindle. The wheel can then be lifted clear of the sorks.

3　To replace the wheel reverse the above procedure. Make sure the brake plate recess locates over the lug on the lower fork leg. Before finally tightening the spindle nut, operate the forks, spin the wheel and operate the brake. Firstly, this aligns the fork leg and secondly it centralises the brake shoes in the drum. Make doubly certain the brake plate recess is correctly located over the lug on the lower fork leg to prevent the plate from turning when braking. Fit a new split pin in the wheel spindle nut.

3.1a Release brake cable from operating lever ... (RM400)

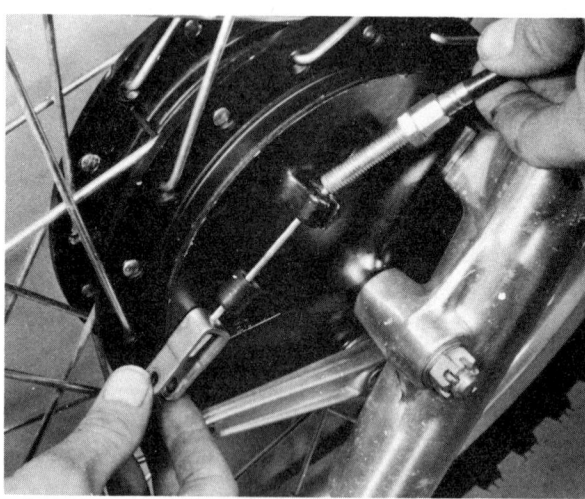

3.1b ... and brakeplate, as shown (RM400)

3.2 Withdraw wheel spindle and lower wheel clear (RM400)

3.3a Check that lug engages during reassembly (RM400)

3.3b Note spacer arrangements, where applicable (RM400)

3.3c Tighten clamp bolt, where fitted (RM400)

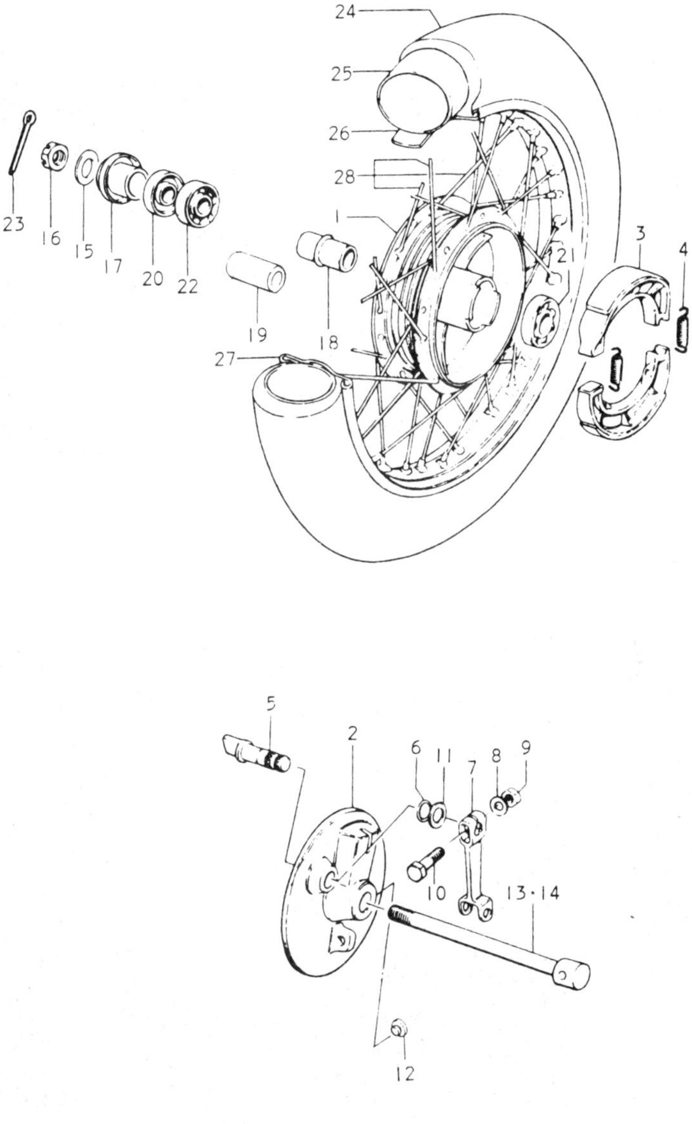

Fig. 5.1 Front wheel – RM 80 models

1   Hub
2   Brake plate
3   Brake shoe – 2 off
4   Brake shoe spring – 2 off
5   Brake operating cam
6   O-ring
7   Brake operating lever
8   Washer
9   Nut
10 Pinch bolt
11 Dust seal
12 Speedometer attachment plug
13,14 Front wheel spindle
15 Washer
16 Castellated nut
17 Spacer
18 Spacer (B model only)
19 Spacer (C and N model)
20 Oil seal
21 Bearing
22 Bearing
23 Split pin
24 Tyre
25 Inner tube
26 Rim tape
27 Wheel rim
28 Spoke set

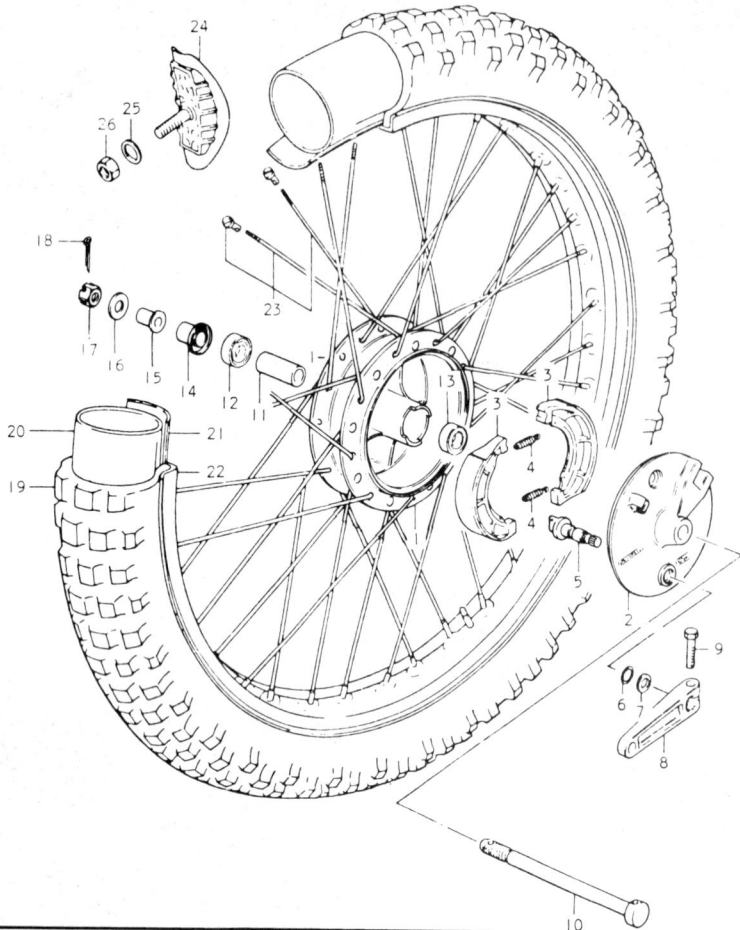

Fig. 5.2 Front wheel – RM 400 models

1   Hub
2   Brake plate
3   Brake shoe – 2 off
4   Spring – 2 off
5   Brake operating cam
6   Dust seal
7   Washer
8   Brake operating lever
9   Pinch bolt
10   Front wheel spindle
11   Centre spacer
12   Right-hand bearing
13   Left-hand bearing
14   Spacer
15   Spacer
16   Washer
17   Castellated nut
18   Split pin
19   Tyre
20   Inner tube
21   Rim tape
22   Rim
23   Spoke set
24   Security bolt
25   Washer
26   Nut

4   Rear wheel: removal and replacement

1   Support the machine on a crate or blocks so that the rear wheel is raised clear of the ground. Remove the rear brake adjuster nut, then depress the brake pedal so that the rod is disengaged from the trunnion in the brake arm. Refit the spring, trunnion and nut to prevent their loss.

2   Release the brake torque arm by removing the split pin or R pin and retaining nut. The torque arm can now be disengaged from the brake plate and placed to one side.

3   Remove the split pin from the end of the wheel spindle and then remove the wheel spindle nut. With luck, there will be sufficient slack in the chain to permit its disengagement from the rear sprocket after displacing the chain adjusters and pushing the wheel fully forward. Failing this, separate the drive chain at the joining link by prising off the spring clip and sliding the chain ends apart. It is a good idea to reassemble the joining link on one end of the chain to preclude its loss.

4   With the chain separated or disengaged from the sprocket, the rear wheel spindle can be withdrawn, freeing the wheel. Lower the wheel clear of the frame, noting that it may prove necessary to twist the wheel to one side to clear the swinging arm and rear mudguard.

5   Replacement is by reversing the removal procedure. The rear brake will need to be adjusted. Before tightening the wheel spindle nut, spin the wheel and apply the brake to centralise the brake shoes in the drum. Use a new split pin after tightening the spindle nut.

5   Brakes: dismantling, examination and replacement

1   Both front and rear brakes are of the single leading shoe type and for servicing purposes can be treated alike.

2   Remove the wheel and brake as described in Section 3 for the front wheel or Section 4 for the rear wheel.

3   Examine the condition of the brake linings. If they are wearing thin or unevenly the brake shoes should be renewed. The linings are bonded to the brake shoes and cannot be supplied separately.

4   To remove the brake shoes, pull them away from the cam and pivot, and then pull them away from the brake plate in a 'V' formation so that they can be lifted away together with the return springs. When they are well clear of the brake plate, the return springs can be disconnected.

5   Before replacing the brake shoes, check that the operating cam is working smoothly and not binding in its housing. The cam can be removed for greasing by detaching the operating arm from the end of the shaft. The operating arm is located on the cam shaft by splines, and is retained by a pinch bolt, mark both the operating arm and the shaft end before removal to aid correct relocation.

6   Check the inner surface of the brake drum, on which the brake shoes bear. The surface should be free from indentations and score marks, otherwise reduced braking efficiency and accelerated brake lining wear will result. Remove all traces of brake lining dust and wipe the drum surface with a petrol soaked rag, to remove all traces of grease and oil.

7   To reassemble the brake shoes on the brake plate, fit the return springs and pull the shoes apart whilst holding them in the form of a 'V' facing upwards. If they are now located with the brake operating cam and fixed pivot, they can be pushed into position by pressing downwards. Do not use excessive force, or there is risk of distorting the shoes. Note: A wear limit is stamped on both cams and an indicator mark is cast on the brake plate.

4.1 Release brake rod from operating lever (RM400)

4.2 Torque arm is secured by nut and split pin or nyloc nut (RM400)

4.3 Remove split pin and wheel spindle nut ... (RM400)

4.4 ... and withdraw spindle to release rear wheel (RM100)

5.3a Brake plate assembly can be withdrawn ... (RM400)

5.3b ... for attention to brake shoes and drum (RM100)

5.4 Fold shoes upwards to release from brake plate (RM400)

5.6 Check brake drum surface for scoring (RM80)

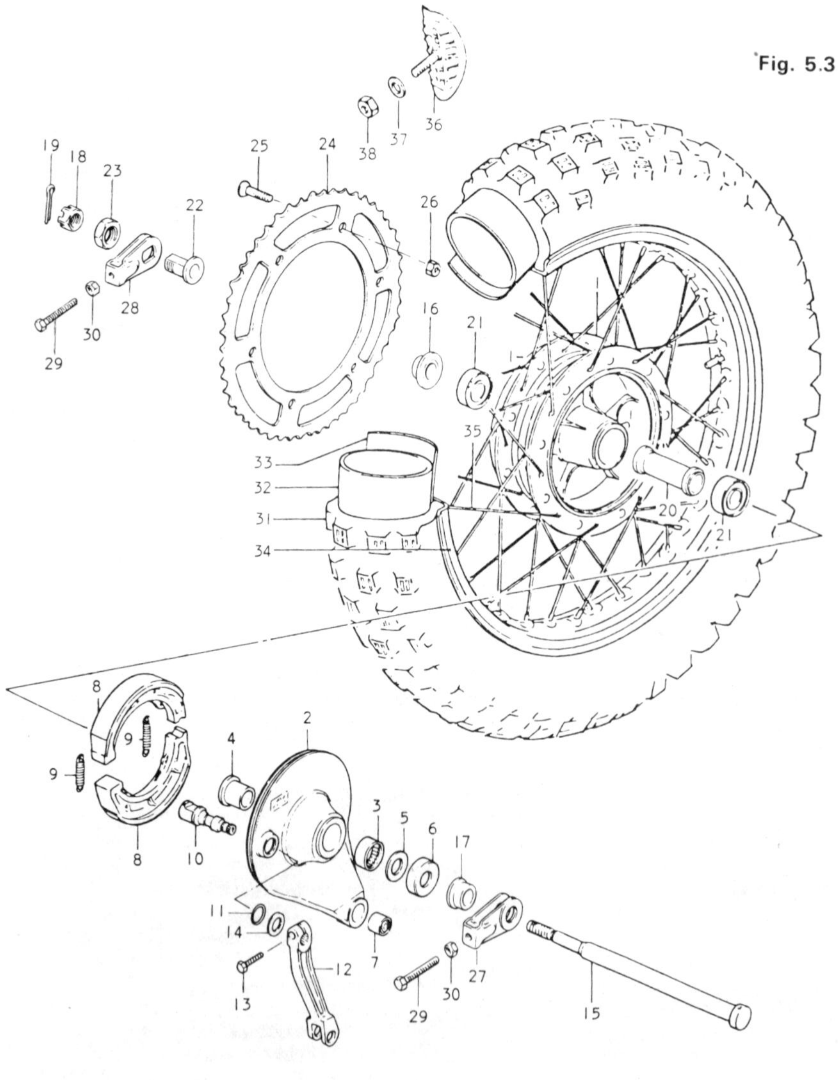

Fig. 5.3 Rear wheel – RM 100 models

1 Hub
2 Brake plate
3 Needle roller bearing
4 Collar
5 Thrust washer
6 Oil seal
7 Bush
8 Brake shoe - 2 off
9 Spring – 2 off
10 Brake operating cam
11 Dust seal
12 Brake operating lever
13 Bolt
14 Washer
15 Rear wheel spindle
16 Left-hand spindle spacer
17 Right-hand spindle spacer
18 Castellated nut
19 Split pin
20 Centre spacer
21 Bearing – 2 off
22 Chain adjuster spacer
23 Nut
24 Rear wheel sprocket
25 Screw – 6 off
26 Nut – 6 off
27 Right-hand chain adjuster
28 Left-hand chain adjuster
29 Adjusting bolt – 2 off
30 Locknut – 2 off
31 Tyre
32 Inner tube
33 Rim tape
34 Rim
35 Spoke set
36 Security bolt
37 Washer – 2 off
38 Nut – 2 off

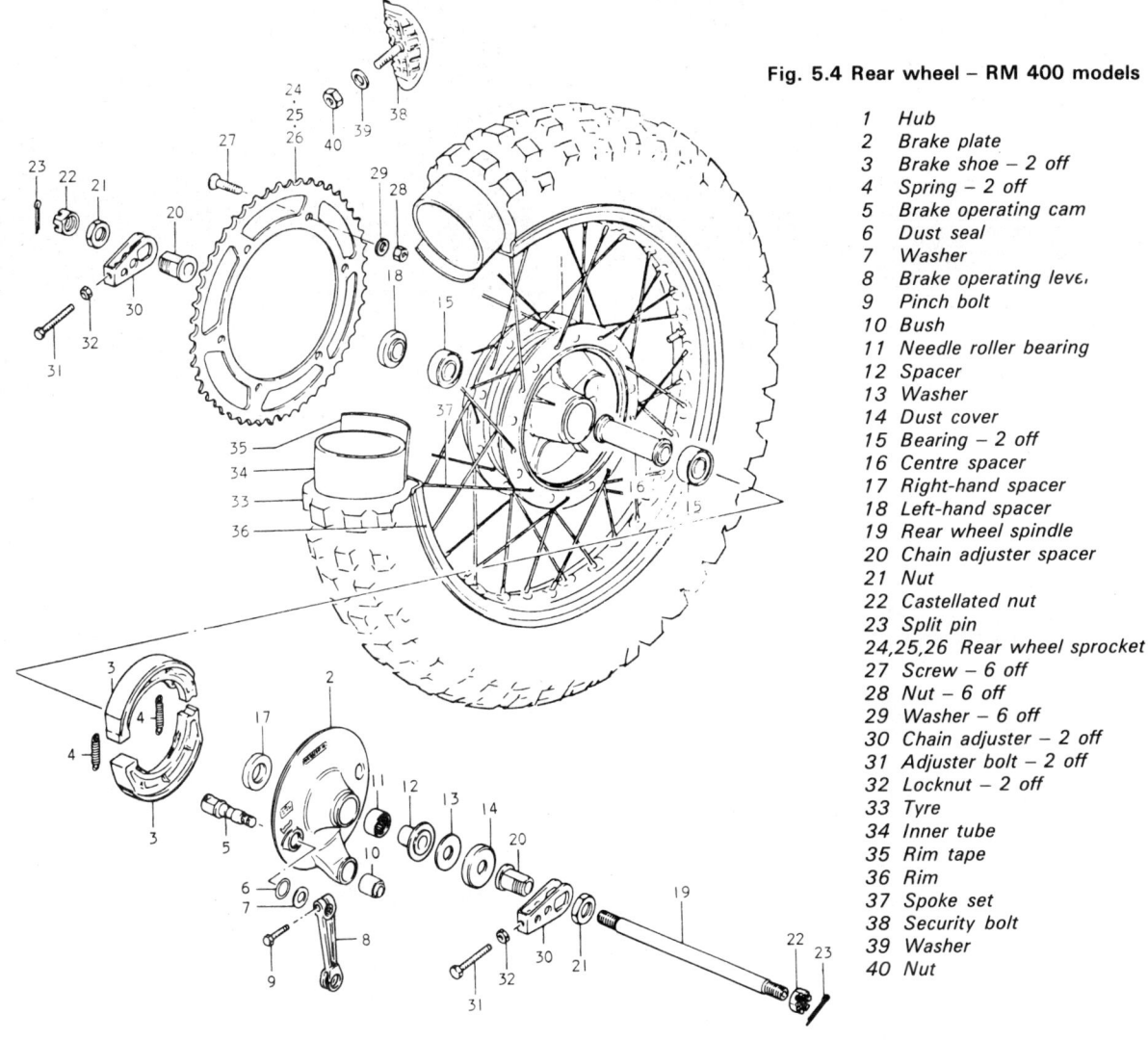

Fig. 5.4 Rear wheel – RM 400 models

1 Hub
2 Brake plate
3 Brake shoe – 2 off
4 Spring – 2 off
5 Brake operating cam
6 Dust seal
7 Washer
8 Brake operating lever
9 Pinch bolt
10 Bush
11 Needle roller bearing
12 Spacer
13 Washer
14 Dust cover
15 Bearing – 2 off
16 Centre spacer
17 Right-hand spacer
18 Left-hand spacer
19 Rear wheel spindle
20 Chain adjuster spacer
21 Nut
22 Castellated nut
23 Split pin
24,25,26 Rear wheel sprocket
27 Screw – 6 off
28 Nut – 6 off
29 Washer – 6 off
30 Chain adjuster – 2 off
31 Adjuster bolt – 2 off
32 Locknut – 2 off
33 Tyre
34 Inner tube
35 Rim tape
36 Rim
37 Spoke set
38 Security bolt
39 Washer
40 Nut

6 Wheel bearings: removal and replacement

1 The ball journal wheel bearings are all fitted with integral oil seals, although an extra seal is located on the right-hand side of the front wheel.

2 The bearings are a drive fit in the hub and are removed by driving them out with a drift, working from each side of the hub. When the first bearing emerges from the hub, the hollow distance collar that separates the bearing can be removed.

3 Remove all the grease from the hub and bearings. Check the bearings for play or roughness when they are rotated. If there is any doubt about their condition renew them.

4 Before replacing the bearings, first pack the hub with new high melting point grease, leaving sufficient room for expansion of the grease when it becomes hot. Drift the bearings into the hub using a tubular drift, contacting on only the outer ring of the bearing (an appropriate size socket will suffice). When the bearing has only one integral seal, make sure this is on the outside. Do not forget the distance collar between the bearings.

5 In the case of the RM100, 125, 250 and 400 models, an additional needle roller bearing is fitted in the brake plate to allow the brake to float in relation to the swinging arm. This bearing is particularly prone to corrosion, as the accompanying photographs show. To prevent its premature demise, it is recommended that the bearing is packed with a waterproof grease each time the brakes are checked. The bearing is removed by driving it out of the housing. As this will almost invariably damage the bearing, it should not be removed unless it is to be renewed.

7 Rear wheel sprocket: maintenance and renewal

1 The rear wheel sprocket is bolted to the left-hand side of the rear hub, and may be removed after the wheel has been released as described in Section 4 of this Chapter. On the RM50, 60 and 80, the sprocket is secured by a total of four bolts, whilst the larger machines employ six Allen screws and nuts as a means of retaining the sprocket to the hub.

2 Like the drive chain, the front and rear sprockets are subject to accelerated wear if not kept clean and well lubricated. This operation should be attended to each time the chain is cleaned and lubricated, preferably after each race. Check the security of the sprocket mounting bolts.

3 Check the condition of the sprocket teeth. If they are hooked, chipped or badly worn, the sprocket must be renewed. It is considered bad practice to renew one sprocket on its own. The final drive sprockets should always be renewed as a pair and a new chain fitted, otherwise rapid wear will necessitate even earlier renewal on the next occasion.

6.1a Note position of front wheel oil seal ... (RM80)

6.1b ... and headed spacer (RM80)

6.2a Drive bearings out to check for wear or damage (RM80)

6.2b Note distance piece fitted between bearings (RM80)

6.3 This bearing has been ruined by water and mud (RM100)

6.4a Sealed side of bearing must face outwards (RM100)

6.4b Do not omit distance piece in hub (RM100)

6.5a Outrigger bearing has been destroyed by water and mud (RM100)

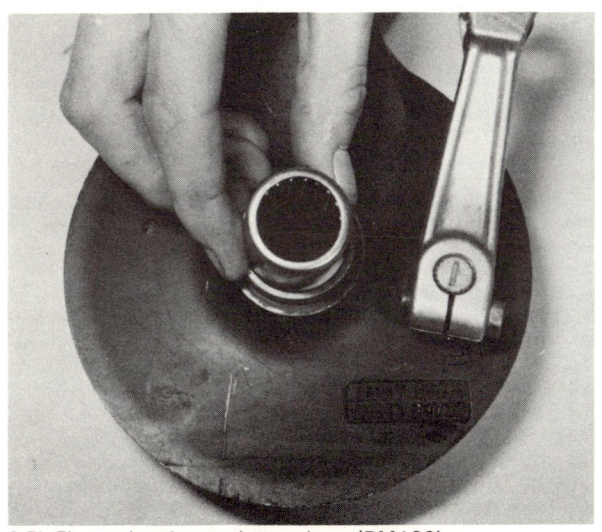

6.5b Fit new bearing as shown above (RM100)

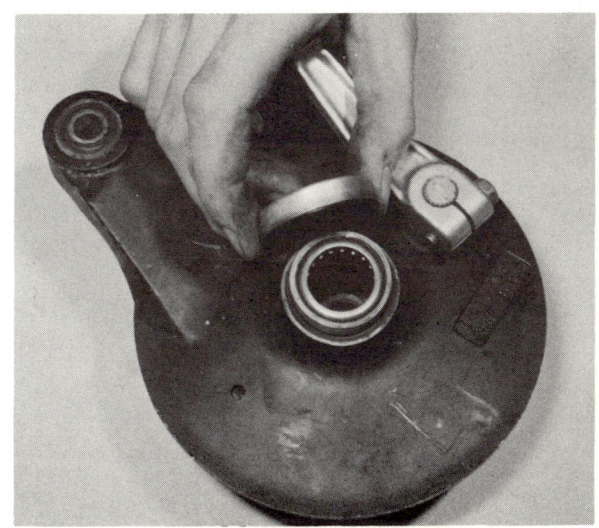

6.5c Do not forget to fit a new oil seal (RM100)

6.5d Headed inner bearing fits as shown (RM100)

7.1a Sprocket may be retained by Allen screws ... (RM100)

7.1b ... or by bolts on smaller models (RM80)

7.2 Check gearbox sprocket for wear or damage (RM400)

7.3 Note condition of old and new sprockets (RM100)

8   Final drive chain: examination and maintenance

1   The final drive chain on all motocross machines is subjected to a constant bombardment of dirt and water, neither of which help to prolong its life. After each race, the chain should be cleaned off using a degreasing fluid, and then relubricated with a good quality chain lubricant. These are widely available in aerosol packs, and can be applied between races to ensure consistent lubrication.

2   To ensure maximum life from the chain, it should be detached for full cleaning at frequent intervals. The chain can be washed out in a cleaning solvent or paraffin (kerosene) and then rinsed in petrol (gasoline) and left to dry. The cleaned chain should then be immersed in a molten lubricant such as Linklyfe or Chainguard. This is fairly thin when hot, and will penetrate the chain links and rollers. As it cools down it sets as a waxy grease, and is thus held inside the rollers rather than being flung off like oils.

3   The chain tension should always be checked after cleaning and lubrication. The required amount of free play varies from model to model, and will be found in the table below. Check the free play in the middle of the lower run, noting that chain tensioner mechanisms, where fitted, should be positioned so that they are not taking up any extra free play. The chain tension should be checked in several positions, as the chain rarely wears evenly. Note the play at the tightest point.

Drive chain free play

RM50, 60, 80	*0.8 – 1.2 in (20 – 30 mm)*
RM100, 125	*2.0 – 2.4 in (50 – 60 mm)*
RM250, 400	*2.4 – 2.7 in (60 – 70 mm)*

4   If adjustment is required, it will be necessary to slacken the rear wheel spindle nut and the nut or bolt which secures the brake torque arm. Move each adjuster by an equal number of flats to preserve wheel alignment. The fork ends are marked with a series of lines which help in checking wheel alignment, but these cannot be relied upon as being totally accurate. Always fit a new split pin to the spindle end after the spindle nut has been tightened, and remember to check the rear brake adjustment, as this may have altered.

5   To check whether the chain requires replacement, lay it lengthwise in a straight line and compress it endwise until all the play is taken up. Anchor one end and pull on the other in order to take up the end play in the opposite direction. If the chain extends by more than the distance between two adjacent rollers, it should be replaced in conjunction with the sprockets. Note that this check should be made after the chain has been washed out, but before any lubricant is applied, otherwise the lubricant will take up some of the play.

6   When replacing the chain, make sure the spring link is seated correctly, with the closed end facing in the direction of chain travel.

9   Chain guides and tensioners

1   The long rear suspension travel of the RM models necessitates some means of preventing the chain from being thrown off the sprockets when the machine is ridden over rough terrain. This is because there is quite a wide variation of chain tension through the operating range of the rear suspension.

2   The solution to the problem varies according to the machine's size. In the case of the RM50 and 60, a small rubber buffer is fitted around the swinging arm cross-tube to fend off attacks by the chain. The RM80 has the added refinement of a spring-loaded jockey wheel mounted below the swinging arm. The larger models have correspondingly more complicated variations to cope with the wider variations of chain tension. The various types are shown in the accompanying illustrations.

3   Little maintenance is required, other than regular checks on the condition of the rubbing strips and tensioner rollers. It is important that these are renewed when they become worn, and care should be taken to avoid the chain rubbing directly on the swinging arm.

Tyre removal: Deflate inner tube and insert lever in close proximity to tyre valve

Use two levers to work bead over the edge of rim

When first bead is clear, remove tyre as shown

Tyre fitting: Inflate inner tube and insert in tyre

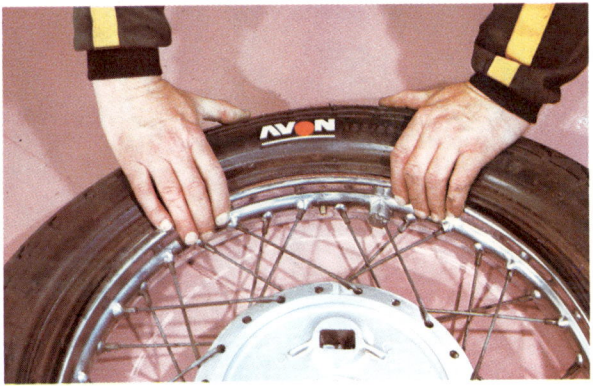

Lay tyre on rim and feed valve through hole in rim

Work first bead over rim, using lever in final section

Use similar technique for second bead, finish at tyre valve position

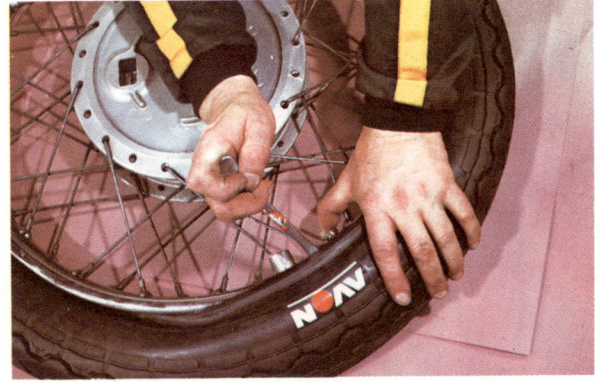

Push valve and tube up into tyre when fitting final section, to avoid trapping

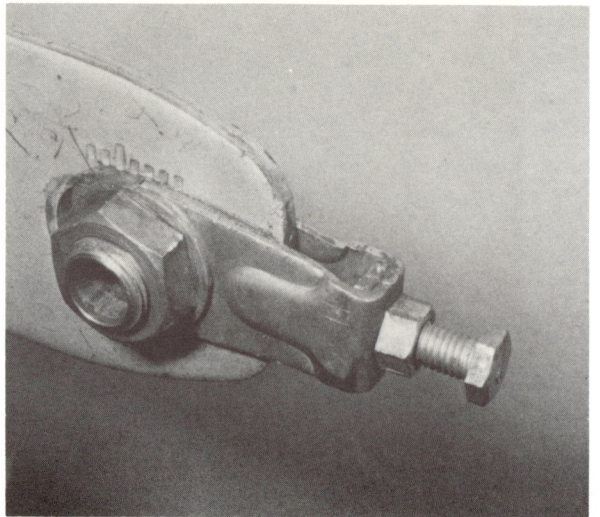

8.4 Marks on adjuster aid wheel alignment (RM100)

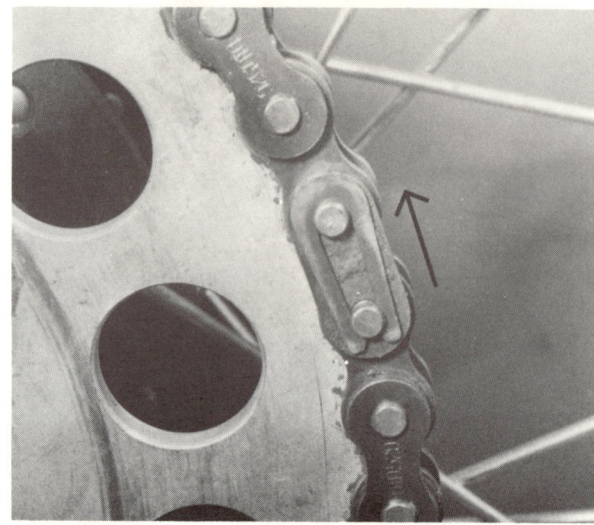

8.6 Closed end of link faces direction of chain travel (RM400)

9.2a Spring-loaded chain tensioner (RM80)

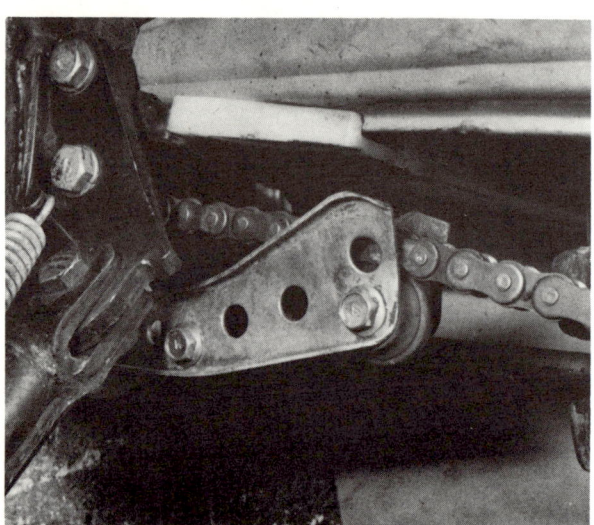

9.2b Similar arrangement on RM100, 125 (RM100)

9.2c Modified (Beamish) chain guide assembly (RM100)

9.2d Check guide rollers for wear or damage (RM100)

9.2e RM250, 400 uses similar arrangement ... (RM400)

9.2f ... for tensioner and guide rollers (RM400)

9.2g This roller required renewal (RM400)

10 Tyres: removal and replacement

1   At some time or other the need will arise to remove and replace the tyres, either as the result of a puncture or because a replacement is required to offset wear. To the inexperienced, tyre changing represents a formidable task yet if a few simple rules are observed and the technique learned the whole operation is surprisingly simple.

2   To remove the tyre from either wheel, first detach the wheel from the machine by following the procedure in Chapter 4 depending on whether the front or the rear wheel is involved. Deflate the tyre by removing the valve insert and when it is fully deflated, push the bead of the tyre away from the wheel rim on both sides so that the bead enters the centre well of the rim. Remove the locking cap and push the tyre valve into the tyre itself. Remove the nut and washer which hold the tyre security bolt, and push the security bolt from position.

3   Insert a tyre lever close to the valve and lever the edge of the tyre over the outside of the wheel rim. Very little force should be necessary; if resistance is encountered it is probably due to the fact that the tyre beads have not entered the well of the wheel rim all the way round the tyre.

4   Once the tyre has been edged over the wheel rim, it is easy to work around the wheel rim so that the tyre is completely free on one side. At this stage, the inner tube and the freed security bolt can be removed.

5   Working from the other side of the wheel, ease the other edge of the tyre over the outside of the wheel rim that is furthest away. Continue to work around the rim until the tyre is free completely from the rim.

6   If a puncture has necessitated the removal of the tyre, reinflate the inner tube and immerse it in a bowl of water to trace the source of the leak. Mark its position and deflate the tyre. Dry the tube and clean the area around the puncture with a petrol-soaked rag. When the surface has dried, apply the rubber solution and allow this to dry before removing the backing from the patch and applying the patch to the surface.

7   It is best to use a patch of the self-vulcanising type, which will form a very permanent repair. Note that it may be necessary to remove a protective covering from the top surface of the patch, after it has sealed in position. Inner tubes made from synthetic rubber may require a special type of patch and adhesive, if a satisfactory bond is to be achieved.

8   Before replacing the tyre, check the inside to make sure the agent that caused the puncture is not trapped. Check also the outside of the tyre, particularly the tread area, to make sure nothing is trapped that may cause a further puncture.

9   If the inner tube has been patched on a number of past occasions, or if there is a tear or large hole, it is preferable to discard it and fit a replacement.

10   To replace the tyre, inflate the inner tube sufficiently for it to assume a circular shape but only just. Then push it into the tyre so that it is enclosed completely. Lay the tyre on the wheel at an angle and insert the valve through the rim tape and the hole in the wheel rim. Attach the locking cap on the first few threads, sufficient to hold the valve captive in its correct location.

11   Starting at the point furthest from the valve, push the tyre bead over the edge of the wheel rim until it is located in the central well. Continue to work around the tyre in this fashion until the whole of one side of the tyre is on the rim. It may be necessary to use a tyre lever during the final stages. Fit the security bolt in position in the rim so that it is only held very loosely.

12   Make sure there is no pull on the tyre valve and again commencing with the area furthest from the valve, ease the other bead of the tyre over the edge of the rim. Finish with the area close to the valve, pushing the valve cap up into the tyre until the locking cap touches the rim. This will ensure the inner tube is not trapped when the last section of the bead is edged over the rim with a tyre lever.

13 Check that the inner tube is not trapped at any point. Re-inflate the inner tube, and check that the tyre is seating correctly around the wheel rim. There should be a thin rib moulded around the wall of the tyre on both sides, which should be equidistant from the wheel rim at all points. If the tyre is unevenly located on the rim, try bouncing the wheel when the tyre is at the recommended pressure. It is probable that one of the beads has not pulled clear of the centre well. When the tyre is correctly fitted the security bolt may be tightened. Do not overtighten the bolt, as it may distort the alloy rim and also the steel tyre bead. In any event overtightening is unnecessary as the security bolt is indented sufficiently to grip the tyre with ease.

14 Tyre pressures should follow recommended pressure for the particular type of tyre utilised. However, experimentation on different terrains will indicate the optimum pressure. Pressures should not be allowed to fall too low, or the risk of the beads escaping the rim edges due to excessive side forces may be run.

15 Tyre replacement is aided by dusting the side walls, particularly in the vicinity of the beads, with a liberal coating of french chalk. Washing-up liquid can also be used to good effect, but this has the disadvantage of causing the inner surfaces of the wheel rim to rust. Particular care should be taken when removing or replacing tyres on alloy rims, as these rims are softer and more prone to damage than their steel counterparts.

16 Never fit a tyre that has a damaged tread or side-walls. A blow-out at high speed will be dangerous to the rider, and a blow-out at any speed may well lose the race, or valuable time.

17 Never replace the inner tube and tyre without the rim tape in position. If this precaution is overlooked there is good chance of the ends of the spoke nipples chafing the inner tube and causing a crop of punctures. For maximum reliability the tyre should be removed, and the protruding spoke ends filed flush, whenever spokes are retentioned.

18 Tyre valves rarely give trouble, but it is always advisable to check whether the valve itself is leaking before removing the tyre. Do not forget to fit the dust cap, which forms an effective second seal.

10.2 Tyre security bolt prevents tyre creep (RM400)

11 Security bolt

1 It is often considered necessary to fit a security bolt to the rear wheel of a competition model because the initial take up of drive may cause the tyre to creep around the wheel rim and tear the valve from the inner tube. The security bolt retains the bead of the tyre to the wheel rim and prevents this occurrence. Similarly, the same device may be employed on the front wheel to prevent tyre creep when the front brake is applied. Security bolts are fitted as standard on the rear wheel of all models except the RM50, and on the front wheel of the RM100, 125, 250 and 400 models.

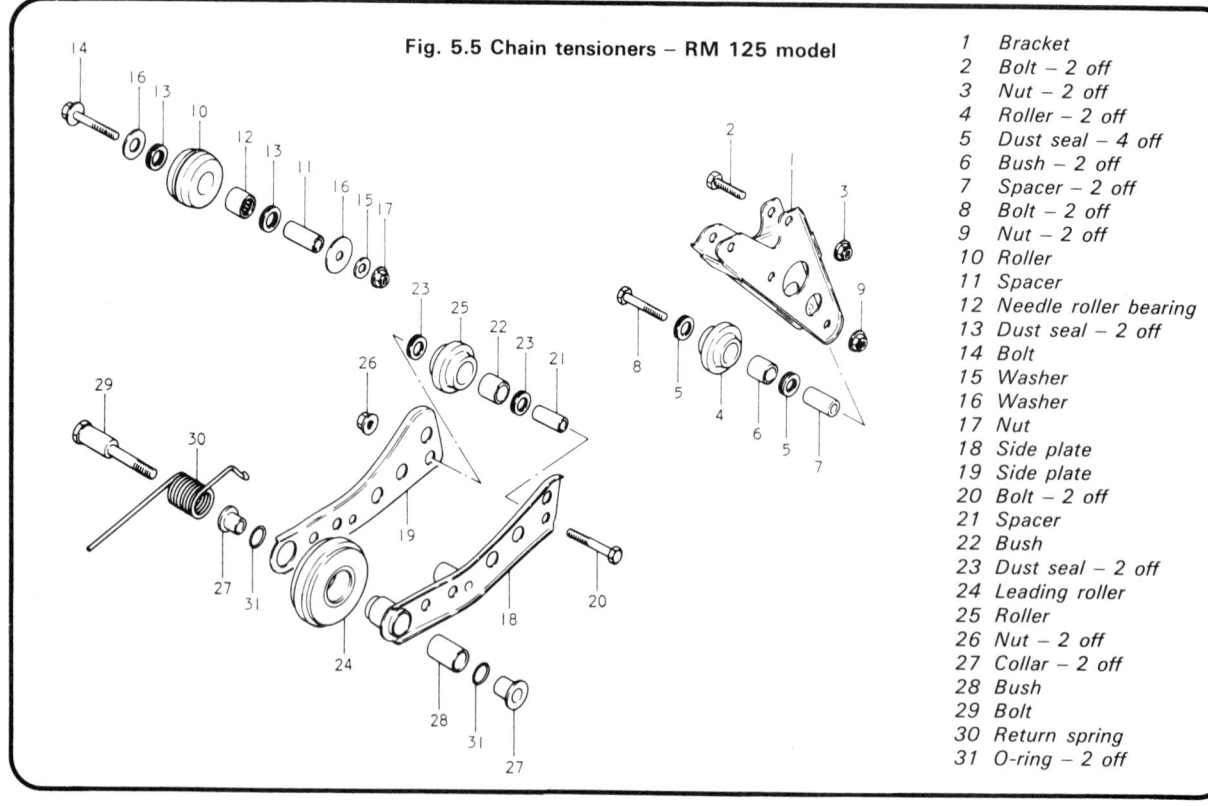

Fig. 5.5 Chain tensioners – RM 125 model

1   Bracket
2   Bolt – 2 off
3   Nut – 2 off
4   Roller – 2 off
5   Dust seal – 4 off
6   Bush – 2 off
7   Spacer – 2 off
8   Bolt – 2 off
9   Nut – 2 off
10 Roller
11 Spacer
12 Needle roller bearing
13 Dust seal – 2 off
14 Bolt
15 Washer
16 Washer
17 Nut
18 Side plate
19 Side plate
20 Bolt – 2 off
21 Spacer
22 Bush
23 Dust seal – 2 off
24 Leading roller
25 Roller
26 Nut – 2 off
27 Collar – 2 off
28 Bush
29 Bolt
30 Return spring
31 O-ring – 2 off

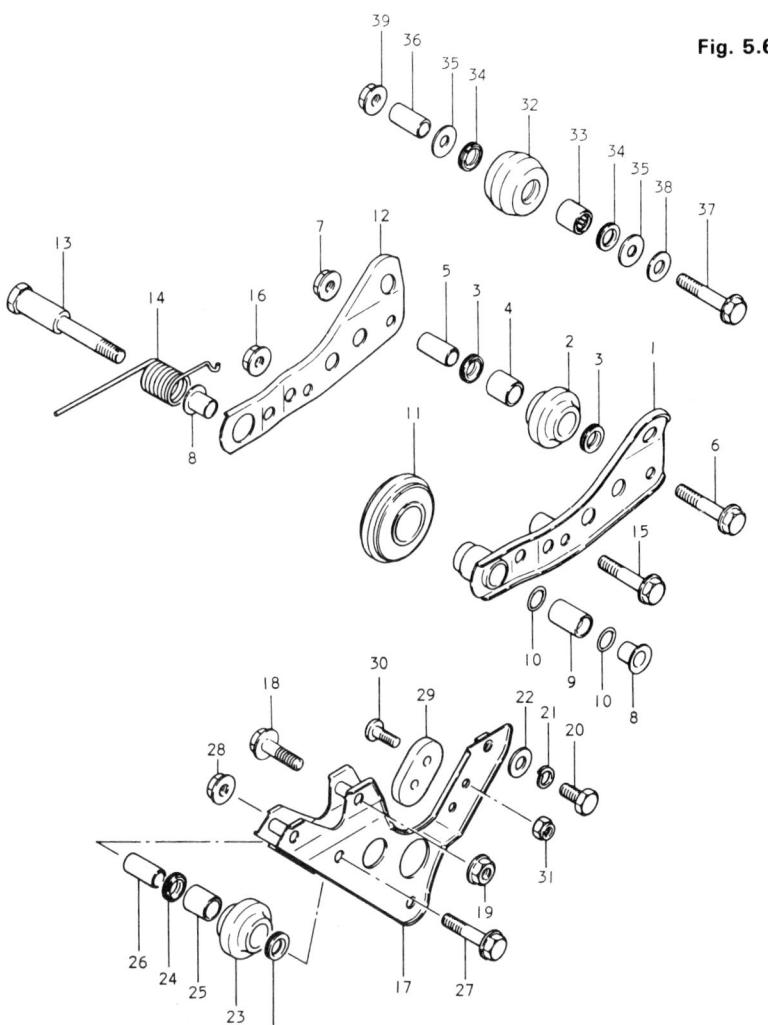

Fig. 5.6 Chain tensioners – RM 250 and 400 models

1   Bracket
2   Roller
3   Dust seal – 2 off
4   Bush
5   Spacer
6   Bolt
7   Nut
8   Shouldered spacer
9   Bush
10 O-ring
11 Roller
12 Bracket
13 Bolt
14 Tensioner spring
15 Bolt
16 Nut
17 Mounting bracket
18 Bolt – 2 off
19 Nut – 2 off
20 Bolt
21 Spring washer
22 Washer
23 Roller – 2 off
24 Dust seal – 4 off
25 Bush – 2 off
26 Spacer – 2 off
27 Bolt – 2 off
28 Nut – 2 off
29 Damping block
30 Screw – 2 off
31 Nut – 2 off
32 Roller
33 Needle roller bearing
34 Dust seal – 2 off
35 Washer – 2 off
36 Spacer
37 Bolt
38 Washer
39 Nut

12 Fault diagnosis: wheels, brakes and tyres

Symptom	Cause	Remedy
Handlebars oscillate at low speeds	Buckled front wheel Incorrectly fitted front tyre	Remove wheel for specialist attention. Check whether line around bead is equidistant from rim.
Brakes grab, locking wheel	End of brake shoes not chamfered	Remove brake shoes and chamfer shoes with rasp.
Brakes feel spongy	Stretched brake operating cables, weak pull-off springs	Replace cables and/or springs after inspection.

Metric conversion tables

Inches	Decimals	Millimetres	Millimetres to Inches		Inches to Millimetres	
			mm	Inches	Inches	mm
1/64	0.015625	0.3969	0.01	0.00039	0.001	0.0254
1/32	0.03125	0.7937	0.02	0.00079	0.002	0.0508
3/64	0.046875	1.1906	0.03	0.00118	0.003	0.0762
1/16	0.0625	1.5875	0.04	0.00157	0.004	0.1016
5/64	0.078125	1.9844	0.05	0.00197	0.005	0.1270
3/32	0.09375	2.3812	0.06	0.00236	0.006	0.1524
7/64	0.109375	2.7781	0.07	0.00276	0.007	0.1778
1/8	0.125	3.1750	0.08	0.00315	0.008	0.2032
9/64	0.140625	3.5719	0.09	0.00354	0.009	0.2286
5/32	0.15625	3.9687	0.1	0.00394	0.01	0.254
11/64	0.171875	4.3656	0.2	0.00787	0.02	0.508
3/16	0.1875	4.7625	0.3	0.01181	0.03	0.762
13/64	0.203125	5.1594	0.4	0.01575	0.04	1.016
7/32	0.21875	5.5562	0.5	0.01969	0.05	1.270
15/64	0.234375	5.9531	0.6	0.02362	0.06	1.524
1/4	0.25	6.3500	0.7	0.02756	0.07	1.778
17/64	0.265625	6.7469	0.8	0.03150	0.08	2.032
9/32	0.28125	7.1437	0.9	0.03543	0.09	2.286
19/64	0.296875	7.5406	1	0.03937	0.1	2.54
5/16	0.3125	7.9375	2	0.07874	0.2	5.08
21/64	0.328125	8.3344	3	0.11811	0.3	7.62
11/32	0.34375	8.7312	4	0.15748	0.4	10.16
23/64	0.359375	9.1281	5	0.19685	0.5	12.70
3/8	0.375	9.5250	6	0.23622	0.6	15.24
25/64	0.390625	9.9219	7	0.27559	0.7	17.78
13/32	0.40625	10.3187	8	0.31496	0.8	20.32
27/64	0.421875	10.7156	9	0.35433	0.9	22.86
7/16	0.4375	11.1125	10	0.39370	1	25.4
29/64	0.453125	11.5094	11	0.43307	2	50.8
15/32	0.46875	11.9062	12	0.47244	3	76.2
31/64	0.484375	12.3031	13	0.51181	4	101.6
1/2	0.5	12.7000	14	0.55118	5	127.0
33/64	0.515625	13.0969	15	0.59055	6	152.4
17/32	0.53125	13.4937	16	0.62992	7	177.8
35/64	0.546875	13.8906	17	0.66929	8	203.2
9/16	0.5625	14.2875	18	0.70866	9	228.6
37/64	0.578125	14.6844	19	0.74803	10	254.0
19/32	0.59375	15.0812	20	0.78740	11	279.4
39/64	0.609375	15.4781	21	0.82677	12	304.8
5/8	0.625	15.8750	22	0.86614	13	330.2
41/64	0.640625	16.2719	23	0.09551	14	355.6
21/32	0.65625	16.6687	24	0.94488	15	381.0
43/64	0.671875	17.0656	25	0.98425	16	406.4
11/16	0.6875	17.4625	26	1.02362	17	431.8
45/64	0.703125	17.8594	27	1.06299	18	457.2
23/32	0.71875	18.2562	28	1.10236	19	482.6
47/64	0.734375	18.6531	29	1.14173	20	508.0
3/4	0.75	19.0500	30	1.18110	21	533.4
49/64	0.765625	19.4469	31	1.22047	22	558.8
25/32	0.78125	19.8437	32	1.25984	23	584.2
51/64	0.796875	20.2406	33	1.29921	24	609.6
13/16	0.8125	20.6375	34	1.33858	25	635.0
53/64	0.828125	21.0344	35	1.37795	26	660.4
27/32	0.84375	21.4312	36	1.41732	27	685.8
55/64	0.859375	21.8281	37	1.4567	28	711.2
7/8	0.875	22.2250	38	1.4961	29	736.6
57/64	0.890625	22.6219	39	1.5354	30	762.0
29/32	0.90625	23.0187	40	1.5748	31	787.4
59/64	0.921875	23.4156	41	1.6142	32	812.8
15/16	0.9375	23.8125	42	1.6535	33	838.2
61/64	0.953125	24.2094	43	1.6929	34	863.6
31/32	0.96875	24.6062	44	1.7323	35	889.0
63/64	0.984375	25.0031	45	1.7717	36	914.4

1   Imperial gallon = 8 Imp pints = 1.20 US gallons = 277.42 cu in = 4.54 litres

1   US gallon = 4 US quarts = 0.83 Imp gallon = 231 cu in = 3.78 litres

1   Litre = 0.21 Imp gallon = 0.26 US gallon = 61.02 cu in = 1000 cc

Miles to Kilometres		Kilometres to Miles	
1	1.61	1	0.62
2	3.22	2	1.24
3	4.83	3	1.86
4	6.44	4	2.49
5	8.05	5	3.11
6	9.66	6	3.73
7	11.27	7	4.35
8	12.88	8	4.97
9	14.48	9	5.59
10	16.09	10	6.21
20	32.19	20	12.43
30	48.28	30	18.64
40	64.37	40	24.85
50	80.47	50	31.07
60	96.56	60	37.28
70	112.65	70	43.50
80	128.75	80	49.71
90	144.84	90	55.92
100	160.93	100	62.14

lbf ft to kgf m		kgf m to lbf ft		lbf/in^2 to kgf/cm^2		kgf/cm^2 to lbf/in^2	
1	0.138	1	7.233	1	0.07	1	14.22
2	0.276	2	14.466	2	0.14	2	28.50
3	0.414	3	21.699	3	0.21	3	42.67
4	0.553	4	28.932	4	0.28	4	56.89
5	0.691	5	36.165	5	0.35	5	71.12
6	0.829	6	43.398	6	0.42	6	85.34
7	0.967	7	50.631	7	0.49	7	99.56
8	1.106	8	57.864	8	0.56	8	113.79
9	1.244	9	65.097	9	0.63	9	128.00
10	1.382	10	72.330	10	0.70	10	142.23
20	2.765	20	144.660	20	1.41	20	284.47
30	4.147	30	216.990	30	2.11	30	426.70

Index

**Printed by
Haynes Publishing Group
Sparkford Yeovil Somerset
England**